Shipwrecked in Paradise

For Rebecca & Derek Smith, PEM members with thanks for your support in sharing this great story.

Paul F. Johnston
SMS #879

ED RACHAL

FOUNDATION

NAUTICAL

ARCHAEOLOGY

SERIES

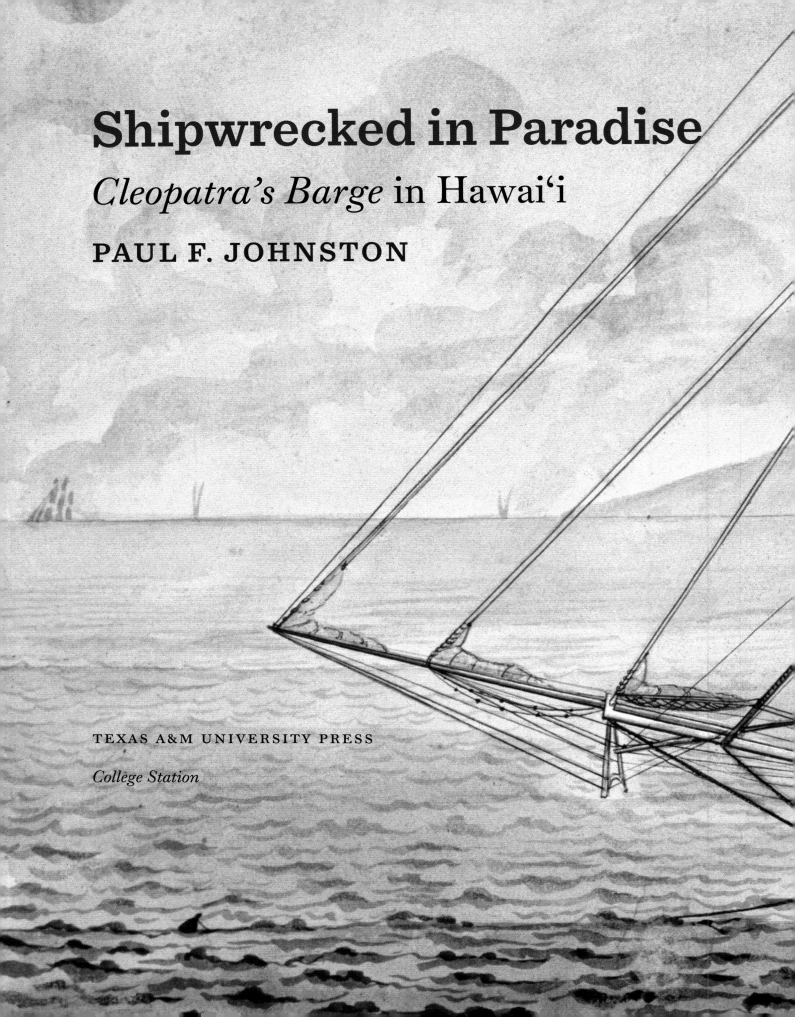

Shipwrecked in Paradise

Cleopatra's Barge in Hawai'i

PAUL F. JOHNSTON

TEXAS A&M UNIVERSITY PRESS

College Station

Manufactured in China by Everbest Printing Co.

through FCI Print Group

This paper meets the requirements of ANSI/NISO z39.48–1992

(Permanence of Paper).

Binding materials have been chosen for durability.

♾ ♻

Library of Congress Cataloging-in-Publication Data

Johnston, Paul Forsythe, 1950– author.

Shipwrecked in paradise : *Cleopatra's Barge* in Hawai'i /

Paul F. Johnston.—First edition.

pages cm—(Ed Rachal Foundation nautical archaeology series)

Includes bibliographical references and index.

ISBN 978-1-62349-283-0 (hardcover (printed case) : alk. paper)—

ISBN 1-62349-283-1 (hardcover (printed case) : alk. paper)—

ISBN 978-1-62349-284-7 (e-book)

1. Cleopatra's Barge (Yacht) 2. Underwater archaeology—Hawaii—Hanalei.

3. Hanalei (Hawaii)—Antiquities. 4. Historic ships—Hawaii. 5. Kamehameha II,

King of the Hawaiian Islands, 1797–1824. 6. Hawaii—History—To 1893. I. Title.

II. Series: Ed Rachal Foundation nautical archaeology series.

DU624.J64 2015

910.9164'9—dc23

2015004800

The Bleeding Edge

I first heard the story of *Cleopatra's Barge* on the first day of my first real job after graduate school, newly hired as curator of maritime history at the Peabody Museum in Salem, Massachusetts, one of the world's foremost maritime collections. I was ushered by a department colleague into a small period room decorated lavishly with dark, exotic woods highlighted in rich red velvet and gold leaf. Small cabinets lining the rectangular room were filled with ancient glass, silver, leather, paper, and porcelain curiosities, and the room itself was a replica of the main salon of the *Barge,* based upon several descriptions contemporary with the vessel's construction in 1816 in Salem (fig. 1.1). Adjacent rooms were filled with ship models, rare furniture, log books from old ships, memorabilia, and beautiful watercolor portraits of those same ships. All the contents of these three rooms—hundreds of artifacts and curios—were related to George Crowninshield Jr. (1766–1817) of Salem, owner of the famous hermaphrodite brig *Cleopatra's Barge* and one of the heroes of this story (fig. 1.2).

The objects relating to the *Barge* were at the museum because they had been removed from the ship before her public auction in 1818 and then passed down to family members or sold off. Over the next 163 years they had gradually made their way into the Peabody's collections, helped in no small part by two proud, dedicated Crowninshield descendants who had cleared out their attics, browbeat their relatives, and closely watched marine art auctions for more than 50 years, snatching up anything to do with their famous ancestors and their large fleet of deepwater trading ships.

As I gradually learned the story of the famous ship—one of the most fascinating and bizarre in our nation's maritime heritage—it sent chills down my spine. I tried to suspend my disbelief at some of the story's less credible turns, but they nearly always turned out to be genuine. It was an authentic tall tale but true, involving such diverse elements as a US president, a pair of Emperor Napoleon's boots, seven lines of Shakespeare, British explorer Captain James Cook's entrails, the respective kings of England and Hawai'i, and the first elephant in America (fig. 1.3).

However, as the story's details began to emerge, much like a Chinese ivory puzzle ball, a gap began to appear. Much was known—and had been published—about the first half of the *Barge*'s life, set mostly in and out of New England. But the second half of her short, eight-year career, prior to her violent loss in 1824, was totally unknown. As I began to investigate the outlines

Figure 1.1. *Filled with authentic furnishings and furniture from the original* Cleopatra's Barge, *this reconstruction of the brig's main saloon was based on contemporary descriptions of the cabin and its contents. Up to 2,600 visitors a day gawked at the luxurious ship as she was being built and fitted out, in a time when people walked or rode horses to reach their destinations. Courtesy of the Peabody Essex Museum.*

of that later phase, which took place in the distant island kingdom of Hawai'i, I learned that this period was equally as strange and exotic as the first.

It was this unknown Hawaiian chapter in *Cleopatra's Barge*'s short-lived but intense career that appealed so strongly to me. For one thing, it was uncharted and unexplored. What might be found in the historical documents left from the period? What might be left from the wreck of the famous ship, and what could it tell us about the material culture of the early Hawaiian monarchy—our nation's only authentic royalty? Almost nothing is preserved from early nineteenth-century Hawai'i (or earlier periods), due to the tropical environment of the Hawaiian Islands and the organic origins of most of their material culture and industries prior to the so-called "discovery" of the Sandwich Islands in 1778 by Captain James Cook of the British Royal Navy.

Further research revealed that not one single artifact existed from the life or reign of the Hawaiian king who had bought *Cleopatra's Barge*—Kamehameha II, nicknamed Liholiho (in formal Hawaiian: Iolani Lunalilo). Son of Kamehameha the Great, who had united the Hawaiian Islands, Liholiho was responsible for the breakup of the royal system of taboos in Hawai'i and for allowing the Christian missionaries to begin their task of religious conversion, changing Old Hawaiian society and culture forever. Yet virtually nothing remained from his brief five-year reign outside the historical legacy, itself written by *haoles,* or foreign traders, seamen, or missionaries. Liholiho's ship and her contents promised to amplify that sparse story and also provide information about early nineteenth-century New England shipbuilding, the origins and development of recreational watercraft in the United States, the transitional historical period between Old Hawai'i and its rapid westernization, and much more.

Figure 1.2. *Oil portrait of George Crowninshield Jr. (1766–1817), attributed to artist Samuel Finley Breese Morse. The portrait was probably commissioned around the War of 1812, when Crowninshield was in his forties. Courtesy of the Peabody Essex Museum.*

Figure 1.3. *The Crowninshields had a family history of eccentric behavior. Dated August 18, 1797, this Boston broadside advertises the first elephant in America, transported by Jacob Crowninshield to New York aboard the family ship* America *in 1796. Jacob reputedly sold the elephant to a New Yorker for $10,000. The broadside invited the ladies and gentleman of Boston to view the female Bengal beast for twenty-five cents. Courtesy of the Peabody Essex Museum.*

Unfortunately, my employment at the Peabody (since merged with the Essex Institute and renamed the Peabody Essex Museum)—the principal source of knowledge about the *Barge*—did not allow more than a sniff around the edges of the subject. For various reasons other research was more important; by the time the subject opened up, it was too late, and I had accepted a position at the Smithsonian Institution's National Museum of American History. However, the *Barge* remained on a back burner as I learned the ropes of the new job and the pleasures and challenges of working within the federal bureaucracy. One of the first tasks I undertook was to familiarize myself with the National Watercraft Collection, whose care I had inherited. Another legacy was some ship wreckage, mainly the power plant and associated machinery from the early Great Lakes steamboat *Indiana,* which the Smithsonian had recovered from Lake Superior back in the late 1970s and pretty much forgotten about since. In all good conscience, I felt obligated to clean up a few of my predecessors' loose ends before I could pursue a new site like *Cleopatra's Barge.* That self-inflicted duty took three years of decompression diving in deep (120 feet), cold (34 degrees) water off Little Lake, Michigan, followed by another year of research and writing (fig. 1.4).[1]

By 1993 the end of the *Indiana* project was in sight, so I submitted a research proposal for *Cleopatra's Barge* upward through the chain of command. It met with little resistance, so I contacted the State of Hawai'i regarding a survey for the wreck of *Cleopatra's Barge* in early 1994. On the basis of earlier experiences elsewhere, I anticipated obtaining a permit through the State Historic Preservation Office and beginning to dive that summer in Hanalei Bay.

The public perception of underwater archaeology commonly embodies a vision of bronzed, swashbuckling heroes diving on shipwrecks in exotic places and recovering massive oak sea chests overflowing with gold, silver, and precious jewelry, all the while fighting off sharks and other denizens of the two-legged variety. However, few of us bear much resemblance to Indiana Jones, and the actual fieldwork of any serious scientific investigation represents only a small fraction—perhaps 5–10 percent—of a real archaeologist's time. The remainder is spent behind a desk either on the telephone, in a library, or blinking at the baleful screen of a computer monitor, and it requires the varied skills and expertise of a professional writer, psychologist, diplomat, detective, surgeon, fund-raiser, general contractor, logistician, cheerleader, and mechanical draftsman. I also frequently exercise the cut-and-paste skills first picked up in preschool and kindergarten. These skills must be leavened with the patience

Figure 1.4. *The steamer* Indiana *was one of the earliest propellers on the Great Lakes. Built at Vermilion, Ohio, in 1848, she was lost in June 1858 off Whitefish Point, Michigan, in 120 feet of 34-degree water. Photograph by Smithsonian National Museum of American History.*

of Job and the persistence of Moses, and it doesn't hurt to throw in a bit of humor as well.

I learned very quickly that my permit application was the first ever received by Hawai'i for a scientific underwater archaeological survey and that consequently there was no procedure in place for processing such an application. Moreover, another underwater scientist wishing to track whales in Hawaiian waters using sonar had just run afoul of environmentalists misunderstanding his methodology, so the state was extremely sensitive to any underwater investigations. As a result, I would need to submit a formal Environmental Assessment for review by twenty-six state and federal agencies as well as the general public, and a separate permit would be required by the US Army Corps of Engineers. In other words, I was required to undergo the same regulatory process for the excavation of a few shallow test trenches in Hanalei Bay's sandy bottom as for the construction of a 500-room hotel on its shores. Moreover, one of the state agencies reserved a year's review period "after receipt of a complete application" and informed me that there were sixty to seventy applications ahead of mine!

A year later I emerged from the process—dazed, amazed, and confused—with five different state and federal permits, one nonpermit, and a total of forty-four discrete conditions for the survey. Among the more interesting—even bizarre—conditions were requirements not to alter the temperature of mile-wide Hanalei Bay by more than one degree Fahrenheit or the bay's salinity by more than one percent. And this round of permits was only for permission to *search* for the wreck—what on earth might be required if we actually *found* something and it warranted fuller investigation?

Hundreds of phone calls, faxes, and letters and an estimated two months of full-time work went into the process, exacerbated by the five- to six-hour time difference and 5,000-mile distance between Honolulu and Washington, DC. It was small consolation to hear from several state agency administrators that my application had set a speed record. Needless to say, we did not conduct the survey in Hanalei Bay in 1994, but I did receive an invitation from the University of Hawai'i to lecture on the Hawaiian permit process, since they were looking into an underwater archaeology program for the future. I was now the world's foremost expert on the topic—however reluctant!

Once all the paperwork was completed, several more important details remained to be addressed: raising funds; finding a research vessel; arranging local accommodations for the dive team; and procuring a reliable air supply for scuba tank refills and other essential supplies for the survey, now rescheduled for July 1995. In the spring of 1995, my wife and I went out to O'ahu for a maritime conference to give the permits presentation. After establishing that no representatives from the state were present in the audience, I gave a fairly graphic portrayal of the trials and tribulations. However, it may have been a bit too realistic, for although it was well received, to date no one else has ever applied to the State of Hawai'i for underwater archaeological excavation permits.

Most of the items on my laundry list were addressed thanks to connections I made through that lecture and others in the state. Captain Richard Rogers of Haleiwa, an avid wreck diver, avocational historian/archaeologist, and pilot for Hawaiian Airlines, volunteered his converted 42-foot surplus Navy utility boat *Pilialoha* (*Circle of Friends*) and a crew of friends and relatives from O'ahu's North Shore for the duration of the project. A cold call from an interested individual in the town of Princeville on Hanalei Bay led to an introduction to the public affairs director at the Princeville Resort (now the St. Regis Princeville) and a generous offer of accommodations for the team. The resort also had a watersports enterprise associated with the hotel willing to provide tank refills at a nominal cost. The Salem Marine Society, dating back to the late eighteenth century and still active, was pleased to support the proposed research on some of its earliest members. My wife and I succumbed to the allure of the Friendly Islands around that time; although we didn't know it, we conceived our first child. All of the rest of the logistics and other plans fell into place relatively easily. However, that may be an oversimplification, for relative to the permit process, anything else connected with the project seemed pretty simple.

Three days before leaving for Hawai'i for the start of the survey, the *Washington Post* announced that the airline on which I had booked my Hawaiian flight had gone bankrupt for the second time. Before departing Washington for Honolulu, I called boat owner Rick Rogers to go over last-minute details. He asked which flight I was taking out there and perked up when I told him. "As an archaeologist, you'll be interested to know that the plane on that flight is one of the two oldest 747s in the world still flying," he said. Although it is generally true that for an archaeologist the older something is, the more interesting, I was not reassured.

First Season

We boarded the research vessel *Pilialoha* twelve hours after my arrival on O'ahu in July 1995 for the twelve-hour voyage to Kaua'i. After she was blessed by a local *kahuna,* sprinkled with sea salt and adorned with fire ginger flowers fixed to various parts of her anatomy with duct tape, *Pili* weighed anchor for the largest stretch of open water in the Hawaiian Islands. The ever-optimistic crew set out fishing lines along the way, and we arrived twelve hours later with two yellowfin tuna that had struck the shotgun lines simultaneously (fig. 1.5). In fact, we arrived lighter than we had left, for the winds and waves robbed us of a sleeping bag and other supplies that went over the side in the high seas. The following morning we offloaded *Pilialoha* and set her up for the survey by wiring in the electronic gear needed for the remote sensing equipment. Along with our black box technology, we had a reliable historical source to guide us in our search for whatever might remain of the shipwreck.

Written in May 1824, missionary Hiram Bingham's eyewitness account of the ship's unsuccessful salvage clearly stated that she had sunk off the mouth of the Waioli River, right near the beach in Hanalei Bay. Presuming the presence of considerable ferrous metal aboard and having been assured by a local marine scientist (who will remain unnamed) that Hanalei Bay's subfloor was not magnetic, I had selected a proton precession magnetometer as the black box of choice, since it measures fluctuations in the earth's magnetic field (such as those caused by magnetic metal). After setting up the mag, we began towing its underwater

Figure 1.5. Pilialoha *beneath a typical Hanalei summer afternoon rainbow. The research vessel is a converted surplus US Navy harbor craft of Vietnam War vintage, which Captain Rogers built into a sportfishing and dive boat. Photograph by Smithsonian National Museum of American History.*

Figure 1.6. *Crewman Mike Reid holds the magnetometer head out of the water to recalibrate for the next tow. This part of the device is towed at the end of a long tether by the boat, and it registers anomalies in the earth's magnetic field caused by metal objects like cannon, iron anchors, cook pots, and the like. At the other end of the tether is the black box operated by Steve James; the box converts the in-water signal into a graphic readout documenting the magnetic fluctuations. Using this technology and Reverend Hiram Bingham's 1824 eyewitness description of the wreck location, we were able to locate the yacht in two days. Photograph by Smithsonian National Museum of American History.*

sensor back and forth across the bay at 50-foot intervals the morning after Independence Day (fig. 1.6). Archaeologist and mag wizard Steve James, whom I had imported from Memphis, Tennessee, to conduct the remote sensing, noted that his instrument went haywire as soon as it received power. After deducting Steve's jet lag from the equation, checking the instrumental calibration, scratching our heads, and muttering numerous multinational phrases of considerable color, the operative characteristic of the malfunctioning instrument was attributed to the indicated presence of background metal in the bay. A few phone calls to some new geologists subsequently confirmed that the entire island of Kaua'i was formed of magnetic basalt and that there was a strong concentration around the north end of the island at Hanalei Bay! This new and unsettling information, combined with relief that his expensive instrument was not malfunctioning, permitted Steve to filter out the background noise sufficiently to read minute magnetic fluctuations, and small targets or "hits" began to emerge almost immediately—clustered right at the spot referenced by Bingham.

Coincidentally, one of our telephone contacts, marine biologist Tom Reed of Honolulu, had just bought an underwater metal detector and was looking for a testing and calibration site, so he flew with it and another operator out to Kaua'i and set it up in parallel with the magnetometer. Sure enough, in a blind test his instrument indicated targets at precisely the same spots as the magnetometer, so we began to reel in his sensor, 50 feet away at the end of its tether to the boxed instrument on our research vessel. Just as the sensor was approaching the boat, a wave pushed it against the stern, and some slack in the tether got caught in the propeller. Before we could cut engine power, the prop sliced through the line and lost the business end of his shiny new and expensive toy in 45 feet of water (fig. 1.7)! Luckily, we heaved a buoy overboard to mark the spot and found the unit just as the light was fading later that same afternoon.

Once found and confirmed, targets were further isolated by manually swimming the mag sensor around each hit and dropping a buoy where the signal was strongest. Each target was then logged into a GPS system and ground-truthed, or visually inspected. In addition, the surrounding reef was visually surveyed by the dive team. In most cases, the signal source was visible, usually turning out to be modern debris such as a reef anchor, piece of tin roofing, steel sign post, or the like, left behind by the 1991 hurricane Iniki. If nothing was visible on the sandy bottom, then *Pilialoha* was anchored directly overhead on a four-point mooring, and a propeller-wash deflector nicknamed *Kai Puhi* (*Sea Blower*) was lowered into place over the target. At this point, the boat engine was turned on at low rpm, and the sand overburden covering the target below was gently scoured off under diver supervision (fig. 1.8).

The prop-wash deflector, also known as a mailbox, is a controversial tool in archaeological excavations, as it was first developed by treasure salvors and is their most heavily used tool for blowing sand overburden off a buried ship-

Figure 1.7. *In a remote location, redundancy can be very useful if something goes wrong. Tom Reed of Honolulu had just purchased a new generation magnetometer for his survey company, and he wanted to test it on a known anomaly. It worked well in Hanalei until the tether was severed by the propeller while backing up. Suddenly an expensive new instrument was lost in 45 feet of water, as the late afternoon was darkening into evening. A quick-thinking crew member tossed a buoy over the side to mark the location, and the mag was retrieved pretty quickly, to everyone's relief. Photograph by Smithsonian National Museum of American History.*

wreck. Essentially, it is a hollow tube with a 90-degree angle that fits over the propeller of a vessel, directing the prop wash straight downward, where it blows away the sand (and anything else in its way). The topside vessel must be securely moored on several points so that it does not move around while the deflector is operating and so that the elbow can be precisely moved to widen or deepen a trench as needed by tightening some lines and loosening others. It is not commonly used by archaeologists as it can be too powerful, blowing cultural material as well as sand out of its path. However, if used carefully, it can dust the overburden away and be shut off when cultural artifacts emerge from the bottom. I could think of no other practical way to remove several feet of overburden, or shifting sands on the bay bottom, that wouldn't alter the topography of the most highly protected classification of public waters in the country, Hanalei Bay. So we obtained a design from another archaeologist who had needed it in the past and tested the device that Rick Rogers built over the winter of 1994–1995 very gingerly at first. Other tools, such as water dredges and airlifts, were more commonly used when the sand covering a site feature was measured in inches rather than feet or yards. For example, against the shallower areas of sand against a sloping reef, the boat could not be backed in safely, and airlifts and dredges were used to excavate the overburden.

We had permission from the state to recover diagnostic artifacts, defined as items that would verify the date and identity of the particular wreck we were seeking. Right from the start of the first test trench, cultural material began to emerge. As expected, however, much of it was modern. The prevailing winds in Hanalei Bay are northerly for nine months out of the year; during the summer, the winds shift and easterly trades blow in. Since we were working in shallow water near the sandy beach in the southwestern corner of the bay at a

Figure 1.8. *Named* Kai Puhi *(Sea Blower), the prop-wash deflector is a shroud that drops down over the boat propeller. The 90-degree elbow directs the prop wash straight downward to remove sand overburden from the wreck features. The boat is on a six- (or more) point mooring like a spider in the middle of its web, so it can be moved around precisely to direct the flow exactly where needed to reveal the site feature below. We limited engine rpms to 1000 for ten minutes at a time to ensure that nothing was damaged or washed away. Photograph by Smithsonian National Museum of American History.*

Figure 1.9. *At first, CON454 appeared to be a short section of broken barrel hoop, but as more pieces emerged of similar size and shape, broader examination revealed that it was an iron adze, heavily oxidized. As the original iron oxidized in the salt water, it bonded with the surrounding sand into a concrete-like object (hence the term "concretion" for this artifact type). Photograph by Harold Dorwin, Smithsonian National Museum of American History.*

little notch in the coral reef, anything and everything ever dropped in the bay would eventually work its way over to our area. In addition, we were working at the mouth of the Waioli River, so anything dropped in the river upstream also would eventually find its way into our survey area.

Both organic and inorganic artifacts from the past two centuries were recovered from the twelve test trenches opened at the wreck site during the 1995 survey. Among the organics were bone, rope, and wood; inorganics comprised ceramics, copper fasteners and hull sheathing, lead patching, glass, ballast stones, and concretions.

Concretions are frequently among the most interesting finds from any underwater archaeological site. They form when iron objects left underwater for any period of time begin to oxidize—the underwater equivalent of the rusting process. The iron oxide, which melts away the surface of the artifact, bonds with the surrounding sand or anything else in the vicinity, forming a hard crust over the original artifact and usually protecting it from further deterioration (fig. 1.9). They frequently contain several objects, and if a delicate artifact was originally deposited beside an iron one, it can be preserved almost perfectly. Sometimes the original iron object is completely oxidized, in which case it leaves a perfect mold of itself that can be cast in epoxy for an exact replica of the original.

After the trenches were excavated and mapped in, they were all backfilled at the end of the season—one of the permit conditions. The backfilling was accomplished with a surplus fire hose and a trash pump; not

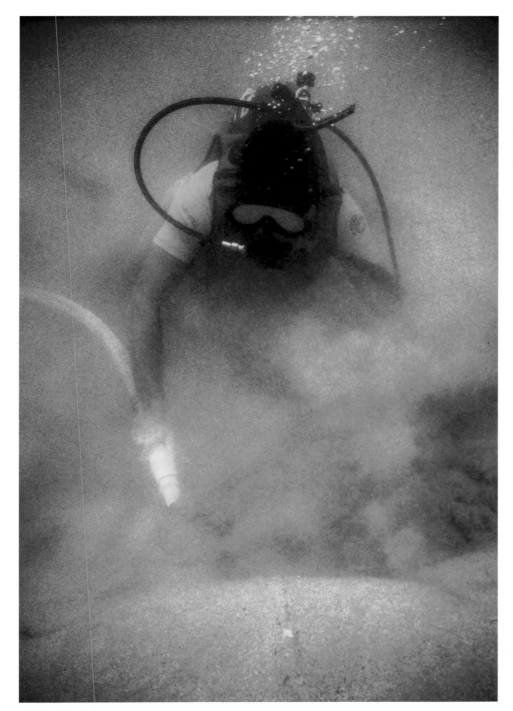

Figure 1.10. *At the end of each field season, our permit required the backfilling of any open trenches. Normally the trenches backfilled themselves naturally within a day or two, but sometimes they needed some help. Here, archaeologist Steve James has donned an extra 20-pound weight belt to compensate for the thrust of the water jet. The hose is directed at the base of the trench to undercut the walls and make them collapse into themselves. Photograph by Smithsonian National Museum of American History.*

only did it restore the bay bottom to its original condition, but it also covered the wreck with sand, enhancing preservation and preventing curiosity-seekers from collecting souvenirs (fig. 1.10). We did not find any of the ship's hull, nor had we expected to. The historical sources were agreed that the wood was teredo-ridden from as early as 1844, and three tsunamis, Hurricane Iniki, and the dynamic surf zone in which the wreck lay also argued against the preservation of hull fabric.

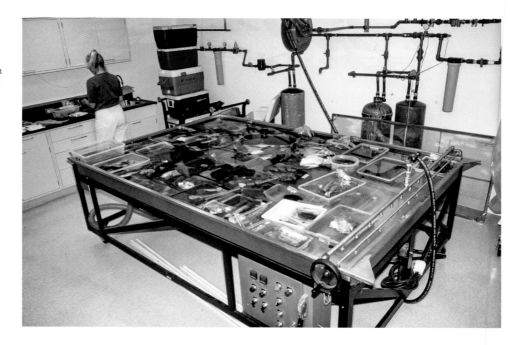

All the artifacts except the ballast stones were shipped back to Washington, DC, for photography, preliminary conservation, cataloging, and desalination (removal of salts from the bay water in which they had soaked for over 170 years). If a waterlogged artifact is simply allowed to dry out without any treatment, the salt in the seawater will crystallize and break apart the object. The artifacts were desalinated using deionized water in an immense stainless steel washing machine with precise temperature and agitation controls, originally acquired for washing the First Ladies' gowns prior to exhibition (fig. 1.11). After the salts had been removed, the real research began.

The concretions with unknown contents were all x-rayed to see what was inside, and other finds were subjected to batteries of scientific tests to ascertain their content and structure. The more complex concretions containing multiple artifacts were sent to the underwater conservation laboratory at Texas A&M University for further treatment (fig. 1.12).

Of the pottery recovered in 1995, only one sherd was contemporary with the wreck (fig. 1.13). Five Chinese brown stoneware sherds (from at least three containers) may be from the wreck, although such wares were made from the eighteenth century well into the twentieth. Similarly, other ceramic sherds were only partly diagnostic, since they also underwent long production runs. A partial brick was originally believed to be ballast or part of the cookstove lining, although another, likelier use emerged later. The presence of Chinese wares was curious and warranted further research, for we had expected to find primarily Euro-American pottery due to the prevalence of these traders in the Hawaiian Islands during the period under investigation. Of the glass fragments, only one—a dark green body sherd with air bubbles from a Dutch

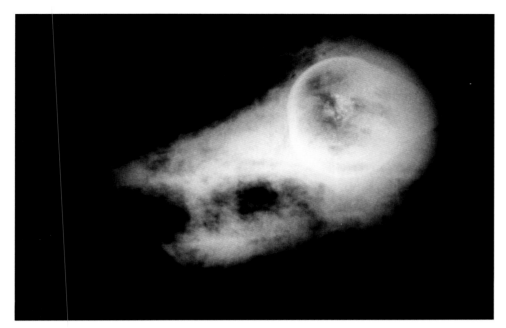

Figure 1.12. *The contents of this x-ray of CON44 were a puzzle that wasn't solved until it was removed from its outer concretion. Looking like the bulb of a turkey baster, it turned out to be the glass bulb from a sandglass or "hourglass." For the final and complete conserved object, see fig. 4.13. Photograph by Hugh Talman, Smithsonian National Museum of American History.*

case gin bottle—dated to the wreck. The remainder (including modern beer and soft drink bottles) were all from a later period.

The sixty-eight concretions recovered that first season revealed a variety of objects through x-ray and mechanical reduction; nearly half turned out to be modern barbed wire, sections of pipe, chicken wire, or other grating/fencing material. These are almost certainly remnants of the 1992 hurricane Iniki, and in fact one of the divers found a large unused roll of rusty barbed wire on the shore on the eastern side of the bay while hunting limpets for dinner one afternoon. Among the more significant concreted finds were a folding (pen) knife, some elements of the ship's rigging, and a two-tined fork of a style that actually predated the wreck by around forty years. Several concretions preserved the forms of various sorts and sizes of ship hull fasteners, ranging from square iron spikes to round metal nails and wooden treenails of various dimensions.

Coincidentally, one flattened concretion contained a thin lens of zinc carbonate (hydrozincite), mixed with smithsonite—the mineral named after James Smithson, founder of the Smithsonian Institution (see fig. 4.72). Hydrozincite is the whitish main ingredient of calamine lotion, used to treat poison ivy. However, there is no poison ivy in the Hawaiian Islands, so it is not clear what artifact this material represents. Three pieces of folded flat sheets of lead patching were re-

Figure 1.13. *This modest, seaworn sherd of annular pearlware or creamware with three brown stripes (CER004) is contemporary with, or possibly even a bit earlier than, the 1824 wreck itself. Photograph by Eric Long, Smithsonian National Museum of American History.*

covered during the survey, ostensibly unused due to the absence of fastener holes or wear marks.

Approximately sixty-seven stones were recovered from the test trenches, ranging in size from 0.7 to 15 oz. Included were granite, tonatite gneiss, quartzite, quartz-bearing breccia, gabbro, limestone, mafic gneiss, granite gneiss, mylonite gneiss, blue schist, tolonite, and basalt. With the possible exception of the last two, all are non-Hawaiian, according to analysis by the Geology Department at the University of Hawai'i, indicating that they were ballast from the wreck site. The blue schist is of particular interest; it is known to originate from only a few places globally, one of which is in the area of Rio de Janeiro. Since the *Barge* made a merchant trip to Rio shortly after she was auctioned in 1818 and before she was sold to Liholiho in 1820, this stone is likely a souvenir of that 1818–1819 voyage.[2]

Two copper hull fasteners also were recovered; one was a bent drift (a long bolt fastening together the major framing timbers), and the other was a long, barbed, chisel-pointed spike that turned out to be for fastening the copper hull sheathing to the outer wooden hull of the ship. Both are almost pure copper. Ten pieces of copper hull sheathing were recovered in various degrees of preservation, ranging from intact to tiny fragments, and most of the larger ones were badly crumpled. This material was used on ship bottoms starting in the late eighteenth century to prevent fouling and penetration by teredo worms. The accounts of such revered explorers as Columbus and Magellan are packed with descriptions of the damage caused to their ships by the voracious teredo, and Columbus lost all four of the ships in his fourth and final voyage to the Western Hemisphere because of the "underwater termite."

In all but a few of our sheathing samples, both interior and exterior surfaces were uncorroded. Another's original 14-inch width was also intact; in its lower right corner of the external surface is preserved the two-line stamp: "W&G/G 24" (fig. 1.14). This 24-gauge copper is of British sizing; before and after the War of 1812, most of America's copper sheet, including Paul Revere's, was purchased from the English either in Bristol or Liverpool.[3] Research indicates that the source of our stamped piece is the Liverpool copper merchants Williams & Grenfell & Co. and that it came from the midship section of the royal yacht. Elemental analysis (x-ray fluorescence and scanning electronic microscopy) of seven of the sheathing samples by the Smithsonian's Conservation Analytical Laboratory (CAL) indicated two different sources or batches for the sheathing, which were almost pure copper (± 97.5 and ± 98.5 percent).

These twisted pieces of copper sheet are the principal evidence for what happened to the ship after she wrecked—the site's "postdepositional history" in archaeological jargon. Virtually all of their edges were punctured with nail holes, through which copper fasteners were driven to attach the sheets to the wooden hull. Significantly, the holes in most pieces were all intact, indicating that they were not torn off the wood but instead fell off it before being battered, twisted, and scoured against the surrounding reef and broken coral at

Figure 1.14. *Several pieces of Haʻaheo's copper hull sheathing were marked with the "W&G/G 24" stamp; this is HS99. Williams & Grenfell were Liverpool (England) copper merchants who had supplied copper to such luminaries as Paul Revere, but they slowed export to the United States drastically during the War of 1812 to avoid aiding the enemy. Photograph by Harold Dorwin, Smithsonian National Museum of American History.*

Figure 1.15. *The pleated or accordioned exterior surface of this nearly intact sheet of copper hull sheathing (HS001) indicates that it was literally scraped off the wooden hull planks by friction against the reef that sank the ship. Photograph by Eric Long, Smithsonian National Museum of American History.*

its foot. This could only have happened in one way—if the teredo worms had consumed the hull planking first (fig. 1.15). Otherwise, the nail holes would display evidence of tearing, as would have happened if Hanalei's 1824 salvors had stripped off the copper for reuse or if powerful wave action had torn it off.

The little nail holes in the copper sheathing tell us even more. They tell us why we found so little of the most famous yacht in history, and during the winter of 1995–1996 they also offered the most compelling reason to return to the site and complete its investigation quickly, before it was lost forever. Commonly, the hull of a wreck is preserved at least to the waterline, even in shallow shoreside conditions such as Hanalei Bay's. This degree of preservation holds the artifact assemblage in a discrete spot, generally relatively intact. However, without the protection of her hull, *Ha'aheo*'s contents dispersed against the surrounding reef, where they mixed with modern cultural material. Now all the mixed-up pieces of the puzzle were being ground into pepper, and this is why we wanted to excavate the *Barge* as soon as possible, before her remains were totally destroyed. In addition, the wreck and its contents represented the only material remains from King Liholiho's reign; as such, they were unique and promised an otherwise unparalleled view into his times and culture.

Six pieces of bone were recovered during the 1995 survey, including an intact button, the lower mandible of a pig (*Sus scrofa*) more than three years old, and domestic dog (*Canis familiaris*) bones. Contemporary Western sources relate that dog and pig were common dietary elements of the Hawaiians and that pigs also were popular pets among the chiefs.[4] However, the maturity of the pig jaw indicated that it was from a pet rather than a food source, as a three-year-old pig was probably too old for eating. Three other bone fragments were cow (*Bos taurus*); this was unexpected, as beef was not part of the Hawaiian diet at this time. The reason for beef bones among the wreck contents would emerge through later research.

Two short segments of three-strand rope were found in a disassociated context; another short strand was found wrapped around an iron thimble, or sail corner reinforcement. Unfortunately, too little cellular structure was preserved to ascertain what the rope fragments from that first season were made of, and this proved the case for all later rope finds as well. Despite the lack of cellular integrity, it is presumed that the rope was made of sisal or hemp, as those were the main materials of rope from this period.

Aside from the artifact work described above, research had to reveal whether the artifacts believed diagnostic in the field actually were so. This involved dozens of letters and phone calls to specialists in various fields ranging from chemists to bone, pottery, lithics (stone), and ceramics specialists. Fortunately, many of these experts are employed at the Smithsonian, but others were farther afield.

Archival research began on several fronts that first winter after the discovery and survey of the *Barge* wreck. For example, we began to develop a set of design drawings for the *Barge* and her theoretical interior arrangements, which the written sources clearly state were unique. However, since no contemporary plans for the vessel exist, we joined its layout from contemporary paintings and drawings of her and similar vessels with educated guesses based on the few contemporary written descriptions of her deck and interior arrangements. However, these accounts were written by tourists and not ship experts, so reconciling their descriptions was challenging and difficult (fig. 1.16).

As mentioned elsewhere, none of *Ha'aheo*'s hull was found in 1995. This

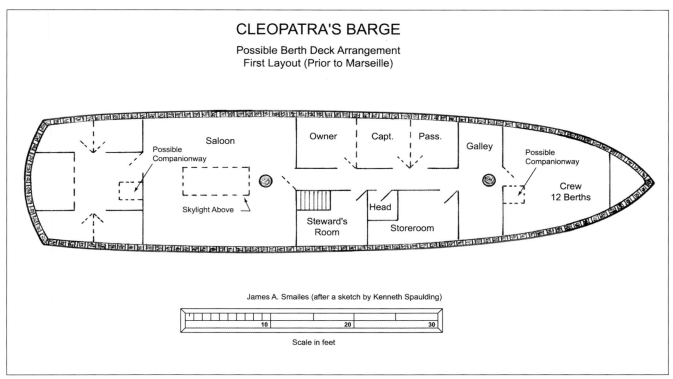

CLEOPATRA'S BARGE

Possible Berth Deck Arrangement
First Layout (Prior to Marseille)

James A. Smailes (after a sketch by Kenneth Spaulding)

Scale in feet

Figure 1.16. *Hypothetical belowdecks plan of the* Barge *in 1817. The layout is based on the few existing journal entries recording various family members or tourists visiting the* Barge *while under Crowninshield ownership; there are no extant plans or a construction contract. See also fig. 2.4. Drawing by James A. Smailes for the Smithsonian National Museum of American History.*

was one of the principal research opportunities we had hoped to pursue, for almost nothing is known of oceangoing ships of the period. The absence of hull remains was extremely disappointing, and when first returning from the survey, I believed that there was not enough left of the famous craft to warrant further field investigations. However, several factors favored a decision to return to Hanalei Bay for another season.

Foremost among these was the harsh environment in which the wreck lay, right at the shoreline in the heavy surf break. This wave action is particularly strong during the winter months, when the waves build all the way from the Arctic before crashing onto Hanalei's beach. The tsunamis and hurricanes endemic to the region also have exacted their toll, along with the shipworms that consumed the ship's wood. If we did not return to the site, there would be an excellent chance that, in a few years, bad weather and local wave action would totally destroy anything at all that remained of the yacht. In addition, it was possible that sport divers, after learning of the vessel's location through our efforts, might attempt to seek souvenirs of the royal Hawaiian yacht.

As a result of these and other factors, I decided to apply for permits to excavate the wreck in 1996. Consequently, I submitted a report of the 1995 survey activities that autumn and applied for another round of permits in the winter to excavate another round of twelve trenches. Getting the second round of permits was much easier than the first ones, and planning and fund-raising occupied much of the spring.

My wife and I had a son in early December, and ten days later the entire federal government shut down. This was actually convenient, as it allowed extra time to help with the new baby. Since he had been conceived around the time of the Hawaiian conference the previous spring and a *kuhina* had blessed the unborn child and urged us to give it a Hawaiian name, his middle name became Kai, which means "sea" or "ocean." A day or two after the government reopened for business, Washington was clobbered with a heavy snowstorm that kept everyone in the city away from work for another week. I got to know my son pretty well, and my wife better.

Second Season

"Hey Paul, you better strap on a tank and come see this," said Steve James, one of the project archaeologists and an incurable practical joker. At the time I was cold, wet, and hungry, having just struggled out of my dive gear after a long morning on the bottom of Hanalei Bay. I didn't know whether to believe him, but something in his tone prevented any questions. Anyway, he hadn't waited around to chat before ducking underwater again. Moreover, we had just started a new trench at a spot directly on the edge of the reef struck by the royal yacht on 6 April 1824, and Steve was the first diver in the trench.

Resigned, I fetched a fresh tank, shrugged into the 30-pound buoyancy compensator and tank combination, belted 16 more pounds of lead around my waist, grabbed the underwater camera, spat in my mask, and giant-stepped into the bay. I was already plotting heinous revenge if Steve had pulled my leg again. Cold before, I shivered anew when I settled on the bottom and saw inside the new trench below. Steve hadn't been kidding, and he was urgently hand-fanning sand from the rapidly collapsing sides of the shallow, conical depression to expose his discovery. A single glance confirmed that my principal research hypothesis for the shipwreck, two years in the making, was totally invalid. And it was a thrilling discovery!

For the first three out of the four weeks of the 1996 excavation, the surface of the bay had been too choppy for Captain Rick Rogers to back RV *Pilialoha* in close to the reef. As a result, we had been forced to set trenches away from the reef edge in the vicinity of the 1995 trenches. Thus far, the finds had pretty well mirrored the 1995 survey artifacts, and we were resigned simply to find more of the same. In fact, the most exciting event of the entire season had been witnessing the failed attempt of a car on the beach one Saturday night to jump the mouth of the Waioli River and watching the resulting formation of a new local wreck site (fig. 1.17). However, the heavy chop vanished during the last week, leaving a flat, glassy surface on the bay's waters. Rick carefully backed and moored *Pili* within eighteen inches of the jagged edge of the reef, which is only five feet under the water surface.

Hindsight, as they say, is twenty-twenty. In retrospect, perhaps I should have expected something unusual in the last trench of the season. For one thing, archaeological lore is filled with such tales, wherein spectacular discoveries found on the last day of a dig season must be covered over and left

Figure 1.17. *The combined police forces from the towns of Princeville and Hanalei met at the site of a wrecked car in the water on the beach to marvel at an example of adolescence gone awry trying to jump an old car across the Waipa River mouth. Photograph by Smithsonian National Museum of American History.*

unexcavated until the following year. In addition, our penultimate trench, which had been opened nearby, had yielded something most unusual in the form of a large, long strip of leather. An inordinate amount of ceramics and glass also had appeared in trench E11.

So I dropped down onto the sandy bottom of Hanalei Bay next to Steve and shook my head in disbelief, for there at the bottom of E12 was an immense jumble of massive hull timbers poking up out of the sand, much like a hyperactive kid's game of pickup sticks (fig. 1.18). There must have been a dozen of them, jammed against and actually under the coral reef itself. It was a shock, since all of the evidence uncovered at the site to date had told us not to expect much in the way of hull remains. Kicking up to the surface, I collected some underwater tapes and slates, slipped new sheets of drawing plastic into them, and we set to work recording and photographing the freshly exposed finds. Halfway through the next day, the downpour began.

Normally, rain has little effect on diving operations. However, these were not normal rains. In a little over an hour a foot of rain fell, flooding the entire eastern side of Kaua'i. The Waioli River swelled up like a recently fed snake and blew out the sandbar across its mouth, dumping tons of fine red and brown silt into the trench and totally obscuring its contents. That afternoon, it was so dark underwater that I got lost at the bottom of E12 and had to abort operations for the day. Time was running out, and we still had to backfill all the trenches over the next three days. The next day, while hand-fanning sand off a timber at the bottom of the trench for photography, a fragmentary piece of red-and-black painted wooden furniture emerged from the silty ooze. Nearly all of its edges were eroded away, but enough remained to verify its overall size and manifest fragility.

It was just too much to handle. Rick dashed off a measured sketch of the delicate find while I shot some photographs, and we were forced to cover it back up

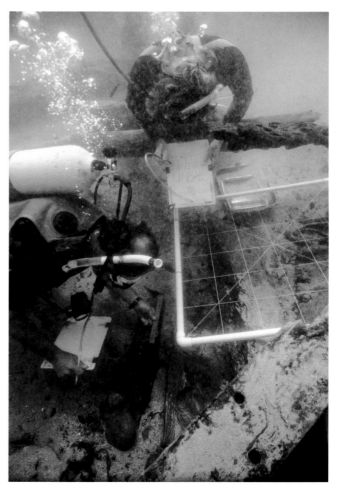

Figure 1.18. *Tom Ormsby (top) and Rick Rogers measuring and drawing the bow timbers in trench E12. These were the first large structural ship timbers found on the wreck site. Photograph by Smithsonian National Museum of American History.*

with a couple of buckets of sterile sand and fill the trench back in. Despite the temptation, there was not enough time to excavate it safely, and it was just too fragile to risk recovery this year.

We spent the last two days of the 1996 field season recovering our moorings, securing *Pilialoha* for the open-water passage from Hanalei back to Oʻahu's North Shore, and backfilling the trenches. The latter is a relatively mindless activity, wherein a diver straps an extra weight belt of at least 20 pounds around his waist, drops like a stone to the bottom of a trench, and spins in slow spirals around the trench while directing a fire hose against its walls, collapsing them inward upon themselves. There is little to see and plenty of time to think, so long as you avoid entanglement in the long, high-pressure hose and avoid reflecting on the tiger shark's documented interest in turbulent water. I started thinking about the furniture piece we'd found and then reburied.

First, it and the hull remains indicated that there was far more left of King Liholiho's yacht than we had believed only a few days earlier. Second, it had a story of its own to tell, if only we could figure it out. Were we excavating in the bow or stern of the storied ship? Was it a table, bed, bench from the crew area, or a chair from the king's cabin? My imagination soared — could it be the actual throne of King Kamehameha II, mute witness to so many of the seminal changes in Old Hawaiian culture during his short but eventful monarchy? One of the fundamental tenets of archaeological fieldwork is that it can pose more questions than it can answer.

That winter, we got to work in the lab. Rick Rogers sent six big, drooling coolers of artifacts back to me in Washington, where they were rid of all their salts. Whenever these coolers were sent from Hawaiʻi and moved around the museum, I was accused of throwing a party and not inviting my accusers. Lolly Vann, a graduate student in underwater archaeology at East Carolina University, was busy in the lab cleaning, sorting, and conserving the more durable artifacts.

The laboratory is a story in itself, for I was loaned a corner of the costume and textile conservation center downstairs in our basement. Along one wall is an immense washing machine that can control regular and dry cleaning times to a second and their temperatures to a fraction of a degree. Over in my corner is a big 6 × 9 ft. stainless steel tray table with agitation controls in two dimensions and two-zone water and spray microprocessor controls. It is in this device that such delicate items as the First Ladies' gowns are washed and treated, and in which all the wet, smelly artifacts from the bottom of Hanalei Bay were first inspected, rinsed, desalinated, photographed, measured, and cataloged. The largest of the concretions were x-rayed out at the CAL. Paint samples were taken from the leather for analysis.

Just before Christmas 1996, ship reconstructor J. Richard Steffy of Texas A&M University foolishly told me he was coming to the Washington area over the holidays to visit his family, and he was kind enough to offer some observations of the hull timbers on the spot. A few weeks later, archaeologist

Susan Lebo from the Bishop Museum in Honolulu made the same mistake and suffered the same fate: she donated a half day to inspect the ceramics and glass finds. Hawaiian and New England archives were asked to send along copies of their relevant holdings; a highlighted find was the original logbook of the 1820 voyage of *Cleopatra's Barge* from Boston to Hawai'i under Captain John Suter. And various federal and state agencies headquartered in Hawai'i and Washington, DC, were contacted to find out about permit renewals for another season in Hanalei.

At the end of our second season of operations, I was faced with a growing list of questions. Would one more year complete the fieldwork and provide answers? The discovery of portions of the hull at the reef, along with the furniture fragment, were unexpected and most welcome finds; nothing observed on the site up to that point had indicated that such features would be preserved in the wreck's dynamic littoral environment. Equally significant was a small assemblage of Native Hawaiian artifacts emerging from the royal yacht, particularly in light of the extreme rarity of material culture directly attributable to the early Hawaiian monarchy. More research would offer further insights into the significance of these and other finds from the 1996 season. As a result, I decided to apply for state and federal permits for at least one more season of excavation.

Third Season

Over the winter, excavation permit renewals came through in record time and the project was well on track, but there was concern on a more personal front. My father had been feeling poorly and had gone into the hospital for some tests in the late spring. The results were not encouraging, and he decided to go into the hospital for some exploratory surgery just as I left for Hawai'i. I went to Connecticut and spent a week with my parents before we flew out. Moreover, I was hearing from Hawai'i that the initial excitement of finding shipwrecks and beginning excavations was beginning to wear thin on the volunteer boat crew from O'ahu's North Shore, and fewer were signing up for the 1997 season than before.

A few days later we were all settled into our expedition headquarters, an embarrassingly opulent house on the Princeville golf course, overlooking Hanalei Bay. Two years earlier I had expressed some concern to the project sponsor, the Princeville Resort, which had donated use of the house—decorated throughout in white—to our project, but I was reassured that it would otherwise be unoccupied (fig. 1.19). By now I had learned not to expect to begin work before the fifth of July, as the boat crew enjoyed partying over the holiday on the previous day. We spent the first day setting the perimeter buoys around the reef edge and setting up the "spider web" over the wreck site. This arrangement, wherein the boat was fastened to as many as nine moorings, allowed it to be precisely moved anywhere on the site to deflect the prop wash precisely onto a particular spot on the wreck. This year there was an extra six

Figure 1.19. *Princeville house and freshwater rinse facility. One of the most critical factors in the success of an underwater expedition in a remote location is maintaining the working gear in good condition. Each day, after ten hours in the salt water, our dive gear needed to be washed thoroughly at headquarters. Photograph by Smithsonian National Museum of American History.*

Figure 1.20. *Captain Rick Rogers performs a float test on the tender* Pili‘iki, *prior to loading on the crew and motoring out to the research vessel anchored in the bay. Photograph by Smithsonian National Museum of American History.*

feet of sand overburden accumulated over the site against the reef as the result of heavy winter storms and surf. There also were new crew both on the boat as well as among the archaeological staff, and it took several days to work into the routine of diving. Project stalwart Steve James had stayed back in Memphis this summer, as his wife Amy was due to have a baby in late July, so I recruited two new archaeologists, Tom Ormsby and Lolly Vann, to fill his place. Tom was a terrestrial archaeologist employed next door at the National Museum of Natural History, and Lolly was an East Carolina University grad student with experience in fieldwork and conservation of underwater finds.

A typical day began by driving down to the beach at the foot of the sugar pier in Hanalei Bay by 7:30, with a pickup of food and ice at the supermarket en route (fig. 1.20). Generally the small boat was already onshore, with the crew filling water jugs, making phone calls, or taking showers. We then would load food, ice, scuba tanks, and people into the small boat for one or more runs out to *Pili*. Once aboard, there would be a short meeting to go over the day's plans, followed by a five-minute ride to the site on the other side of the mile-wide bay. The small boat would leave early, pick up the main bow mooring, and hand it up on deck for securing. Then it would run the other mooring lines out to the mooring buoys, after which we would crab the big boat over to the spot chosen for that day's work by hauling in on some lines as we let out others. Once the boat was secured, the divers would suit up and *Kai Puhi* would start blowing, normally for ten minutes at 1,000 rpm. This would go on all day, with the divers going down, recording, photographing, and recovering any finds uncovered by the shifting sands at the bottom of the trench. The centers of the trenches and any significant finds were triangulated from benchmarks or datum points—short stainless steel posts driven into the reef—so they could be entered onto the site map. We normally stopped work a bit after 5:00, drove home via the supermarket for the evening's dinner or the dive shop to fill tanks, followed by a shower, swim, nap, or whatever. Few were awake past 10:00 p.m., excepting only on the one day off per week (Sundays). On Sundays the crew usually went touring, fishing, or surfing around Kaua'i, slept, had a beach barbecue, or wrote postcards.

The first area we excavated in 1997 was the area last seen during the prior season—trench E12, at the reef's edge where we had found the timbers and leather piece at the end of the previous season. Immediately we hit a problem, caused by the extra sand overburden. *Kai Puhi* did not generate enough thrust to push the sand up and out of the trench; instead, it formed a ridge or berm on the top rim of the circular trench that effectively trapped the sand inside. Extra power was applied gingerly, but ineffectively. As soon as the blower was turned off, the steep sides of the trench immediately began to slump or fall in, covering the bottom and preventing excavations from exposing any new wreck features. A water dredge was hastily assembled, lowered over the side, and started, but its volume was inadequate to move the sand any faster than it was backfilling by itself. Captain Rick finally thought up a means by which the berm was blown off with a fire hose and high-volume water pump before resuming the deflector, but it took considerable extra time to rig and deploy this device each time the berm grew high enough to restrict sand removal.

Then, midway through the season, *Pili*'s engine started knocking. It took an entire day to diagnose and repair the problem—a loosened flange between the diesel engine's transmission and the prop shaft that was not only letting the shaft flail around in its stuffing box but also letting seawater into the bilges. During the resultant idle time one of the *Pili*'s crew told one of the archaeologists a bit too much about his recent background for comfort. A word to the captain resulted in one less mouth to feed; unfortunately the lost crewman had been enthusiastic, hard-working, and experienced around boats. Around that same time, the daily routine was broken by a morning visit out to the boat from local resident and writer Michael Crichton, his wife, and some friends. That same afternoon a local boatman took two of us out to the mouth of the bay to try to relocate and record a large stockless anchor hooked on a coral head in 45 feet of water. Tradition attributed it to *Cleopatra's Barge,* and I had seen and photographed it in 1994 during a reconnaissance visit with two University of Hawai'i marine biologists working in Hanalei Bay (fig. 1.21). It was a good candidate, about the right size for a *Barge*-size ship, measuring 9 ft. 5 in. long with a 5 in. thick shank and 3 ft. 7 in. long arms with 1 ft. 7 in. flukes. However, we were unable to relocate either it or an anchor chain we had promised to find in payment to the boatman for taking us out to the anchor. A wasted afternoon, made worse by an incident at the end of the workday as we were leaving *Pili* for a ride to the beach. We loaded six empty scuba tanks, five people, and assorted gear into the small boat and were headed ashore when the driver suddenly gunned the engine. Down went the bow of the little boat,

Figure 1.21. *Large stockless anchor lodged beneath a coral head 59 feet deep in the Hanalei Bay anchorage. Missionary Samuel Whitney said that the parting of the* Barge's *anchor cable was one of the causes of the ship's loss, but unfortunately there's no way to link this anchor to the royal yacht. Photograph by Alan Friedlander, Fisheries Ecology Research Lab, University of Hawai'i.*

Figure 1.22. *People often brought artifacts that they wanted some help identifying to the shipwreck lectures. Usually someone could help, but this bronze item found on a beach on Kaua'i's south shore was a mystery. Photograph by Smithsonian National Museum of American History.*

which promptly swamped. "GET OUT!" ordered the captain, and everyone dutifully abandoned ship, very nearly causing another shipwreck in Hanalei Bay in full view of all onlookers on the beach and water. There was more trouble later that day—best forgotten—but the small boat engine never was the same after that.

Toward the beginning of the third week, my mother called to say that my father was fighting a losing battle; my sisters were with her when he died at home on the 23rd. I shut down diving operations and laid out work for the crew for a few days. My wife stayed behind in Hawai'i with our son; I flew back to Connecticut, helped with the funeral arrangements, and returned to Kaua'i a few days later, having lost a father, friend, mentor, and my biggest fan.

By that point there were only a few days left in the season, and that was when we always had the most visitors. Family, friends, journalists, Hawaiian television stations, students from the University of Hawai'i, interested locals, and others came out to the *Pili* and toured the finds; snorkelers were able to watch us work below. We excavated for a few more days and then backfilled the trenches, pulled the site buoys, stowed the boat gear for the journey home, and finished cataloging and packing the artifacts over the last couple of days. We had the final cookout on the beach at Hanalei, overlooking the site. Sponsored by the Kaua'i Historical Society, I presented the season's finds at a lecture at the Hanalei School, and that is always fun as we take along a large bucket of artifacts from the site for a show-and-tell. The questions at the end are the best part (fig. 1.22), and this year there were lots of kids from the school itself, who had actually set up their own website for the wreck.

Packing the artifacts at the end of the season was the last thing we did each year. First, all the artifacts were sorted into types, and it was a good chance to review the season's finds. We had spent ninety-nine hours underwater during the 1997 excavations, and most of that time was spent recording the hull timbers we had found this season and the previous year. Although we had permission to open twelve trenches, in 1997 we dug only three, and one of them had been a leftover from the previous year. One reason for the shortfall was the extra sand that had accumulated over the site during the winter before; removing this extra overburden from each trench slowed us down considerably. In addition, we had found a large number of small finds this season, the recording and recovery of which took more time than in prior seasons. And finally, my absence for nearly a fifth of the project on account of my father's death had meant that diving was curtailed for that period.

Figure 1.23. *The artifact coolers containing the finds from each season were carefully packed, partially filled with brackish water, caulked shut, and sealed with duct tape to keep the moisture in. Back at the museum in Washington with a Hawaiian tan each summer, presenting the coolers as containing artifacts and not Hawaiian fish fillets or beer was a hard sell. Photograph by Smithsonian National Museum of American History.*

The finds were carefully packed into coolers for shipment to Washington. This was a ticklish process, as the express mail service had a 75-pound weight limit per container (fig. 1.23). And as Rick Rogers had discovered in 1995 when trying to send the first batch of artifacts back to DC, shippers did not appreciate sending wet, drooling coolers on their expensive planes. A casual conversation with the shipping clerk revealed that the company had been involved in an expensive and drawn-out lawsuit over a human heart shipped once in a leaky cooler. The fluid had leaked out, which not only destroyed the heart but also damaged some of the electronics aboard the plane. So we drove the dozen or so coolers to the Lihue airport, and as fortune was smiling on us, we pulled into the freight depot right after the floor had been washed. We carefully set the coolers into the middle of the largest still-drying puddle, hoping to camouflage any leaks.

Once back in Washington, the artifacts were desalinated, further cataloged, and photographed. That fall I took the concretions and wood samples out to the CAL for x-rays and wood-typing respectively. Microbotanist Harry Alden set to work analyzing the wood samples, and in the process I remembered the seeds we had casually put into a film container during the fieldwork. While he was looking at them under the microscope, senior furniture conservator Mel Wachowiak strolled by and did a double-take at the two small, nondescript round objects with stems. He checked more closely and declared that they were not seeds, as we had thought, but beads and that furthermore he saw gold on them. It turned out that they were gilded beads that would have been set into something like a picture frame or bulls-eye mirror from the early nineteenth century, just right for the period of the wreck (fig. 1.24). Mel went on to describe their manufacturing method: first the beads were turned on a long line separated by the little stalks. Then they were separated and coated with an adhesive. A sheet of gold leaf was floated in a bucket of water, and the bead

Figure 1.24. *When these two tiny wooden artifacts were recovered, they were initially described as seeds. While we were looking at them more closely for analysis at the Smithsonian's Conservation Analytic Lab, furniture conservator Mel Wachowiak recognized them as wooden beads. Under a microscope, traces of their original gilding was visible, making this the first gold discovered on the wreck site. The beads probably decorated a bull's eye mirror or other artwork frame. Photograph by Hugh Talman, Smithsonian National Museum of American History.*

was twirled between two fingers from below, up and into the gold leaf, which covered it completely. Then the gilded bead was glued into its final resting place in the picture frame or mirror. It was the first gold we had found on the wreck, and although there wasn't much left of the precious metal, it was exciting to find it nonetheless.

The following fall and winter were spent preparing a report of the summer's work and findings for the Army Corps of Engineers and the State of Hawai'i—one of the major conditions of our permits. Time also was spent in preliminary artifact research whenever it was available. More questions arose, but one of the biggest concerned the hull of the ship. Were there only a few timbers left, jammed against and beneath the reef that had caused the wreck in the first place? Where was the rest of the hull? Had it simply vanished from salvage, teredo damage, 170 years of winter seas and storms, the three recorded tsunamis that had hit Kaua'i's North Shore in the recent past? Another year of excavations were called for, and I broke the news to Rick around the new year.

Fourth Season

The 1998 season started a bit differently. When archaeologist Tom Ormsby and I showed up at Washington National Airport early on the Fourth of July for the first leg of our journey out to Hawai'i, Tom went inside and was told that TWA had canceled the flight; this created a bit of low-level panic. However, a brief chat with the airline personnel resulted in a taxi voucher over to Dulles for a flight to St. Louis leaving at exactly the same time as the one from National. Even with the extra travel we made the flight in plenty of time. TWA went bankrupt not too much later and no longer exists.

As soon as we arrived at the Lihue airport on Kaua'i, we picked up the rental car, loaded our gear aboard, and drove up to the Princeville Hotel to pick up the house keys. This year the usual house was in use by resort hotel VIPs for the first two weeks, so the hotel had arranged for a nearby smaller house for the first half of the season. Captain Rick, a crew of five, and *Pilialoha* arrived later that evening, just in time to grill the fish they'd caught on the passage and participate in the Independence Day celebrations in and along the shores of Hanalei Bay. Rick brought along his father for the first time.

Fortunately for us, Mr. Rogers cared little for boat work; as a retired executive with the Boy Scouts of America, he turned out to be an excellent cook, and he plied his culinary skills for the onshore project crew for a week before returning to his job as a state park manager on O'ahu. The next morning we set buoys and moorings for the excavation as usual. We met Sunrise Nitrox Divers owner Richard Neumann to borrow his spare emergency oxygen kit. Even though we were diving in very shallow water on this site, oxygen is required on all Smithsonian diving projects, and Richard was kind enough to loan us his spare DAN unit so we wouldn't have to empty one, lug it out, and refill it on Kaua'i.

Steve James showed up this season with a six-month-old son to keep his wife and teenage daughter busy. Diving began a couple of days after our arrival on Kaua'i, and we quickly discovered that the winter had been very good to us, putting very little sand overburden onto the wreck. This in turn meant there was less sand to move, making the digging easier and far more efficient. On the other hand, the first half of the season was very rainy; this not only affected morale but also the underwater visibility. Early one morning after about a week, a pod of around twenty dolphins entered the bay looking for an easy breakfast, and they stayed around long enough to escort us over to the site before moving on. A few days later Steve earned his berth by coming up from a dive and noticing that the *Pilialoha* was oriented in a new position. It turned out that she had broken her main mooring line and was slowly dragging on the smaller lines, gradually being blown closer and closer to the reef. Lots of shouting resulted in the small boat running a new line out to the main mooring buoy, and all was well again.

My wife, son, and in-laws arrived on the 17th, and that afternoon I drove into Lihue to help pick them up. Luckily, I had been humping full scuba tanks for the past couple of weeks in preparation for their arrival, so all that baby paraphernalia seemed much lighter than it normally had back on the mainland. For some reason, 20 July was an especially dangerous day that season. Loyal crewman Don Pace began by walking the plank, quite literally walking off the side of the boat while focused on coiling a heavy line. Later that day, Tom became a poster boy for looking around as a diver ascends to the surface. Distracted by what he had found during a long dive, he ascended without looking up and attempted to leave an impression of the top of his head on the bottom of the small boat. The impact made a very distinctive, unforgettable sound, as did Tom himself when he finally managed to break the water surface.

Few on the mainland know it, but Hawai'i has the highest per capita consumption of Spam in the country, probably on account of its relatively low cost. Perhaps not coincidentally, Hawai'i also has the highest relative number of welfare recipients in the nation. Since we rotated food duties, one night I dusted off and prepared an old family recipe from World War II—Spam, spinach, and egg casserole—one which, incidentally, had won me the prize of least expensive meal in my first excavation season as a graduate student. Despite some creative remarks from the crew about its content, there were no leftovers, and one crewman even left the *Pilialoha* for the first time in several days to sample the cuisine.

At the start of the last week we held a press conference at the Princeville Hotel, at which the divers were introduced and the season's finds displayed. It was well attended, and all proceeded smoothly. At one point, a Hawaiian

Figure 1.25. *Hanalei Bay survey post, used to mark shoreline lots in the 1920s. How one ended up offshore in the middle of Hanalei Bay is a mystery. Perhaps an unhappy beachfront lot owner wanted to rearrange his property line? Photograph by Smithsonian National Museum of American History.*

in Old Hawaiian costume came out of the back door of the room and blew a long note on a conch shell, or *pu*. None of the journalists turned around for the first blast, but they did for the second. It was a terrific photo opportunity for one of the artifacts we had recovered earlier that week: a shell horn or trumpet, complete with tonal hole that we were calling "The Royal *Pu*." The photograph of a Hawaiian blowing the shell overlooking Hanalei Bay where it had been found made the covers of all the state's largest newspapers.

That afternoon a couple of the television reporters came out on the boat with us to film the project at work; one of them was kind enough to share her last meal over the side with the local fish. While excavating a new trench in the middle of the site, we discovered and recovered a heavy concrete post, 30 in. long and $4\frac{1}{4}$ in. on a side, with an "X" on one end. This was a baffling discovery, solved by a call to Wagner Surveying in Hanalei. It turned out to be a property marker that had been set along the shore of the bay and the Waioli River back in 1920 (fig. 1.25). How it made its way into the center of the wreck site, a few hundred feet offshore, was mute testimony to the dynamic power of nature's forces working in the area. According to Wagner, a few of the markers were still in place on the shore and beach area of the bay.

On the last day of July, I lectured again at the Hanalei School to a full house. Although they had not asked any questions, two men stayed afterward and asked me to come out to their car in the parking lot. I was curious at first but then upset when I learned that they had been snorkeling around the site after hours and had picked up a few pieces of wood from the wreck that they wanted me to look at. After advising them that no one but us had permission from the state to recover artifacts, they willingly surrendered their finds with profuse apologies.

Things took a turn for the worse the very next day. *Kai Puhi* self-destructed by breaking a chain and jerking one of its spars out of the fiberglass shroud; luckily no one was hurt when it whipped off its mount on the swim step and banged against the stern. With our main excavation tool out of commission, we decided to start backfilling the trenches a bit early. So we broke out the water pump and fire hose, but the pump's casing cracked after only a short time, spewing cold bay water against the engine housing and cracking that also. So we started to break down and stow the gear in preparation for the long voyage back to Oʻahu's North Shore. While moving *Kai Puhi* around from the stern of *Pili* to the bow, it dropped on a crewman's finger, bloodying it. After mooring, we began offloading our dive gear from the boat, and in washing it back at the house later that afternoon a fundamental part fell off my buoyancy compensator, rendering it useless. All in all, a day of massive equipment failure, fortunately all on the last day. Rick took it as a sign that we were finished with excavations on the site and began telling that to all who would listen. Our total bottom time that season was 177 hours.

Figure 1.26. *Angel Spielman's Hanalei Bay cake, complete with blue bay water, our research vessel* Pilialoha, *and the shipwreck. Photograph by Captain Richard W. Rogers.*

The next day was Sunday, our day off, and we celebrated the season's end with a big cookout at the Princeville house of project friends Debra and Rick Drayton. Temporarily underemployed the prior summer, Rick had volunteered much of his free time that year for the project, and Debra had kept us well supplied with her remarkable cooking in gratitude for keeping her husband occupied. Boat cook Angelique, one of the more unusual characters Rick had recruited from O'ahu's North Shore, had prepared an immense sheet cake for the event, decorated with a scale image of Hanalei Bay complete with a rainbow, the *Pilialoha* anchored onsite, waterfalls down the mountains in the background, dolphins in the blue water, and more (fig. 1.26). There was even a miniature wreck in the middle of the cake, with broken chopsticks for the hull frames. A dozen or so friends also contributed to the party, and we took the boat crew down to the vessel late that evening. They left early the next morning for O'ahu.

Later that day, Tom and I had a scare while we were preparing the bucket of artifacts for show-and-tell at the last public lecture. The conch shell horn, or *pu,* was missing! The last time anyone had seen it was at the Hanalei School lecture the other night. A quick call to principal Nick Beck yielded an invitation to visit the school, talk to the custodial staff on duty, and look around, without any luck. At that point I called the state archaeologist on Kaua'i, Nancy McMahon, to let her know of our loss. She suggested we keep looking and file a police report just to go on record with the authorities about the problem. We did that and despondently began cataloging the last of the finds and packing them up for shipment back to the mainland.

Normally, the process of cataloging the artifacts was a long, occasionally boring but generally interesting process overall. As they were recovered from the site trenches, the artifacts were placed into buckets marked with the trench number. Then each object was measured, described, and entered into the master artifact catalog. The catalogers were the first to really study the objects and see trends or patterns developing in the excavation trenches as the objects were closely inspected and written up (figs. 1.27 and 1.28). We also had archaeological ceramic expert Susan Lebo from the Bishop Museum and glass experts Steve Gould and Celeste Le Seur come over to Kaua'i from O'ahu nearly every year to examine their respective artifact types and assist

Figure 1.27. Artifacts were set in buckets of salt water on site and cleaned superficially. Their buckets corresponded to the findspots in each trench. Each day, the finds were transported to the shore where they were inspected, documented, measured, and put in half salt and half fresh water to initiate desalination without shocking the artifacts. Here Rick Rogers is sorting and inspecting at the buckets at the house before cataloging. Photograph courtesy of Captain Richard W. Rogers.

with the general listings. Since we found nearly 250 concretions in 1998, we had to go to Walmart and buy some more large seventy-gallon coolers (for a total of thirteen that year). In the process of filling them to distribute the weight evenly among them, we discovered that one of us had transferred the conch horn into one of the other coolers. So that mystery was solved, though it raised the vexing question of whose memory was so derelict that he couldn't remember moving the conch—to the exclusion of all else in the bucket—from that container into another one.

One other problem developed at the other end, back in Washington. Although we had overnight express–shipped a total of thirteen coolers from Kauaʻi on 5 August, only twelve had arrived by the 8th. One was missing, and in the process of emptying them out and placing their contents into a freshwater bath for the first stage of desalination, it became apparent that some of the Hawaiian artifacts were in the missing cooler. I called the shipper and provided the shipping label number and a description of the cooler. I also explained that the contents looked like rocks but were actually the property of the king of Hawaiʻi, conveniently omitting that the artifacts were stored in several inches of forbidden water (if it hadn't already leaked out). I checked into the shipper's website, watching the progress of our coolers across the country. They had all stopped in Long Beach, California, en route back east, but no. 8 had not been checked out of that airport. "I'm sorry, sir, that's not how we trace our misplaced shipments. Please wait while we investigate this matter further."

A week passed with daily calls; however, still no cooler, and I had to catch a ferryboat on the other side of the country to an even smaller island than Kauaʻi. Finally, after a full ten days, the cooler showed up, and guess where it resurfaced? That's right—Long Beach! Luckily for me (but unluckily for the artifacts), the bay water had dried up so that the artifacts were still damp within their wet packing towels, but they were no longer submerged. This meant that the shipper was willing to continue no. 8's cross-country marathon. The final outcome was that the contents were all present and undamaged; the sole consolation was the shipper's agreement not to charge for shipment of that container.

We found our first human remains in the third season, and their presence could have caused a slowdown at best, a shutdown of the excavations at worst. Whenever human remains are found on a Hawaiian archaeological site, work is usually stopped until the site can report to the burial council, which decides the method of disposal and other issues. However, the wreck site was

Figure 1.30. *Mauna Ala, the Royal Mausoleum, overlooking downtown Honolulu. Before the Christian conversion of the Hawaiian monarchy, the bones of the* aliʻi *or high chiefs were commonly burned of their flesh, and then the skull, arm, and leg bones were buried in secret or sacred places. Specific burial practices varied from island to island. Photograph by Smithsonian National Museum of American History.*

transported—and the chronology of the second chapter in her life had taken on some breadth, depth, and shape—a life of its own. I lectured on the 1998 and earlier finds a few times on Oʻahu and Kauaʻi, renewed some acquaintances, and the last morning hiked at sunrise to the top of Diamond Head, overlooking the shore and city of Honolulu. I also tried hard to convince Rick that another—final—season was required, and asked him about leasing his boat and crewing it myself. While I did not extract a commitment from him for another season's excavations by the time I left, he did promise to think about it.

The Final Season

Over the following winter I did manage to convince Rick that his boat was needed for another season—with or without him. He decided that he would take only two weeks' vacation, work with us for that period, and join us on weekends, leaving the boat in our hands for two weeks. This was fine, as all we were doing each day was driving the boat a half mile, mooring, and then turning on the engine every few minutes. Some of the volunteer crew even might have enjoyed it! However, a few other problems surfaced the spring before our final season.

Figure 1.31. *Mauna Ala, the Royal Mausoleum. Many of the most important chiefs in Old Hawaiʻi found their final resting place at Mauna Ala. Liholiho and his wife Kamamalu are buried here, along with twenty-one other members of the royal family. Photograph by Smithsonian National Museum of American History.*

Two weeks before the team was scheduled to convene in Hanalei for the excavation season, all of the discretionary funds at the Smithsonian back in Washington were frozen. This included most of the money I used for the project, and it was the precise point in time when I had finalized the boat charter, obtained the requisite insurance waivers, and ordered traveler's checks for the season's food, fuel, supplies, and other expenses. And suddenly I had no money.

There were also some issues with the permits. As always, I had sent in applications to the various appropriate local, state, and federal agencies at the end of January. Then I tracked them very carefully, ensuring that they were received and processed. By the last month before departure, all but one—from the US Coast Guard, traditionally the easiest of them all—were in hand. The permit I needed was to place a few buoys around the site perimeter and thus notify the local *Notice to Mariners*. It seemed that the Coast Guard had not received the original application, so I faxed another immediately. That one vanished, too, as did the next copy. Finally, however, the fourth one took, and I secured a verbal permit in time for the season to begin. Just a week before departure, through the grapevine I learned of yet a new permit needed, and this one had teeth: it was a local anchoring permit for which the County of Kaua'i reputedly wanted $180. I decided to take care of this one when and where necessary, rather than in advance.

Thankfully, the flight out to Hawai'i was uneventful this year, and the usual routine of picking up the oxygen kit and house keys, checking in with the boat, celebrating the Fourth of July with the crew, setting mooring and site buoys, relocating the reef markers, shaking down the small engines, and so forth kept us occupied for the first two days. This season, the plan was to simply test the outer fringes of the site, along with a few inside spots, to ensure that we had not missed anything. One of the site moorings broke on the first day of use, sending *Pili* toward the reef. Totally ignoring the divers under the boat for nearly a half hour, the topside crew finally managed to get the situation under control, but not without Captain Rogers falling overboard in his zeal to handle the situation. The earliest finds of the season were the usual sort of things: rusty barbed wire concretions, some modern beer bottle glass, and a few copper fasteners. Unique were a pair of pierced cowrie shells, which the Hawaiians used for octopus lures by poking a stick between the two holes and dangling a bit of ribbon or feather at the ends as an item of curiosity. When dangled before an octopus lair, they lured the occupant out and around the lure, whose line was then jerked up.

Sundays were our day off, and on the first one, a few of the crew took scuba tanks off to a wet cave on the road to Haena and went diving in it to check out a local legend of buried treasure. Tom was reacquainting himself with his fiancée, who had just flown in for a visit, and I went over to the Princeville Hotel to check in at the dive shop and inspect a site on the hotel's grounds that the island's archaeologist had said might be appropriate for the reburial of the human bones we had found in 1998. The following day Tom took the day off to go to Princeville with his bride-to-be for a wedding license; crewman Bob MacMillan returned from an O'ahu surfing contest with a sixth place in the "Weekend Warrior" category, and we were told a story of tiger sharks in Hanalei Bay by a local. We had noticed that very few swimmers were in the water the first few days we were out there, and asked project supporter Mike Reid why. It seemed that a few days before our arrival a fishing boat had come into the bay and set a net for some baitfish. Then the boat left, apparently forgetting to recover the net. The net did its job, filling with lots of tasty baitfish, and an enormous group of tiger sharks had come in and camped out in the bay to feast on the bounty. A call went out from the Coast Guard to the fishermen urging them in no uncertain terms to retrieve their nets, and the beaches had been closed until the sharks left. Of course, we didn't hear this story until we had already been diving for four days—luckily without incident. That evening, I called home and learned that my mother was back in the hospital for tests, the air conditioning had quit in our house, and our eldest son had been bitten by a friend's little brother. I went to bed late that night of a fairly typical day, trying to shake off feelings of déjà vu from the summer of 1997.

The next several days were rainy. It is hard to describe the effect of this sort of weather on a project like ours, for which the entire purpose is to become—and then to remain—wet for long periods of time. I probably wouldn't get much sympathy anyway, so suffice it to say that anything more than a light morning misting followed by a brilliant rainbow is pretty unusual in Hanalei for this time of year, and anything more than that tends to dampen spirits and everything else in its way. Leather shoes and belts are transformed into mold-blotched lumps overnight.

The next several trenches, all along the reef edges outside of where we had last found artifacts, did nothing to raise our communal mood, as they were either empty or absolutely typical in the amount and nature of their content. Actually, this was a good sign, as I was constantly reminding the crew. The best indication that we had found everything there was of the royal yacht would be to dig empty trenches for the last two weeks of the season.

Then, about midway through the season, things changed. It began with the setting of a trench along the side of the reef, but well outside the area where we had found anything, a bit south of the artifact-rich area. We came upon a rectangular wooden box sunk into a large bed of black river-rounded stones sprinkled with randomly scattered whole bricks. The entire lot was cemented into place by a black substance with a sandy surface, rendering the whole into a giant concretion. At first, the box appeared to be empty with only the bottom showing, but closer inspection revealed that its top was actually in place, but crushed flat into the bottom. Even closer examination indicated that what we had thought was the top actually must have been the bottom, for there was no sign of a lid, clasp, or hinge to be seen on the upper, visible surface.

That same day, I came up around midday for some air and lunch. While stripping off my wetsuit, I heard a faint noise from the general vicinity of the engine cover that sounded like a handful of crescent wrenches rattling in a box. I reported it to the captain, who shut down the engine, lifted the cover, and sent Robert below into the hot, confined, greasy space abaft the engine. There he found a problem in the stuffing box, where the propeller shaft pierced the hull. It seemed that the bolts holding the box together had backed out from all the sustained engine and shaft vibration, allowing water to gush into the bilges of the boat. This explained the presence of gradually increasing amounts of bilge water, and also accounted for why the sump pump had kept working more and harder over the past few days. Both of these gradual changes had been noticed earlier in a philosophical sort of way, but a root cause not sought until now. Anyway, the repairs, restuffing, and resealing of the stuffing box assembly occupied most of the rest of the afternoon, and the underwater wooden box below had to wait another day, leaving that evening to inflame our imaginations as to its contents. The lightweight construction of the box left no doubt in my mind that it was not a strongbox or treasure chest, but I did nothing to disabuse the other crew members and divers of the idea that it might contain treasure—the layman's fantasy was too powerful.

Tom and I dove the next morning; as he measured and drew the box, I excavated it. Carefully removing the bottom, inside I found the box filled with sand. Aside from a silt slightly darker than the surrounding sand at the top (which was not the bottom), there was nothing in it beyond a small piece of charcoal and a sliver of green glass. This, however, did not disappoint the crew topside as much as I had thought it would when I broke the news to them after the dive. I guess it was a little like a lottery ticket, in which the fantasy of winning and spending all that money is far more rewarding than the reality of losing. Anyway, after recording and photographing the box, we backfilled it and covered it with a plastic container covered with rocks to prevent it from being damaged by *Kai Puhi*.

Moving southward from the wooden box toward the shore, some interesting new finds began to appear. Foremost among these was a line of vertical timbers tight against the reef (fig. 1.32). After four seasons, we were all so conditioned to the belief that nothing of the ship's hull was preserved that at first I thought that something like a section of wharf or some telephone poles must have washed in and lodged against the reef face. However, the regularity of the timbers' size and spacing, as well as their increasing numbers, soon indicated otherwise, and the presence of a sizeable section of the ship was confirmed by a test along the outside surface that revealed horizontal planking along the outer sides of the vertical timbers as well as copper hull sheathing fastened to the outside surface of these hull planks, or strakes. These sheets of copper were identical to the pieces we had found all over the site, but this time they were fastened to the timbers instead of floating free.

At the same time, some interesting new sorts of small finds began to appear in our trenches, including an intact copper gunpowder flask; a round disk of glass that turned out to be a deck light (a horizontal window set into the deck to admit light below); a red checker (board game piece) and the copper top of an inkwell-like object with a beautiful Greek meander pattern circling its lip. A bone clothing button also emerged, as well as two large flat fine-grained basalt stones with worked surfaces that turned out to be grinding stones for

*If you want to know how Religion stands at the Islands
I can tell you—All sects are tolerated but the King worships
the Barge.*

— Charles B. Bullard to Bryant & Sturgis,
  1 November 1821

A Million Pounds of Sandalwood

Built at Salem, Massachusetts, in 1816 by Retire Becket for George Crownin-shield Jr., the hermaphrodite brig *Cleopatra's Barge* occupies a unique spot in maritime history as the United States' first oceangoing yacht. Costing nearly $100,000 to build and fit out, she was so unusual that up to 2,600 visitors per day visited the vessel even before she was completed.[1] Her owner was no less a spectacle.

George Crowninshield Jr. and the Origins of *Cleopatra's Barge*

Even to the Crowninshields, renowned throughout the region for going their own way, George Jr. was a bit odd. Unburdened by much of a formal educa-tion, the eldest of five sons worked in his father's shipping firm in Salem, ship-ping out as a captain by the age of twenty. However, he preferred shore duty and gradually took over the construction, fitting out, and maintenance of his family's considerable fleet of merchant ships, carefully grown from successful privateering during the Revolution and subsequent international trade under the new US flag (fig. 2.1). In his leisure time, George drove his custom yellow horse-drawn carriage around Salem (fig. 2.2), embarked upon several lifesav-ing missions at sea (for one of which he won a medal), recovered the bodies of US military heroes from the British after a famous naval loss in the War of

Figure 2.1. *Crowninshield's Wharf in Salem, Massachusetts, as depicted in 1806 by artist George Ropes Jr. The family ships* America, Belisarius, Fame, Prudent, *and* John *are tied up along the wharf; another of their vessels is hove down for repairs at the head of the wharf near three pump makers and a smithy. Courtesy of the Peabody Essex Museum.*

Figure 2.2. One of George Jr.'s great pleasures was tearing around the town of Salem in his little yellow curricle, or two-horse cart, as shown in this detail of Ropes's portrait of Crowninshield's Wharf. Courtesy of the Peabody Essex Museum.

1812, dressed in flashy clothing of his own design, and generally behaved in a fashion quite at odds with his diminutive stature, portly proportions, and local perceptions of good taste.

Despairing of his sons ever getting along and mindful of the Jeffersonian Embargo of 1807 preventing international commerce from US ports, in 1809 George Sr. dissolved the firm of George Crowninshield & Sons. His fleet resumed privateering during the War of 1812, fielding (among others) the ship *America,* also built by Retire Becket and the single most successful privateer in that conflict (fig. 2.3).[2] He died in 1815, leaving his three surviving sons wealthy and idle.

Soon afterward, George Jr. headed down to Becket's shipyard in the northeast corner of Salem Harbor and ordered up a radical new vessel: a private yacht. At the time, the concept of a ship built for pleasure was unknown on the western side of the Atlantic, where ships were built solely for trade or war, and the yacht attracted considerable local attention. The new ship was a hermaphrodite brig, square-rigged on the foremast and fore-and-aft rigged on the main, and with a hull modeled after the Crowninshields' privateer *America.* No expense was spared, and the final product cost an astonishing $50,000 to build and another estimated $50,000 to fit out and furnish in the high style demanded by the owner, who planned to live aboard his private yacht as well as sail in her. Initially named *Car of Concordia,* the brig measured 83 feet in waterline length and 100 feet on deck, half an inch under 23 feet in breadth, and 11 feet $5\frac{1}{2}$ inches deep and weighed $192\frac{41}{95}$ tons (fig. 2.4). Crowninshield built her using the finest materials available, and he incorporated several innovative ideas he had developed while managing the family fleet into *Car*'s fittings, capstan, rigging, and other features. She even had plumbing, as noted by one of her distinguished Mediterranean visitors.[3] Her lavish furnishings included custom silver, glass, and china services (fig. 2.5), and her interior decor rivaled that of the wealthiest homes, stimulating several contemporary descriptions (fig. 2.6).[4] Her exterior was distinguished by a herringbone paint scheme on the port side and multicolored horizontal stripes to starboard; a life-size painted wooden Indian on deck; velvet-served quarter-deck lines; considerable gilding; and the latest patent windlass, pump, and rudder technology. In November, immediately after receiving her passport autographed by Secretary of State James Monroe, the ship was renamed *Cleopatra's Barge* (fig. 2.7). The reason for this was never revealed but may have been due to a reading of some lines from William Shakespeare's romantic tragedy *Antony and Cleopatra:*

The barge she sat in, like a burnish'd throne,
Burn'd on the water: the poop was beaten gold;
Purple the sails, and so perfumed that
The winds were love-sick with them; the oars were silver,
Which to the tune of flutes kept stroke, and made
The water which they beat to follow faster,
As amorous of their strokes. (02.2.191–197)

George Crowninshield's love of a spectacle was displayed as he launched the *Barge* on Monday, 21 October 1816, fully rigged and with all sails set (figs. 2.8–2.10). That winter was a harsh one in which Salem Harbor iced over, and while waiting for open water George entertained the admiring crowds with rides in his boat, perched atop a sleigh, out to the *Barge* for tours and other entertainments. Finally, on 30 March 1817, all conditions—personal and meteorological—were adjudged adequate for departure, and *Cleopatra's Barge*

Figure 2.3. *George Crowninshield Sr.'s War of 1812 privateer* America, *painted by the famed French watercolorist Anton Roux. Cut down a deck or razed from her days as a merchant vessel,* America *became one of the swiftest and most successful privateers of the War of 1812. The eighteen-gun ship took twenty-eight prizes in her first three privateering voyages. Built by Salem shipwright Retire Becket in 1804,* America *served as the model for* Cleopatra's Barge. *Courtesy of the Peabody Essex Museum.*

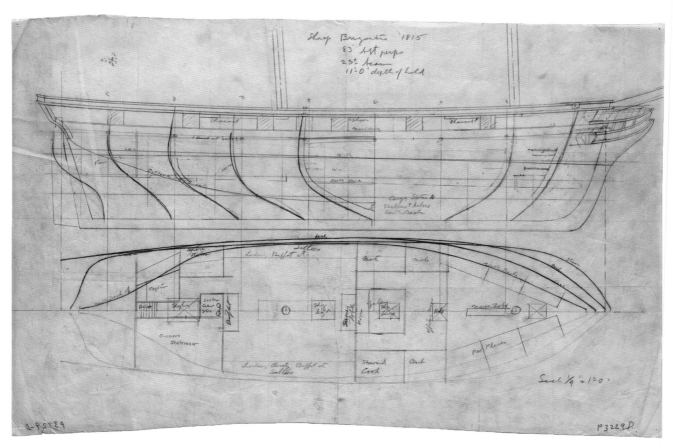

Figure 2.4. *Naval architect Howard I. Chapelle drafted a preliminary and hypothetical set of lines and belowdecks arrangement for* Cleopatra's Barge *in the early 1950s; they were never finalized into an inked drawing. See also fig. 1.16. Courtesy of the Peabody Essex Museum.*

Figure 2.5. Barge *owner George Crowninshield Jr. commissioned custom china and silver services just for his private yacht. Some of the ship's original Sheraton Fancy chairs are on display in the Reception Rooms of the US Department of State in Washington, DC. Courtesy of the Peabody Essex Museum.*

Figure 2.6. *George Jr.'s stateroom aboard the* Barge *was not especially opulent, as shown by its comparatively modest contents. This is not a formal reconstruction of the owner's quarters, but it does contain original stateroom furnishings. Courtesy of the Peabody Essex Museum.*

cleared Salem on a voyage of pleasure "To one or more ports, places, cities, islands, townes, boroughs, villages, bays, harbours, basins, rivers, creeks, lakes, inlets, outlets, situated in the known world, between the latitude of the Cape of Good Hope, and the artic [*sic*] Circle, once or more times."[5] Accompanying the owner were more than 300 letters of introduction from the likes of James Monroe, Admiral Sir Isaac Coffin of Britain, and Commodore William Bainbridge. Also aboard were George's yellow cat Pompey and a crew of fourteen men and boys (fig. 2.11). Among the latter were George's cousin "Sailor Ben" Crowninshield as master, along with the captain's footloose son "Philosopher Ben" Crowninshield (figs. 2.12 and 2.13). Two African Americans—the steward and the cook—also signed on. In a bizarre foreshadowing of Hawaiian things to come, cook William Chapman claimed that he had sailed to the Sandwich Islands with Captain James Cook and later settled there. One day it was revealed by a neighbor that shortly after Captain Cook's death on the Big Island, he had been wandering through the woods when he came upon the freshly slaughtered entrails of a pig. After cooking and eating them, he learned that they were actually Captain Cook's intestines.[6] Altogether, the crew was an unlikely, quixotic, and colorful group of individuals, and shortly after the *Barge* cleared Salem, George's sister-in-law Mary Crowninshield wrote of them rather candidly: "I am sorry—but they may appear better abroad than at home."[7]

Despite the *Barge*'s boundless sailing plan, she headed straight for the Mediterranean. To the alarm of the crew, the Atlantic passage and sailing directions were guided to no little extent by the owner's dreams. Over the next six months, she visited fifteen ports, undergoing a series of unparalleled adventures and misadventures (fig. 2.14). One day in Barcelona, a crowd of 8,000 "genteel and well dressed people" was so intent on inspecting the "wonders of Cleopatra's Barge" that "several fell overboard at the foot of the

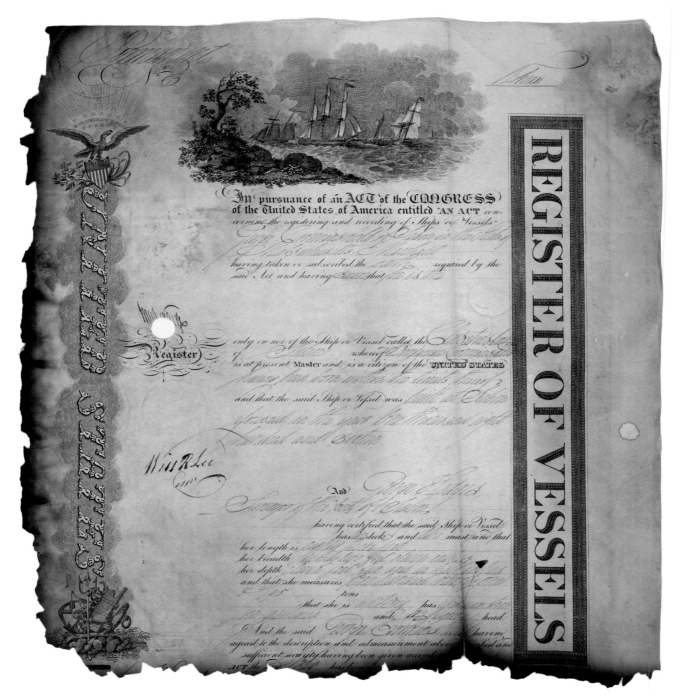

Figure 2.7. *Certificate of Registry for Cleopatra's Barge, Salem, Massachusetts. By the time George Crowninshield Jr. registered his yacht, he had changed her name from* Car of Concordia *to* Cleopatra's Barge. *Dated January 11, 1817, this is the earliest registration, burned along the bottom and side edge. Courtesy of the National Records and Archives Administration, RG 41, Bureau of Marine Inspection and Navigation.*

Figure 2.8. *Historic naval architect and Smithsonian curator Howard I. Chapelle started a reconstruction of* Cleopatra's Barge *with this spar plan (P-3229). Dated November 16, 1954, the drawing notes referenced original paintings of the brig, modified with Fincham's rigging tables. Courtesy of the Peabody Essex Museum.*

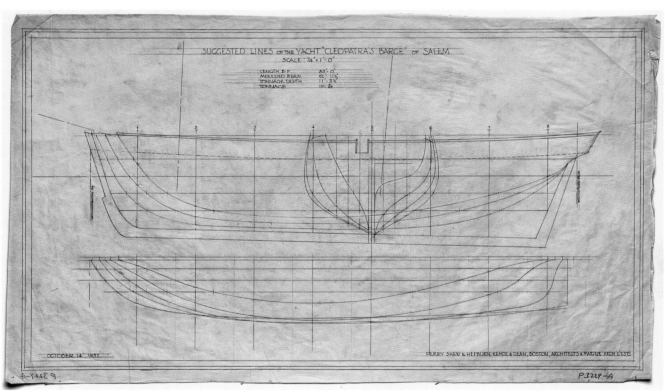

Figure 2.9. *Chapelle developed a set of hypothetical lines for the* Barge *for the architectural firm that designed and built the replica main salon off the Peabody Museum's East India Marine Hall. Courtesy of the Peabody Essex Museum.*

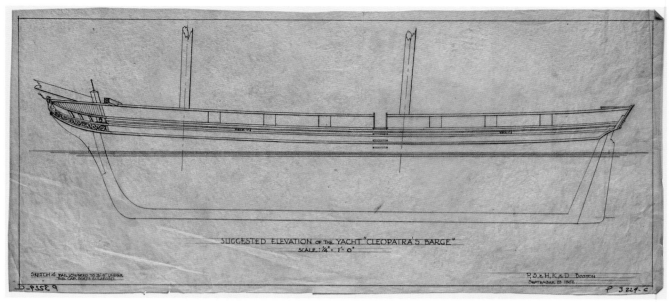

SUGGESTED ELEVATION of the YACHT "CLEOPATRA'S BARGE"
SCALE: ¼" = 1' 0"

Figure 2.10. *Chapelle's hypothetical waterline elevation of the* Barge, *commissioned in 1952 by the architectural firm of Perry Shaw, Hepburn, Kehoe & Dean of Boston. Courtesy of the Peabody Essex Museum.*

ladder." A military officer felt compelled to force his way aboard with drawn pistol, and a pregnant woman was so overcome by the experience that she went into labor. That same day, "1800 to 2000 of the ragamuffin class were turned away."[8] In Genoa, Chapman the cook astonished a prominent German astronomer with a discourse on four different methods of deriving lunar distances for determining longitude, presented with "a white apron around his waist, a fowl in one hand, and a carving knife in the other." (fig. 2.15) In late May, at Majorca, George Crowninshield embarrassed his crew (and his brother Ben, secretary of the navy at the time) by begging supplies from the US frigate *United States,* and then running his hands through a small keg of copper nails he received as though they were golden doubloons.[9] George's admiration for Napoleon was so outspoken at French and Italian ports that a French warship began shadowing the *Barge,* especially after he spent a week in Rome with relatives of the exiled emperor (fig. 2.16). One of his most ardent wishes had been to find an exotic foreign princess and bring her back on the *Barge* to his hometown Salem, where she would be the source of envy and admiration by all who beheld her.[10] But in none of the countries visited was George able to lure a European princess aboard, much less talk her into accompanying him back to the United States, and he was forced to leave Europe in August without female companionship. *Cleopatra's Barge* arrived back at Salem on 3 October 1817, and her owner died of a heart attack six weeks later, well into plans for his next voyage to the Baltic via England.

The Sandwich Islands

Since those days in the early nineteenth century, no fewer than three books and dozens of articles have told and retold parts of the story of *Cleopatra's Barge.* However, all of these secondary sources—even those by Crowninshield

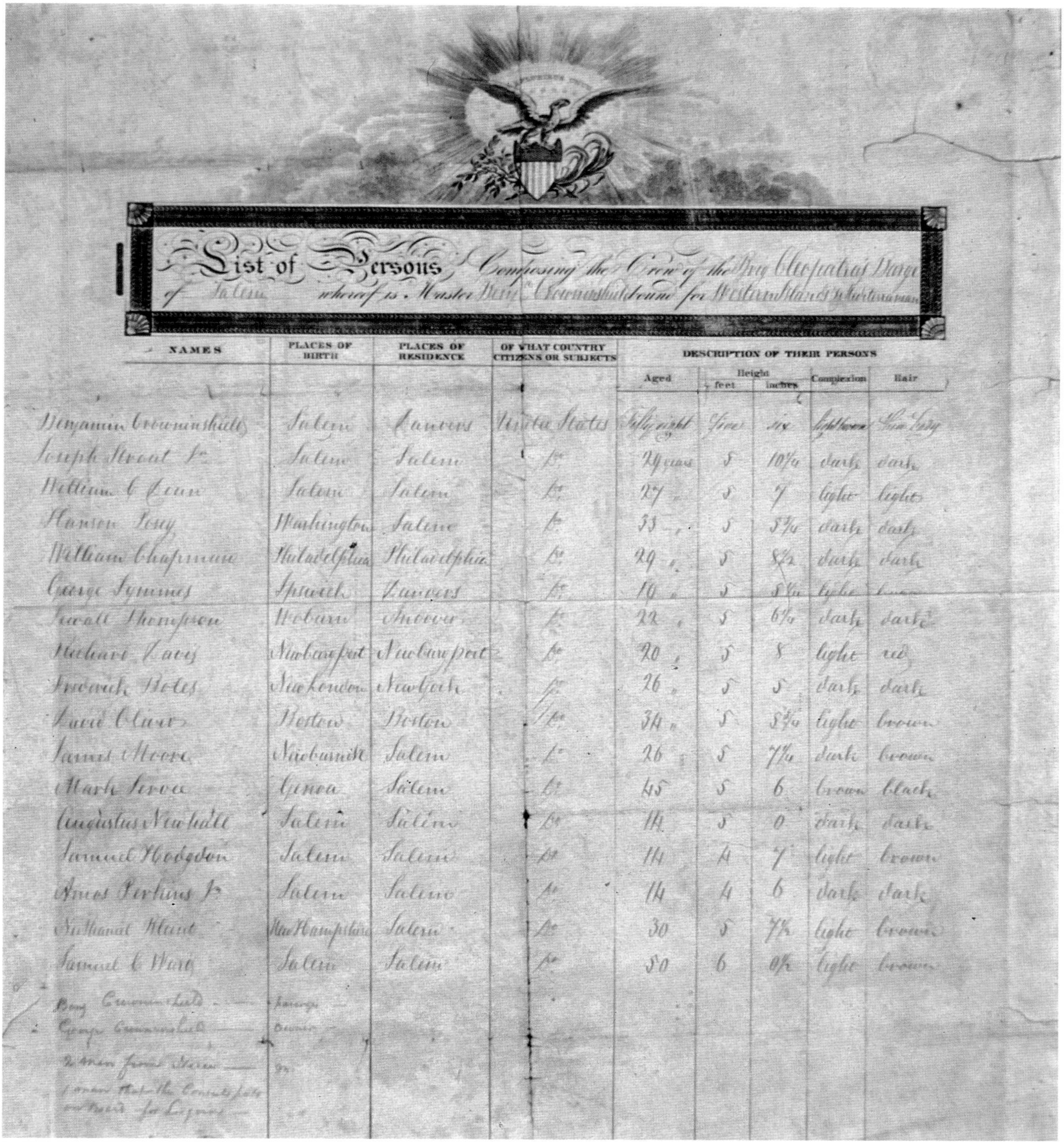

Figure 2.11. *The crew list for* Cleopatra's Barge's *first voyage detailed seventeen men under Captain Benjamin Crowninshield, George Jr.'s cousin and an experienced family mariner. The steward and cook, who knew celestial navigation, were African American, as were two of the deck crew. Courtesy of the Peabody Essex Museum.*

Figure 2.12. *"Sailor Ben" Crowninshield (1758–1836), master of the* Barge. *He was master of the Crowninshield ship* America *on a famous 1804–1805 voyage to Sumatra for pepper. Midway through the trip he broke owners' orders and sailed to Mocha for coffee instead. Although disobeying his owners' explicit written directive, he earned the family a fortune. Courtesy of the Peabody Essex Museum.*

family members—share a significant gap. While they all recount the famous vessel's New England history in great detail, they all end with only a few lines about the four-year interval between the *Barge*'s sale to the king of Hawai'i in 1820 and her 1824 loss.[11] None investigate or recount the ship's rich Hawaiian history—equally as strange and amazing as the New England chapter of its story.

What follows attempts to bridge that gap and tell the peripatetic story of a remarkable vessel's second life in a distant and exotic locale, about as far away from New England as a ship can sail. It is replete with whimsical meanderings, lengthy digressions, manifold backtrackings, and tall tales. In short, George Crowninshield Jr. would have been proud of his favorite possession's later life, for many of her later adventures echoed his own eccentric experiences aboard her. Despite his unrequited royal aspirations, little could he

Figure 2.13. *"Philosopher Ben" Crowninshield (1782–1864), Barge diarist, son of "Sailor Ben," master of the* Barge. *His personal diary recounts all of the gossip and daily life detail aboard the* Barge *on her Mediterranean cruise until he left the homeward-bound brig in Gibraltar, disgusted at his cousin George's excessive behavior. Courtesy of the Peabody Essex Museum.*

have known—nor could he have ever imagined—that one day kings, queens, princes, and princesses would walk her decks, or that a king—second in the line of the United States' only authentic royalty—would own his yacht before her remarkable loss in a tropical paradise on the other side of the world.

This history picks up where others begin to conclude—with the ship's 1820 registration to new owners.[12] Richard Crowninshield, younger brother of the first owner, purchased the *Barge* at auction in August 1818 from his late brother's estate for $15,400—a fraction of what she had cost only two years earlier (figs. 2.17 and 2.18). On 27 April 1820, she was reregistered to John Bryant and William Sturgis, principals of the Boston China traders Bryant & Sturgis.[13] The price Bryant and Sturgis paid for the famous ship is unknown, but the registration certificate does record that they had a partner who also

Figure 2.14. *The Genoa port painter Antoine Pittaluga painted this watercolor of the* Barge's *starboard side, showing the horizontal stripes just below the gun ports on the main deck. Courtesy of the Peabody Essex Museum.*

Cleopatra's Barge of Salem

Figure 2.15. *Antoine Pittaluga painted this watercolor of the* Barge *at the harbor of Genoa, Italy, showing the port side of the ship with its contrasting herringbone paint scheme. Courtesy of the Peabody Essex Museum.*

CLEOPATRA'S BARGE OF SALEM

Figure 2.16. *Napoleon's boots, a lock of his hair, a cameo, and a sample of rock from Elba collected by* Barge *owner George Crowninshield Jr. Many Americans at the time were Bonaparte partisans. Courtesy of the Peabody Essex Museum.*

Figure 2.17. *Classified ad in the 21 July 1818 edition of the* Salem Gazette *newspaper announcing the forthcoming auction of the* Barge. *The ship's contents, valued at $7,000 to $8,000, were first removed and distributed among family members. Then the brig was sold at auction to George's brother Richard for $15,400 and converted into a coastal trader for a short time. Courtesy of the Peabody Essex Museum.*

SHIP NEWS.

1817

PORT OF SALEM.

Sunday, March 30.—Sailed the brig "CLEOPA-
TRA'S BARGE," Capt. Benj Crowninshield, on a
voyage of pleasure, observation and improvement.

SALES BY AUCTION.

THIS DAY, at 11 o'clock,
Will be sold at Public Auction,
The late Mansion House of
George Crowninshield, sen. Esq. deceased,
together with all the Out Buildings and Fen-
ces adjoining, situate on Derby street: the
whole to be removed in the course of the then
ensuing week; reserving however all the
rocks and bricks; and also, (for a future sale)
the Carriage House and Stable.
Terms made known at the sale.
T. DELAND, Auct.

Brig Cleopatra's Barge.
On Monday, the 27th inst. at 12 o'clock,
AT INDIA WHARF,
Will be sold at Auction, per order of the
administrators to the estate of the late
Geo. Crowninshield, deceased,
The elegant, well built
and fast sailing brig Cleopatra's Barge, burthen about 200
tons. As this vessel has been
so frequently viewed by the people of this vicinity and strangers in general, a more particular description is unnecessary.

—ALSO—
One half of the ship A-
merica, armament and appur-
tenances. This Ship was a
successful cruiser in the last
war with Britain.

—ALSO—
One half of sloop Jefferson, and appur-
tenances.
These vessels, with their inventories, may
be examined at any time previous to the sale.
T. DELAND, Auct.
Salem, July 14, 1818.

Next MONDAY, at 9 o'clock,
At Thordike Deland's Office,
FRANKLIN PLACE,
(Per order of the administrators to the estate
of Geo. Crowninshield, deceased)
$39,566 64 in the United States
Six Per Cent Stock.
26 Shares Union Marine Insurance Company.
11 do. Salem Marine do.
5 do. Massachusetts State Bank Stock.

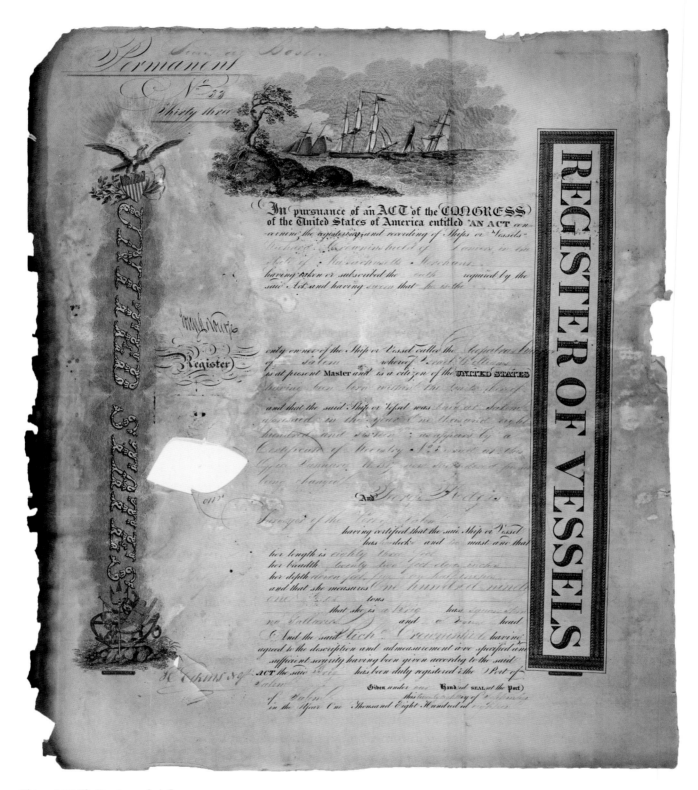

Figure 2.18. *The* Barge *was briefly reregistered to George's brother Richard for a coastal voyage or two. Courtesy of the Peabody Essex Museum.*

happened to be its master of record at the time, Captain John Suter of Boston (fig. 2.19).

Captain John was well suited to the task. Born near Norfolk, Virginia, on 20 March 1781, he and his brother were orphaned and separated at a young age. At eight, John was sent to Boston on a schooner and apprenticed to a Boston pilot.[14] Uninterested in formal education, he nevertheless flourished in and around the waters of Boston Harbor, surviving a shipwreck aboard a pilot boat when she was run down and sunk one night. Shortly after the Quasi-War with France began in 1796, Suter was serving aboard a privateer off the French coast when she was captured in the English Channel; he secured his release and even managed to hold on to his savings of 100 gold dollars hidden in his clothing.

In 1799 Suter made his first voyage out to the Pacific Northwest as third mate aboard the vessel *Alert;* subsequently he found himself in the West Indies, where he was captured by the British near Martinique and impressed into service aboard an English frigate. In 1804 he signed on the Boston ship *Pearl* as first mate for a long voyage back to the Pacific Northwest and China; he served in this capacity for three years and returned to Boston from Canton in 1807 as her master. His first documented voyage to the Sandwich Islands was as master and supercargo of *Pearl,* leaving Boston in autumn 1807 and arriving at Hawaiʻi in January 1808. This voyage may have initiated his relationship with Bryant and Sturgis, as they owned one-sixth of *Pearl*'s outbound cargo. Suter became master of the Boston ship *Atahualpa* in September 1811 and returned to the Pacific Northwest shortly afterward, in concern for an impending embargo. Under Suter, *Atahualpa* left Sitka, Alaska, in August 1813 with a large fur cargo and arrived at Oʻahu in October; in mid-December she was sold to US interests for $4,700, then sold again to the Russian-American Company and renamed *Bering.*[15] Suter left Hawaiʻi for Canton with his furs aboard the privateer schooner *Tamahamaha,* in which he had a part share, and the cargo brought nearly $50,000 in Canton. However, the British detained the vessel and Suter in China for nearly a year before they were able to escape and return to Boston.[16]

Suter took command of the Bryant & Sturgis ship *Mentor* in July 1816; as with many of his earlier commands, he took her to the Northwest Coast. Although furs were scarce by this time, Suter made a successful and very profitable trip, returning to Boston in June 1819 and then resigning his command.

Figure 2.19. *A miniature portrait by an unknown artist of Captain John Suter, part owner and master of* Cleopatra's Barge *on her voyage to Hawaiʻi. Courtesy of Suter descendant Deborah Rood Spencer. Photograph by Hugh Talman, Smithsonian National Museum of American History.*

From Boston to Lahaina

On 22 June 1820, less than two months after Bryant, Sturgis, and Suter bought her, *Cleopatra's Barge* cleared Boston for the Sandwich Islands under Captain Suter. Although she bore a general cargo of "Axes, Brandy, Cottons, Gin, Hats, Hard Ware, Lead, Looking Glasses, Molasses, Muskets, Swords, Rum, Dry Goods, Sugar, Tea, Wine, Boots," copper, umbrellas, and a wagon,[17] she left New England with a far different purpose in mind than general trade. In their letter of instruction to their partner Captain Suter, dated two days before he departed, Bryant and Sturgis wrote: "The Cleopatra's Barge of which you have the immediate command is inttended [*sic*] to be Sold Vessel & Cargo at the Sandwich Islands . . . in this case you must endeavor to make your agreement with the King in the clearest manner—Stating how many Pikels of wood you are to Receive what the quality is to be & when it is to be delivered to your agent."[18]

The partners intended from the outset to sell the famous yacht to Hawaiian king Kamehameha II, son of Kamehameha the Great, who had united the Sandwich Islands and only recently died in May 1819, leaving his eldest son in power. Although the same letter to Captain Suter contained elaborate backup plans should the *Barge* fail to sell in Hawai'i, several subsequent letters to Suter sent aboard other vessels indicated the owners' total confidence that the famous yacht would be irresistible to the king.

Two different logbooks are preserved for the *Barge*'s outbound voyage from Boston to the Sandwich Islands; differing only in small details, they tell the tale of an uneventful voyage whose monotony was broken only by frequent sail changes and an occasional squall.[19] The most interesting aspect of these records begins when *Cleopatra's Barge* was about a month out of the Sandwich Islands, as the crew began preparing her for sale. Activities include scraping the masts, unbending old sails and bending newer ones, "ratling & taring the riggin," painting the spars and hull, scraping the deck, cleaning the hold, and sundry other "jobs of ships duty." After 138 days at sea, the *Barge* arrived at Lahaina, Maui, on 6 November 1820; the very next day Kamehameha II, better known as Liholiho,[20] was welcomed aboard along with some family members and attendants (fig. 2.20). The *Barge* must have left for O'ahu sometime over the next few days, for on the 11th, Captain Suter sent ashore at Honolulu all of the *Barge*'s spare spars (totaling twelve masts, gaffs, yards, and booms).[21] The following day the local Christian missionaries were permitted to collect their "61 letters, a box of tea, a bag of coffee, a box of medicines, a box of clothing, &c," providing they kept secret anything in the letters that could affect Bryant & Sturgis trade. Other items were delivered to the Governor (Chief Kalanimoku) and to Captain Babcock, master of another of the king's brigs, *Neo*.[22] On the 12th, the *Barge* sailed for Maui with passengers, a large boat for the king, and some missionary letters. Liholiho was still at Lahaina, and Suter did not want to let his prey stray too far. The

Figure 2.20. *This flattering watercolor portrait of King Kamehameha II (ca. 1797–1824) was painted ca. 1890 by an unknown artist, around sixty-five years after the king's death. Painted in the Western "portrait bust" style, it shows the young king at the height of his early manhood and powers, dressed in a Western outfit of gold-braided red coat with fur collar. Courtesy of the Bishop Museum.*

next day, he anchored at Lahaina in 15 fathoms and hosted the king for dinner on the 15th, saluting his royal guest's arrival aboard with a five-gun salute.[23]

On the following day, 16 November 1820—just ten days after his first visit to the ship—Liholiho purchased the *Barge* and her (remaining) cargo for 8,000 piculs of sandalwood, worth $80,000 at the time.[24] Although Bryant & Sturgis had written very detailed "reminders" to Captain Suter regarding contract terms for the potential sale of the yacht, Suter seems to have "broken orders" and ignored them.[25] Despite an undated draft sale contract preserved among his papers, no signed bill of sale existed. This absence of a written, signed contract for the quality and delivery dates for the sandalwood payments was to haunt Bryant & Sturgis and its agents in Hawai'i for the remainder of the company's enterprise there.

However, the Boston China traders had gauged their royal prospect well. Liholiho's father, Kamehameha I, had loved foreign ships; over time he had collected a sizeable fleet of Western vessels, which, with guns and training by the *haoles* (foreigners), were a major asset in creating and maintaining his far-flung kingdom of islands.[26] Liholiho inherited his father's love of ships; one of his childhood companions remembered seeing Liholiho frequently sailing a boat model "like a real man-of war" on a pond and also recalled that their favorite boyhood pastime was drawing ships in the sand at the beach.[27]

Liholiho inherited the monarchy upon his father's death in May 1819. Although he ruled for only four and a half years, his short reign had a greater impact upon Hawaiian culture and society than any other earlier or subsequent monarch. Chief among his royal deeds (backed by his father's favorite wife and his own co-regent Ka'ahumanu) was the formal abolition in November 1819 of the *kapu* (taboo) system of political and social power, which created a vacuum in the belief system of Native Hawaiians—already corrupted by considerable contact with Euro-American explorers and traders at least as early as Captain Cook in 1778. Second was his allowance of the Pioneer Company of Protestant American missionaries to stay in his kingdom (initially for a year) upon their arrival from Boston in April 1820. These evangelical missionaries stepped into the breach only a few months after the *kapu* abolition and found fertile grounds for spreading the Gospel and replacing the old beliefs with Christianity.[28]

The missionaries, informally headed by the Reverend Hiram Bingham (fig. 2.21), quickly dispersed around the Hawaiian Islands, establishing mission stations and schools. In the course of these efforts, they generated a considerable volume of correspondence and activity reports between themselves, their families, and their central office back in Boston, the American Board of Commissioners for Foreign Missions (ABCFM).[29] These papers, viewed through the filter of early nineteenth-century missionaries proselytizing "savage" peoples, provide a wealth of information about *Cleopatra's Barge* and her movements, as everything from the climate to the geography and people was new to the missionaries, and their eyes were wide open to every event of even

One guest, Karl Gillesem, provided unique details on the *Barge*'s royal armament at the time, although he apparently overcounted the gunports: "The king had bought this yacht from some American merchant for 80,000 piastres. Though the vessel was finished internally with gilt mirrors and did mount sixteen brass twelve-pounders, she was certainly not worth that huge sum."[43]

Lieutenant Aleksei Petrovich Lazarev of the Russian sloop *Blagonamerennyi* observed the *Barge* at greater length than any other contemporary author of any nationality:

there appeared, at about noon, the royal fleet of four brigs and the same number of schooners . . . Ahead of the fleet entering the harbor went the yacht carrying the king. She fired a five-gun salute, to which the fort and other craft all replied with the same number of shots . . . the royal yacht having dropped anchor in the harbour, we had sought permission to present ourselves to the king, but the latter told us, through an official, that because of the untidiness and disorder on his yacht he would be unable to receive us that day . . .

On reaching the yacht, the king informed Captain Vasil'ev that we were to receive a five-gun salute . . . both our sloops should respond to the royal salute with an equal number of guns . . . whereupon the yacht fired off another five rounds, in response. As well as by the yacht, guns were fired by the fort, the flotilla, and even a few minutes later, on several American vessels.

The king invited us into his cabin, where we were asked to be seated round a large table covered with a cloth. He himself sat at the head, placing Captain Vasil'ev at his right hand and Captain Shishmarev at his left, while the rest of us sat without any distinctions of rank. For the king's favorite wife, a chair was placed beside him; and behind them, on the floor, sat a fly chaser and a functionary with a spitoon [*sic*].

Several chiefs, probably of the highest nobility, likewise entered the cabin but had no place at the table. Conversation began with our praising the royal yacht, which was in fact justified, while an African Negro was bringing several tumblers, wine-glasses and, finally, four carafes full of liquid to our table . . . He was dressed only in a white shirt. Saying, "Rum, brandy, gin, wine," he went off. The king then began to regale us, offering us our choice of drink and pouring a glass of wine for himself. We followed his example and drank his health.

The queen . . . was a woman of unusual height and size. Although a chair had been placed for her, she did not sit on it long. Instead, she constantly paced about the cabin and struck the seated chiefs with her heavy hand . . .

The yacht on which we found ourselves would have done honour to an owner other than a half-savage Islander. She had been built in America by a wealthy citizen and, on his death, had been sold to other Americans then trading with the Sandvichane. These new owners in turn then sold her to the local king for 80,000 piastres, or 400,000 roubles. The sum was indeed an appalling one, but it must be noted that the Americans did not receive hard cash for the yacht, but rather sandalwood . . .

The yacht of which I speak was built of solid oak as a schooner and had all the qualities of a good sea-going vessel. She was armed simply and well, and beautifully fitted out on the exterior, with fine carving on bow and stern. She had fourteen gunports, only eight of her guns being loaded while we were there. We also much admired her internal arrangements. At her stern were a salon finished with pink and deep blue mountings and gilt, a bed-room, a buffet, and a stairway leading up to her deck. Midships was a cap-tain's cabin and, forward, quarters for a crew, a storage area for tackle and so forth, a galley above and, finally, a spacious lounge containing tables of the finest workmanship, inlaid with palm and lacquered redwood. The walls of this lounge were embellished with a number of carved gilt designs, and the floor was spread with good English carpets. Seeing all this painstaking work and fitting, one could only regret that such a beautiful craft had fallen to the Sandvichane and not to devotees of order and cleanliness; for the in-terior of that yacht no doubt resembled a stable shortly after our departure.

On the 24th, the king visited both [Russian] sloops at our invitation . . . the Otkrytir . . . like our own vessel, saluted him from five guns. The royal yacht, the fort, and the entire Sandvichanskii flotilla responded with an equal salute.[44]

Either the royal yacht had a somewhat different layout from the original Crowninshield arrangements, or Lieutenant Lazarev mistook a few details (like the *Barge*'s brig rig). Crowninshield's grand salon toward the stern remained gilded but was now decorated with pink and blue "mountings" (probably hanging textiles). Liholiho also may have enlarged the space, as the Russian naval officer does not mention the aftermost officers' cabins from Crowninshield's days. Forward of the salon remained the owner's quarters. Many of the other spaces also remained, with the principal exception of a large and opulent "lounge" up forward. This must have been created through open-ing and joining of some of Crowninshield's smaller forward spaces—possibly the original crew's quarters and adjacent areas, as Lazarev states that the crew now had midships space instead of forward berthing, as in the original design. This forward lounge, richly decorated with gilding, expensive English car-pets, and fancy inlaid tables, presumably served as the royal family's quarters, as the reception for the Russians was in another cabin with different, more modest furniture (mere chairs and a covered table). Liholiho displayed his ap-preciation of Euro-American protocol in seating his foreign guests to either side of himself, leaving room at the table only for his favorite wife, Kamamalu. The exotic African steward and his tray offering choices of strong alcoholic beverages must have made a powerful impression even on Western guests and conferred high status on the king when among his other chiefs. Lieutenant

Lazarev counted the number of gunports correctly and added the detail that only eight cannon were mounted, leaving six ports empty at the time.

After this episode, once again the *Barge* dropped out of sight for several weeks. She was sighted off a small island on the south side of Maui on 25 June and then vanished again for a time. It was almost certainly during this interval that Liholiho was developing his bold plot to confirm Kaua'i as part of his kingdom, unite all the islands under one king, and thereby achieve a goal at which even his illustrious father Kamehameha had only partly succeeded. Under the circumstances, it would have been essential for him to confer with the greater and lesser chiefs of all the other islands—perhaps several times—to enlist and maintain their support for his ambition. Moreover, a degree of secrecy would have been desirable, as many of the kingdom's chiefs did not support his abolition of the *kapu* or his reign in general, and several were related by blood or marriage to Chief Kaumuali'i, who ruled Kaua'i.

Nevertheless, word of Liholiho's possible intentions had leaked as far as the foreign community in Honolulu by 14 July, and three days later the *Barge* sailed for parts unknown (at least to those who wrote about it). Perhaps to disguise his true intentions, on or around 21 July Liholiho set out from O'ahu in a small, open sailboat with just two other chiefs and two women, crossing the largest stretch of open water in the Hawaiian Islands and arriving on Kaua'i at 3:00 a.m. the following morning. He immediately placed himself in the care of Kaumuali'i, the wise, powerful, and wealthy chief who enjoyed island-wide loyalty. Declining the opportunity to rid himself of his unexpected and totally unprotected rival, Kaumuali'i reaffirmed his allegiance to Liholiho, as he had done earlier with the king's father. Two days after Liholiho's arrival, the *Barge* arrived as well, carrying his wives and others. The two chiefs and their parties then sailed around Kaua'i in their personal vessels for several weeks, visiting the island's sites of interest. John Coffin Jones Jr., commercial agent for the United States and business agent for Marshall & Wildes (a business competitor of Bryant & Sturgis), had a distinctly sour view of this royal junket and the *Barge* in particular, complaining to his employers back in Boston:

the next day they landed at Atooi [Kaua'i] . . . there they commenced their round of dissipation and put a stop to all business on that Island, every man was recalled, from cutting wood . . . Had the Cleopatra's Barge never have come to these Islands we should in all probability have made as great a voyage as ever was performed in these seas, that vessel is so superior to any of ours, that they will scarce look at them, had the sale of the Barge been managed right, she would have sold for 12000 piculs as quick as she did for 6000 [*sic*], they almost adore her; Suter has done everything to injure us, and succeeded in some degree, he has persecuted our concern to an overbearing degree; every foreigner in this country is ready to cut his neighbours throat, truth is a stranger here, the Sandall [*sic*] wood fever will deprive some of their reason.[45]

John Jones was not Captain Suter's only critic. Charles Bullard, Bryant & Sturgis's own agent in Hawai'i, echoed his rival's sentiments in a letter written a few weeks later to his employers from aboard their ship *Tartar* en route to Canton from Honolulu:

—as regards that, Capt. Suter acted hastily, both as to *price* and *terms*—... I must once more refer to the sale of the Barge particularly the terms— Here a most grand mistake was made, but it would require ten pages to go into the particulars, that . . . with such a vessel as the Barge, it was not at all necessary to deliver her before payment—the King would have "found no rest for the sole of his foot" until he was in possession of her, and had Suter held on, a Cargo [of] Wood would have been brought forward very soon—According to Suter's own interpretation of the contract he was to have no wood until Lewis & Babcock were paid . . . If you want to know how Religion stands at the Islands I can tell you—All sects are tolerated but the King worships the Barge.[46]

Bullard's *ex post facto* condemnation of Captain Suter's conditions of sale is suspect, to say the least. It is difficult to believe that a part owner of the *Barge,* and one of the most successful Pacific sea traders, would not have tried to arrange the very best terms for himself and his partners, under whatever particular circumstances prevailed in the Sandwich Islands at the time. Suter may have believed that the king was overextended in sandalwood payments at the time and that there was no point or need in demanding full payment prior to taking possession of the *Barge.* However, as later events showed, Suter did make a mistake in the *Barge* sales transaction, as he never obtained a signed contract for the sale.

During their lengthy visit to Kaua'i, Liholiho, his family, and his chiefs enjoyed the generous hospitality and protection of their royal host. That changed, however, on the evening of 16 September, when Liholiho invited Kaumuali'i aboard *Cleopatra's Barge* after a day sail. No sooner had the Kaua'i chief settled into a seat in the main cabin around 9:00 p.m. than Liholiho weighed anchor and set sail for O'ahu. Perhaps to disguise his intentions, the event occurred on the Sabbath, and Liholiho's wives and a number of his chiefs were left behind on shore.

Suspecting the worst, Kaumuali'i called out to his brig *Tamaholalahna* (*Kamaholelani*) to come after him, but the *Barge* was quickly lost in the darkness and was not seen again for a week. On the following Sabbath the yacht reappeared at Waianae on the western side of O'ahu, where Kaumuali'i was dropped off, presumably under armed escort, to make his way to Honolulu; Liholiho himself did not return to Honolulu until 30 September.[47] Said Sybil Bingham in a letter to her friends back in East Windsor, Connecticut, "You may judge of the excitement this event produced in the minds of those thus deprived of their King."[48]

Thus, in one stroke, *Cleopatra's Barge* kidnapped the ruling chief of Kaua'i and provided the means by which Liholiho achieved the one goal that even his powerful father Kamehameha the Great had been unable to attain despite repeated attempts. Meanwhile, back on O'ahu, Liholiho's co-ruler Ka'ahumanu took a liking (both personal and political) to Kaumuali'i; they were married by 10 November 1821, cementing his exile from Kaua'i. The former Kaua'i chief returned to his former kingdom only once before he died in late May 1824.[49] However, by that date the island of Kaua'i already would have avenged the *Barge*'s treacherous act.

Around the same time that Liholiho returned to Honolulu, Captain Suter seems to have suffered a moral setback. Both in the Sandwich Islands as well as back home in Boston, he had a reputation as a bible-toting Baptist always ready to lend a helping hand to the missionaries whenever possible.[50] Just six months earlier, he had earned praise in Mercy Partridge (Mrs. Samuel) Whitney's journal for giving the Waimea mission "a barrel of hard bread, a barrel of molasses, part of a barrel of beef & pork, a considerable quantity of tea, several hams, a pot of pickles, a large pitcher of cranberry preserves, a bottle of pepper & some mustard seed." He also offered to loan the Whitneys his ship carpenter to build some furniture for their house, and the following month, when the mission was contemplating a trip to the Society Islands, Suter had offered a crew to man the ship offered them by Kaumuali'i.[51] However, around the beginning of October, the missionaries noted in their official record that physician Dr. Blatchely had chastised Reverend Bingham for telling "Manooea (a girl who had lived in the mission family) that she had done wrong to leave the school to live with Capt. Sutor [*sic*]."[52] Although it is within the realm of possibility that the Hawaiian girl left school to serve as Suter's housekeeper, considering the terse language of the official mission's journal entry, it seems likelier that Suter succumbed to the allure of the islands like so many other seamen before and after him. Interestingly, no one seems to have said anything to Suter himself, perhaps because he had been so generous and helpful to the mission in the past. Surely by coincidence, he left Kaua'i for Canton aboard his old ship *Mentor* on 13 October and never returned to Hawai'i—or the Pacific Ocean—again.[53]

The next appearance of the *Barge* in the historical record represented a milestone event for the American missionaries. As mentioned above, the Pioneer Company had been granted permission by King Liholiho to remain in his domain for only one year. Seeing fertile and receptive ground for their mission, as the end of the year approached, they hoped to extend their stay beyond the initial period. On 15 October missionary physician Dr. Thomas Holman and an unidentified ship captain ("Captain C.") visited the king "to get land, cows, oxen and horses." Liholiho, Ka'ahumanu, and Kalanimoku received them on the quarterdeck of the *Barge* for what must have been a pivotal moment for the brethren. The request was granted, in effect endorsing an indefinite stay for the missionaries (through the land gift), and the king left for Hawai‘i Island and Kalanimoku for elsewhere on O‘ahu respectively, leaving Ka‘ahumanu to work out the grant amounts and other details.[54]

Two months later Liholiho and his wives voyaged to Honolulu from Hawai‘i aboard the *Barge* specifically to visit Ka‘ahumanu, who was sick at the time. Although a few other 1821 *Barge* voyages may be inferred from documented Honolulu arrivals, the last mention of her that year was on 27 December, when she arrived at Honolulu from Hawai‘i bearing the king and his men and retinue. The vessel was towed into the harbor with the obligatory cannon salutes "and loud crying" announcing his arrival.[55]

A Pivotal Year

The first 1822 record of the *Barge* was the surrender document of her Boston registration; dated 16 March, it documents the sale and property transfer by William Sturgis, John Bryant, and John Suter, "Sold to the natives of the Sandwich Islands."[56] (fig. 2.24). The comparatively late date of this document is probably attributable to the long, drawn-out sandalwood payments that frustrated Bryant & Sturgis agent Charles Bullard so greatly. However, he was about to become even more frustrated and disturbed on the famous ship's account. On 18 April during a routine overhaul, *Cleopatra's Barge* was found to be almost completely rotten abaft the mainmast. Bullard wrote a lengthy account of the unfortunate discovery and its remarkable results to his employers in Boston:

Register
Cleopatra's Barge
rec'd at Boston
March 16. 1822
Surrendered to Com
Agent of U.S at
Woahoo Vessel sold
to the natives of the
Sandwich Islands

Figure 2.24. *Surrender of Registration for* Cleopatra's Barge, *March 16, 1822, Boston, Massachusetts. The obverse of the* Barge's *1822 registration surrender document is too faint to reproduce; this is the reverse. Although the ship was sold to Liholiho in 1820, the New England registration was not surrendered until 1822, around the time the vessel was rebuilt and renamed. Courtesy of the National Records and Archives Administration, RG 41, Bureau of Marine Inspection and Navigation.*

> my business was in the best possible terms until 18th April when the Carpenters who were overhauling the Barge reported she was *rotten;*—This I could hardly credit, but on examination found it was too true:—From the main chains aft above water, *She was a complete mass of dry rot.*—The effect produced by this can hardly be conceived;—Their disappointment was great in proportion to their previous expectations—When I went to *Court* where I before received every attention, I found nothing but frowns . . . They informed me that Capt. Suter represented the Barge as a first rate vessel, nearly new, and *guaranteed* she would wear ten years without repair & etc. But *they* said she must be 15 years old, and that she was sent out on purpose to deceive them, and that the concern were a set of liars and villians [*sic*] . . . A grand consultation of chiefs was held, and it was at first determined not to pay any more wood, on which I took a decided stand,

and after three weeks gained the majority in my favor, and I have after much vexation and *expense* recd. 1984 Peculs—I had the greatest difficulty in obtaining any thing like decent wood or fair weight—Before this took place, they were better pleased with the bargain than any they ever made, and would have given me the best lots of wood . . . The animosity of the King's party and some others is so great on account of the Barge, that they are determined if possible that I shall not buy any wood; and I am obliged to keep on as good terms as possible with them on account of the old debts.

About ten days since the King informed me that he should not pay any more wood; That an *allowance* ought to be made for the rottenness of the Barge etc . . . The rottenness of the Barge while it has operated so much against me, has been of great advantage to other concerns . . . I am in a bad predicament, the contract for the Barge not being *endorsed* nor half made . . . The Barge blew up at a most unfortunate moment.[57]

Perhaps the most intriguing aspect of Bullard's account is that he was somehow able to persuade the king to resume sandalwood payments for the *Barge* despite her condition and that he was even able to collect another 1,984 piculs for her sale under the circumstances. Exactly how he did this was only revealed later. Rumors and misinformation immediately began circulating among the resident foreigners and missionaries, and thence back to the rest of the world. Marshall & Wildes agent John Jones, who only one letter earlier had openly envied the *Barge,* now wrote spitefully and with no little schadenfreude to Boston: "the Barge has proved good for nothing, every timber aloft [i.e., abaft] her mainmast is so defective that you can pull out any of her bolts with your fingers, her transom, &c. is all punk. she is now hauled up and condemned and will never leave the harbour again. So much for the famous Barge. Sturgis may hang up his fiddle here, it is a fortunate thing that the Barge did not belong to our concern."[58]

English visitor Gilbert Mathison, who must have talked with Liholiho right after the discovery of the *Barge*'s condition, even went so far as to state: "She was called the Cleopatra's Barge, and to catch his Sable Majesty had been fitted up in a style of considerable elegance; but she had not been long in his possession, when the timbers on one side were found to be decayed, and the ship altogether not seaworthy. He had therefore no alternative but to dismantle and break her up, and in that way endeavor to make the best of a bad bargain. The King, in allusion to this transaction, told me one day, that the Americans had cheated him, by selling rotten ships."[59]

On 3 May a group of missionaries went aboard the storied yacht to see her condition for themselves, mournfully recording, "we went together on board the Cleopatra's Barge, or Moku Haheo (The Proud vessel) as the natives call it, to examine this admired flower of the Ocean, now exceedingly defaced & going to decay."[60]

This journal observation is of interest not only because it indicates the high regard of the missionaries for the ship, but it is also the earliest reference to a Hawaiian name for the *Barge.* Liholiho must have renamed his flagship in recognition of her new status as his personal craft. On 8 October agent Bullard informed his employers that he had met with Kalanimoku and was still encountering difficulties collecting the last 800 piculs of sandalwood due on the *Barge,* but remained optimistic of the outcome.[61] Just two days later, the missionaries dryly recorded the absolute low point in the working life of the famous ship, writing in the official mission journal for that and the following day:

> The brethren went on Board the Ship Wellington now condemned and offered in sale to us. We concluded to purchase her hull at 600 dollars, to accommodate the mission with plank & timber for building & with fuel . . . The king and Pitt [Kalanimoku] refusing us permission to haul the Ship ashore, because they now wished to buy her for their own use, Capt. G. very readily allowed us to decline taking her. The king takes the ship's hull, main mast, fore mast and bowsprit, in barter for 10 guns which belonged to the Cleopatra's Barge.

The ship referenced was actually a brig that arrived at Honolulu 21 July, discharged her cargo of cloth and timber over the next ten days, and was then surveyed for condition on 7 August. The missionaries needed Liholiho's permission to haul *Wellington* ashore on the high tide to break her up, but the king had finally decided he wanted her for himself. So he bartered ten valuable guns from his erstwhile favorite for portions of a condemned hulk, worthless for anything but firewood and timber suitable for recycling.[62]

However, just two days after this apocalyptic journal entry, *Cleopatra's Barge* arose like a phoenix from the ashes. On 13 October, in a letter to his employers, Charles Bullard further analyzed the yacht's condition and the presumed reasons for it: "The rottenness of the Barge was probably occasioned by the close work aft which prevented a proper circulation of the air—she is perfectly sound foreward [*sic*] of the Mainmast." In that same letter, he noted that Captain Thomas Meek had contracted to repair her with "timber and plank from Norfolk Sound" in Alaska and that Meek "will probably make a profitable job of it."[63] Meek, an experienced seaman from Marblehead, Massachusetts, had made several voyages as captain to the Pacific Northwest for sea otter skins and other goods and knew his way around ships and the coast.

Meek had recently sailed his brig *Arab* to the Queen Charlotte Islands (south of Sitka), arriving there in early August and spending five weeks there trading as well as cutting "timber" and firewood. He sent boat crews up the sound to cut the raw logs, which were either loaded onto the boats or rafted down to the shore point nearest *Arab.* There, under the supervision of the ship's carpenter, they were hewn into planks, beams, and spars for stowage and returned to Hawai'i in late September.[64] Unfortunately, there is no men-

was time for Rives to seek new friends and new horizons, and he seems to have found both in *L'Aigle*'s Captain Starbuck.

So the king and his entourage left for England without *Ha'aheo* after all, and the famed ship was mentioned only twice in passing for the rest of the year. The first was a journal entry by Levi Chamberlain for 2 December, in which he records that the royal yacht traveled from Honolulu to Maui in another mission: "Stephen Pupuhi accompanied Karaimoku [Kalanimoku] in the Barge. He will remain at Lahaina to assist the brethren in their work." Now that the king was away at sea, Kalanimoku resumed his rank as master of *Ha'aheo*. The year's last reference is a brief and obscure diary entry by American merchant Stephen Reynolds in Honolulu—"Barge came."[90]

With the king gone, the kingdom was left in the hands of co-regent Ka'ahumanu, with Kalanimoku as her prime minister.[91] In early February 1824, *Ha'aheo* resumed transport duties with the carriage of a missionary party to Waiakea (then and now part of Hilo) on Hawai'i Island's eastern shore. On the 7th, *Ha'aheo* arrived from Kailua, Hawai'i (via Kawaihae) with Hawaiian chief Kouhou. Reverend Samuel Ruggles and Joseph Goodrich were pleased to find the chief friendly and helpful to their cause, which was further supported by the arrival on the 12th of *Ha'aheo* with all the supplies they were expecting (excepting only some fish).[92] On the 15th, *Ha'aheo* cleared Waiakea for Lahaina, where she spent four days before arriving at Honolulu on the 19th, bearing letters from Messrs. Goodrich and Ruggles regarding the latter's house-raising. She also transported 118 piculs (7.86 tons) of "very superior" sandalwood to Honolulu for Captain Blanchard, in partial payment for the sale of the schooner *New York* (to Kalanimoku)—a rare reference to the use of *Ha'aheo* as a cargo ship.[93] Another followed soon after, when the royal brig cleared Honolulu for Kaua'i on the 21st. Her arrival there the following day was noted by Reverend Bishop; he and his wife took leave of Reverend Samuel Whitney at Waimea (where they had wintered) and boarded the brig, lying a mile offshore, via a double canoe. The Bishops' new orders were to proceed to O'ahu and thence to the Big Island, where they were to join the Thurstons at the Kailua mission. Accompanying the Bishops aboard *Ha'aheo* for the thirty-six-hour journey was a house frame for Kalanimoku, sold him by a Mr. Crocker of Marshall & Wildes.[94]

Kalanimoku originally planned to sail *Ha'aheo* to Waiakea on the Sabbath (29 February), and he had generously offered to alter her itinerary to accommodate the Bishops' plans to go to Kailua. However, Hiram Bingham persuaded him to wait a day to take along the new Hawaiian hymnals, then being printed. A further delay was caused by the death and funeral of Chief Ke'eaumoku, but early in the morning of 4 March a messenger informed the Bishop and Richards parties that the brig was ready to sail. The missionaries hurried down to the waterfront, only to find that the ship had left the harbor and was already out at the roadstead in company with two others of the king's brigs. At first the missionaries thought they had been left behind, but it turned out that Kalanimoku had decided to take advantage of a fresh morning breeze to get out of the harbor and had left the ship's boat on shore to ferry their baggage out to the brig. Captain Blanchard loaned his boat for the passengers, and by 11:00 a.m. the missionaries were comfortably aboard *Ha'aheo* en route to Hawai'i via Lahaina. The brig arrived at Lahaina on the 7th, spent two days there, and left for Kailua on the 9th. She arrived there the following morning and disembarked the Bishops. However, the winds were high that day, and consequently *Ha'aheo* stood offshore with their baggage. Bishop proposed to leave most of it aboard, including that destined for Waiakea; however, Kalanimoku urged the missionaries to take everything off the ship that they did not want the crew to pilfer. Another reason that the Waiakea-bound cargo had to be offloaded from *Ha'aheo* was that she was heading back to Honolulu before resuming the Kailua-Waiakea voyage. Moreover, the brig had anchored some distance offshore due to the high winds, and the missionaries had been unable to find any Hawaiians willing to go out until the late afternoon, when the winds abated.[95] As a result, most of their effects were offloaded by means of a double canoe. Only a barrel of beef, some bricks, three barrels, and possibly a box of *waiwai* (treasure/specie) destined for Waiakea were left aboard due to the heavy weather. *Ha'aheo* cleared Kailua the evening of the 11th for Honolulu, arriving there on the late morning of 13 March. This is the last known voyage of the ship, for she dropped out of sight for the next three weeks. When she finally reappeared, she was lost forever (fig. 2.25).

The next reference to *Ha'aheo* was contained in an 8 April 1824 diary entry by Reverend Whitney, then stationed at the Waimea mission on the south shore of Kaua'i:

> News has just arrived that the Cleopatra's Barge was driven on shore night before last at Hanarei [*sic*], a district on the northern side of this Isle, and completely wrecked. This beautiful vessel cost king Rihoriho three years ago, eight thousand pickle of Sandal-wood estimated at ten dollars per pickle, eighty thousand dollars. She was managed wholly by natives, all of whom except the Capt. was intoxicated at the time. She parted her cables, had this not been the case they might have put to sea, and survived the gale.[96]

Whitney attributed the loss to three factors. One was that the ship was crewed by Hawaiians, all but one of whom were intoxicated. Unfortunately, neither he nor anyone else ever identified any of the Hawaiian crew. This indicates that Kalanimoku, who was invariably mentioned by name when he was aboard *Ha'aheo,* may not have been aboard for this voyage. Secondly, the ship parted her cables, possibly indicating that she was secured in Hanalei Bay with more than one anchor.[97] And thirdly, there was a gale that night, which exacerbated and possibly even caused the cable parting. Whitney further suggests that there may have been a connection between the gale and the cable problem—not unlikely—and that had there not been bad weather,

the ship might have survived one or more of the other factors. But he offers no insight as to why the brig was at Hanalei, or even on Kaua'i at all, and he may not have known.

Kaua'i in general was geographically and politically isolated from the rest of the Sandwich Islands, and Hanalei was quite remote even to Whitney in Waimea. By the time any new information about the shipwreck was available, the trail was either cold, invisible, or insignificant to the singularly focused missionaries. Perhaps she was on a simple pleasure cruise, and the crew was merely relaxing at anchorage when a squall arose, strained the anchor cable,

Figure 2.25. *In 1992, artist Raymond A. Massey painted this realist portrait of the* Pride of Hawaii *entering Hanalei Bay in early April 1824, on what would turn out to be her last trip. The Ship Stores Gallery of Lihue, Kaua'i, was kind enough to donate proceeds from print sales of the artwork to the Smithsonian excavations. Courtesy of the Ship Stores Gallery, Lihue, Kaua'i, Hawai'i.*

and snapped it. Under such meteorological conditions—not uncommon on Kaua'i's North Shore—the crew's intoxication might or might not have affected the outcome, depending upon where in the bay they were anchored and how much time they had between losing their anchor(s) and striking the reef.

But there is another likelier and more sinister explanation for the brig's presence on Kaua'i in early April of 1824. Liholiho's rule over his kingdom of islands had gradually decentralized, either voluntarily or because he lacked the power to enforce his father's political will. This had placed more power into the hands of the chiefs.[98] Certainly his abolition of the *kapu* had destabilized the old Hawaiian sociopolitical system. Moreover, Liholiho's departure a few months earlier had resulted in kingdom-wide unrest among the chiefs, especially those of Kaua'i, which had never taken well to the Kamehameha rule. It must have been clear to the ruling chiefs back on O'ahu around this time that Kaua'i needed attention.

It is far likelier that *Ha'aheo* was on Kaua'i in April for reconnaissance and intelligence-gathering purposes, to see what could be learned about possible unrest there before it actually broke out. Perhaps her crew had heard rumors when they visited the island just a few weeks earlier. The fact that her whereabouts for her last three weeks were unrecorded argues for a Hawaiian mission for the ship; had she been transporting missionaries or engaged in other, more normal inter-island activities, her voyages probably would have been recorded. And if in fact the yacht was reconnoitering the local political climate, it is equally possible that people in Hanalei deliberately cut her cables under cover of darkness and a storm, perhaps with some thought of avenging her role in Liholiho's successful plot to kidnap their chief two and a half years earlier.

Later events advocate a reconnaissance mission for *Ha'aheo*'s last voyage. Chief Kaumuali'i was to die the following month in Honolulu, and some signs of illness may have been evident earlier. As soon as Kaumuali'i died, Kalanimoku's nephew Kahalaia was appointed governor of Kaua'i, over both sons of the late chief. As might be expected, this did not sit particularly well with the people of Kaua'i. Kalanimoku planned to visit shortly after Kaumuali'i's death to monitor the island's affairs but was unable to make the trip until late July. In August 1824, just four months after *Ha'aheo* sank, Kaua'i revolted under the nominal leadership of Kaumuali'i's son George Humehume, and a short but bloody battle resulted in the suppression of this revolt.

On 24 April, Whitney recorded in his journal that all of the chiefs and people in Waimea left for Hanalei that morning to attend to the wreck, blaming their hesitation and delay of nearly three weeks on the "stupidity of their Governess"—Debora Kapule, Kaumuali'i's favorite wife. A week later, Hiram and Sybil Bingham left Honolulu for Kaua'i to join the Whitneys, on account of "the state of the island which they now occupied alone." Accepting a free passage from Captain Swain on the schooner *Washington,* the Binghams arrived the morning of 3 May and must have learned of *Ha'aheo*'s fate immediately, for Bingham left for Hanalei just two days after his arrival. According to his memoirs, Bingham went to Hanalei not out of curiosity or concern for the safety of the island's growing Christian flock, but instead to use the loss of the royal yacht as an entrée for preaching to the Hawaiians on the dangers of intemperance:

As most of the leeward chiefs, and many of their effective men also, were at that time assembled on the opposite side of the island, being called there for a new lesson on the evils of intemperance; I started soon to meet them, and to explore and preach . . . The lesson which some yet needed to learn more thoroughly, was, that if the free use of intoxicating drinks is allowed in kings, or commanders of nations, it must be equally allowable in commanders and mates of vessels, and if a ship cannot well be commanded by a drunken captain, much less a nation by a drunken ruler. But who could trust a fine vessel to an inebriate maniac; and what sane passenger could risk himself with him? But through the mismanagement of a drinking captain and crew, the beautiful Cleopatra's Barge, the favorite vessel of the monarch of the Hawaiian archipelago, was wrecked in the bay of Hanalei, and lay not far from the beach, dismantled and ruined. The people had assembled there for the purpose of hauling her up, and saving what could be saved from the wreck.[99]

It is interesting to visualize Bingham sermonizing to the assembled Hawaiian chiefs and commoners—by now, in their own language—on the shore at Hanalei Bay, with the graphic example of the wrecked royal yacht within sight just a hundred yards or so away (fig. 2.26). He clearly had access to new information in Hanalei that Whitney down in Waimea lacked, for he repeats—three times just in this one short passage—that the captain was as drunk as his crew. His account further strengthens the hypothesis that the officers and crew were anonymous rather than well-known chiefs. Noticeable by their absence is any mention of the gale or cable parting, which Bingham likely would have cited as earthly manifestations of God's wrath upon sinners had they applied. He also mentions that the ship was partially dismantled for her salvageable parts and contents, and in a remarkable passage he provides a highly detailed description of the attempted recovery and salvage of the royal yacht on 7–8 May 1824. It is long, but quoted in its entirety here, since it is the only known local account of the loss and subsequent salvage attempt for *Cleopatra's Barge:*

After the people had, with commendable activity, brought on shore from the wreck, spars, rigging, and other articles, they attempted to draw up the brig itself. This furnished one of the best specimens of the physical force of the people, which I ever had opportunity to observe for more than twenty years among them—indeed the most striking which I ever saw made by unaided human muscles. They collected from the woods and margins of the river, a large quantity of the bark of the *hibiscus,* and with their hands

Figure 2.26. *Rick Rogers' watercolor of the Reverend Hiram Bingham's sermon in Hanalei Bay in early May 1824 combines all of the details of Bingham's historical account with the archaeological evidence into a single image. Courtesy of Captain Richard W. Rogers.*

without any machinery, made several thousand yards of strong rope, such as is in common use at the islands. Twelve folds of this they made into a cable. Three cables of this kind were prepared for the purpose of dragging up the wreck of the Cleopatra's Barge on shore.

These three cables were then attached to the mainmast of the brig, a few feet above the deck, leading some distance on the shore towards the mountains, nearly parallel to each other. At the sides of these the multitudes were arranged as closely as they could conveniently sit or stand together.

The brig lay in about ten feet of water, and partly on her side which was furthest from the shore, and very near to a reef of rocks rising nearly half way to the surface. Over this reef they first proposed to roll the vessel. Everything being arranged for their great muscular effort, an old but spirited chieftain, formerly from Oahu, called Kiaimakani (Wind-Watcher), passed up and down through the different ranks, and from place to place, repeatedly sung out with prolonged notes, and trumpet tones, "*Nu—ke—hamau i ka leo,* be quiet—shut up the voice." To which the people responded, "*Mai pane,* say nothing," as a continuance of the prohibition to which they were ready to assent when they should come to the tug. Between the trumpet notes, the old chieftain, with the natural tones and inflections, instructed them to grasp the ropes firmly, rise together at the signal, and leaning inland, to look and draw straight forward, without looking backwards towards the vessel. They being thus marshalled and instructed, remained quiet for some minutes, upon their hams.

A man called a *kaukau,* son of a distinguished *kaukau,* whose office it was to rehearse for the encouragement of the drawers, an ancient and popular song, used for a tree when a canoe was to be drawn from the mountains to the shore, rose, and with great rapidity and surprising fluency, commencing with an address to Lono, an ancient god, rehearsed the mythological song, of which the following are the better parts:—

"Give to me the trunk of the tree, O Lono—
Give me the tree's main root, O Lono—
Give me the ear of the tree, O Lono.
Hearken by night, and hear by day,
O Poihiihi—O Poahaaha—
Come for the tree, and take to the sea-side.

"My husband heard at the Pali,
Heard at the Pali at Kailua—
Koolau was filled with the stench of smoke
By burning men to cinders—
The dogs followed the scent.

"My feet have led on and are weary,
I am come from inland,
From the land of distress where I stayed.
My dwelling was on the mountain height,
My talking companions were the birds,
The decaying leaves of the *ki* my clothing."

These passages constitute about one tenth of the whole song, some of which is adapted only to a gross heathen state, and is unfit to appear in an English dress.

The multitude quietly listening some six or eight minutes, at a particular turn or passage in the song indicating the order to march, rose together, and as the song continued with increasing volubility and force, slowly moved forward in silence; and all leaning from the shore, strained their huge ropes, tugging together to heave up the vessel. The brig felt their power—rolled up slowly towards the shore, upon her keel, till her side came firmly against the rock, and there instantly stopped: but the immense team moved on unchecked; and the mainmast broke and fell with its shrouds, being taken off by the cables drawn by unaided muscular strength. The hull instantly rolled back to her former place, and was considered irrecoverable. The interest of the scene was much heightened by the fact that a large man by the name of Kiu, who had ascended the standing shrouds, being near the main-top when the hull began to move, was descending when the mast broke, and was seen to come down suddenly and simultaneously with it in its fall. Strong apprehensions were felt on shore that he was killed amidst the ruins. Numbers hastened from the shore to the wreck, to see the effects of their pull and to look after Kiu. He was found amusing himself swimming about on the seaward side of the wreck, where he had opportunely plunged unhurt, when he was in imminent danger.

At this time the king of Kauai, then at Honolulu, was dangerously ill. The chiefs and people assembled to recover the lost brig, being apprised of it, soon dispersed, some to hasten to him, and some to return to their dwellings to wait the result.[100]

As Bingham says at the outset of this unsuccessful salvage, he never saw greater human effort expended on a single task in his entire life. The main cables, made of hibiscus fiber, must have been harvested, processed, and woven in the two short weeks between the departure of the chiefess from Waimea and the application to *Ha'aheo*'s mainmast.[101] Had the mainmast not broken, the Hawaiians might have been able to draw *Ha'aheo* high up enough onto the reef for repairs. As it was, they recovered the sails, spars, and everything else useful before (and probably after) the unsuccessful salvage attempt, finally abandoning the wreck to the shallow bottom of Hanalei Bay.

Word of the royal loss at Hanalei did not reach the other islands for more than a month, with the return of the schooner *Washington* from Kaua'i on 12 May. Missionary business agent Levi Chamberlain added further details associated with the loss in his journal entry for that same day: "The loss to government is thought to be considerable not only of the vessel, but of specie on board, of which it is said there was considerable. There were also in her a few articles belonging to the mission." However, he investigated the matter overnight and the following day was able to record that at least the mission's *waiwai* was safe, having been removed from the yacht when she was last at Lahaina.[102] Reverend Artemas Bishop summarized the mission's losses on the *Ha'aheo* shipwreck early in June, writing from Kailua to Chamberlain in Honolulu, "The articles left on board of the barge were the barrels destined for Waiakea, bricks for both this & W.[aiakea] station, and a barrel of beef for this place. We had not heard of the loss of the barge until the arrival of our friends . . . I have had no occasion to use the waiwai destined for Waiakea. Shall expect to forward it by the first conveyance."[103]

Kalanimoku did finally visit Kaua'i in late July aboard his schooner *New York,* but before going to the seat of government at Waimea, he "touched at Waioli first, to look after the wrecked Cleopatra's Barge."[104] It is unclear what he may have been after with this unusual detour, but it may have been *Ha'aheo*'s leftover guns or other armaments. He also may have collected what-

ever was left behind on the beach by the Kaua'i salvors or what he could recover from a local notification. In any event, there may have been enough
salvaged materials to fill his schooner, for he arrived at Waimea not aboard
New York but upon the brig *Tamahololani,* formerly owned by Kaumuali'i,
to address land settlements and other political activities during this normally
unstable political transition. *New York* may have taken whatever remained of
value from the *Ha'aheo*'s remains back to Honolulu.

Thus ends the contemporary record of the famed ship, for after she wrecked,
she was no longer of any use or interest to those in the Sandwich Islands who
kept written records. The island of Kaua'i—possibly with human interven-
tion—had exacted revenge upon the famous ship for her part in Liholiho's
kidnapping of its beloved chief only a few years earlier, and the island buried
her bones in the sand at the bottom of a little mile-wide bay on its north shore.

Liholiho never learned of the loss of his most prized possession. After clear-
ing Honolulu on 27 November 1823, *L'Aigle* sailed for England via Rio de
Janeiro. By the time of her arrival at Rio ninety-four days later, Rives had
been replaced as interpreter by Hawaiian James Young, one of Liholiho's
punahele along for the voyage.[105] However, under mysterious circumstances
(believed by the Hawaiians to have been engineered by Jean Rives and Captain Starbuck), Young was left behind at Rio with all of the royal party's official papers.[106] *L'Aigle* arrived unannounced at Portsmouth on 17 May 1824,
but the Hawaiian plans for a royal audience were embarrassingly thwarted
until Young's arrival on a coal ship some weeks later, as he carried official
proof of the king's identity and mission along with the requisite letters of
introduction.[107] The royal party made its way to London, where Liholiho's
money chests were opened and found to be missing $12,000. When ques-
tioned, Captain Starbuck indicated only that $3,000 had been spent at Rio,
and apparently the matter of the missing specie was dropped without further
question.[108]

While awaiting an audience with His Majesty King George, Liholiho and
his party amused themselves with sightseeing tours, visits to the opera, tai-
lors and dressmakers, and other diversions (fig. 2.27). In early July he and
Queen Kamamalu contracted the measles, to which the Hawaiian Islands had
not been exposed; the queen died on 8 July, followed quickly by Liholiho on
13 July. Boki, governor of the Big Island and de facto successor to the royal
Hawaiian party, dismissed Rives immediately following Liholiho's death "for
repeated ill behavior"; Rives promptly stole the king's gold pocket watch
and made off for Paris. After the surviving chiefs returned from England to
Hawai'i with the royal corpses on HMS *Blonde,* they revoked Rives's land
grants and he never returned to the islands.[109]

Later History of the Wreck

Despite her total loss and abandonment, *Cleopatra's Barge* would not stay
down. Twenty years after the wreck occurred, the thread was picked up again

THEIR MAJESTIES
KING RHEO RHIO; QUEEN TAMEHAMALU; MADAME POKI;
OF THE SANDWICH ISLANDS, AND SUITE.
As they appeared at the Theatre Royal Drury Lane, June 4th 1824.

Figure 2.27. Their Majesties King Rheo Rhio; Queen Tamehamalu; Madame Poki; of the Sandwich Islands, and Suite. As they appeared at the Theatre Royal Drury Lane, June 4th 1824, *by J. W. Gear. While awaiting a royal audience with King George of Britain, the Hawaiians had little to do beyond sampling the London entertainments. They created a sensation wherever they went because of their exotic demeanor and clothing. Courtesy of the National Portrait Gallery, Smithsonian.*

by a local Kaua'i correspondent identified as Kekau, who submitted a brief article from Kaua'i to the Honolulu newspaper *The Polynesian:*

> Waioli, Feb. 1st, 1845. To the Editor of the Polynesian:—Arrival Extraordinary. On the 30th of Dec. a part of the hulk of the Haheo [*sic*] or "Cleopatra's Barge," wrecked in this bay some 15 or 20 years, started from its watery bed and washed upon the shore. Many of the oak timbers are in quite a sound state, except so far as perforated by the teredo or ship-worm. From the quantity of iron and copper bolts, we judge she must have been framed for *strength* as for beauty.—[110]

Thirteen years after the 1844 storm that tossed a section of the *Barge*'s hull ashore, a serial article on the ports of Hawai'i in *The Pacific Commercial Ad-*

vertiser added a new twist to the story, stating, "The wreck is supposed to have occurred solely through the incompetency or negligence of the master, a foreigner."[111] However, this 1857 story offers no source for its supposition and would appear to be suspect, as it is much later and contradicts all of the contemporary accounts. That same year, human agents disturbed the grave site, as recorded in the Hawaiian-language newspaper *Ka Hae Hawaii:*

> in the year 1824 in the month of April, a ship was wrecked at Wai'['] oli, Ha'[']aheo was the name, it was Kamehameha II's ship, and its cannons were found this month. Two guns were retrieved by two men diving at the wreck, and are deposited on shore with some other iron objects, and the divers say two more cannons remain in the sea. The age of this ship, from its sinking to this day, is 33 years. That's how long these guns have stayed in the sea, not the least damage, very good [condition], no parts missing, no dents, no rust, they are both shiny to see. Although the outsides are covered in coral, they were all done, [and are now] truly fine. Written on the outside of these guns is the year 1813, and I believe that's the year they were made. This is a new sight, many natives have come to look, and Haole, too. Some copper plate has also been found, unrusted. Some iron and copper nails, too, unharmed.[112]

A 1919 article detailing an oral history taken of A. S. Wilcox, a member of an important *haole* family on Kaua'i, sheds further light on the 1857 salvage of the wreck. Wilcox, who was a boy in the 1850s, recalled that it was local Hawaiian A. S. Nu'uanu who salvaged the wreck from a scow anchored overhead. His divers recovered two iron cannon and some wooden wreckage, "perhaps part of a capstain [*sic*]," from a piece of which his brother Edward made a wooden ruler. He further recollected that the two cannon were around Hanalei for several years and he tried to find them much later to adorn his own yard but learned from another local *haole* that they had been carried off by a British man-of-war (fig. 2.28). He then arranged with a local Hawaiian to find and raise the other brass cannon said to be lodged in the reef by the wreck, but was unsuccessful.[113] Wilcox's brother Edward, in a 1920 letter from Kaua'i to his nieces in Connecticut, added yet more detail to the story in remembering that a vessel was under construction at Waioli in the 1850s, and some Hawaiians were told that there was a brass gun in the wreck. There was a considerable reward if they recovered it, so they hooked the wreck and recovered at least one iron gun, an oak capstan, and the iron post on which it revolved. Edward had an oak ruler made from part of the capstan barrel, blackened (he supposed) from the rusting iron around it and with a white streak through it. When he had looked for the ruler in 1900 he was unable to find it and wondered rather plaintively if his nieces had seen it.[114]

Once again, interest in its most famous shipwreck waned on Kaua'i, where it remained undisturbed for 138 years after the Nu'uanu salvage. In 1991 author Clive Cussler, founder of the National Underwater and Marine Agency,

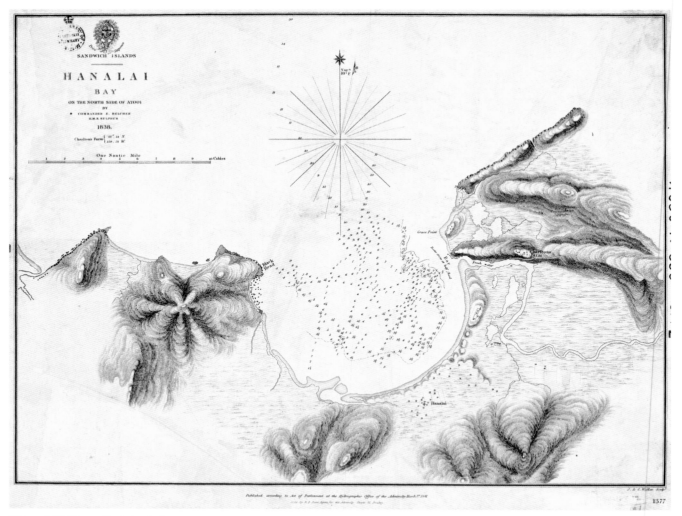

SANDWICH ISLANDS

HANALAI
BAY
ON THE NORTH SIDE OF ATOOI
BY
COMMANDER E. BELCHER
H.M.S SULPHUR
1838.

One Nautic Mile

Figure 2.28. The earliest chart of Hanalei Bay was surveyed in 1838 by Sir Edward Belcher, commander of HMS Sulphur, *and published in 1841 by the British Admiralty.* Sulphur *was likely the "British warship" mentioned as having removed one of* Haʻaheo's *cannon from the Hanalei shore; the ten-gun ship had been converted from war to survey duty in 1835 and was working in the Pacific Ocean in the late 1830s. Courtesy of the State Library of New South Wales, Sydney, Australia.*

visited Hanalei Bay for the express purpose of finding the storied yacht, but left after a short time. In 1994 the author, under the auspices of the Smithsonian's National Museum of American History (NMAH) first visited the bay, and the rest (as they say) is history . . . and archaeology.

In 1995 the NMAH received the first underwater archaeological permits ever granted by the state of Hawaiʻi to search for the wreck of *Cleopatra's Barge* in Hanalei Bay. Using a combination of Hiram Bingham's contemporary account of her loss and modern electronic remote sensing equipment, the wreck was located in the southwest corner of the bay and surveyed for condition and scope. Excavations began that year and were completed in the summer of 2000, yielding more than 1,250 lots of artifacts from the famous ship. These artifacts represent the only material culture from the brief reign of King Kamehameha II, a member of our nation's only authentic royalty. A catalog of the artifacts, a chronology of the ship in Hawaiʻi, and associated materials are available on the Smithsonian website americanhistory.si.edu/cleopatrasbarge.

The Ship Structure and Equipment

There are three sources of information for *Cleopatra's Barge* before she was sold to Boston owners and left New England for the Sandwich Islands in 1820. In descending order of quantity, the first category is the written word, followed by the pictorial evidence. The last is the collection of artifacts that remain from her first life in New England. This latter material, first cataloged for a 1916 exhibit and again for an exhibit of Crowninshield period rooms that the Peabody Museum of Salem opened in 1959, displays everything from the ship's flag to her special-order furniture, silver service, and custom china settings.[1] No expense was spared in outfitting the private yacht with the most elegant and luxurious furnishings available, reflective of Crowninshield family wealth and power in the growing country. Souvenirs collected during the single Mediterranean voyage undertaken by her first owner also speak to the life of leisure that he adopted upon completion of the *Barge,* his personal tastes, and what that meant to a wealthy and eccentric individual of the time.

A few paintings and drawings of *Cleopatra's Barge* are preserved from her New England days and are now at the Peabody Essex Museum in Salem, Massachusetts. Most of the drawings are from owner George Crowninshield's journal, kept for him by clerk of the *Barge,* Samuel Curwen Ward (fig. 3.1). A few more sketches are from the journal of "Philosopher Ben" Crowninshield. So nicknamed to distinguish his name from his father's, he was the son of the *Barge*'s captain, nephew to *Barge* owner George Crowninshield Jr., and a passenger during the Mediterranean cruise. A ne'er-do-well who had been expelled previously from two prestigious institutions of higher learning for personal preferences deemed inappropriate by their administrators, Philosopher Ben had little better to do than tag along on his uncle's yacht. In fact, it is to him we are indebted for the colorful descriptions of the *Barge*'s daily life during the Mediterranean cruise. Within his detailed diary are sprinkled a few drawings of the vessel in various ports. Unfortunately, these port sketches are common to their time in showing shoreline features and shoreside and port facilities, to the general exclusion of any harbor or shipping details. When they show the *Barge* at all, they display her in so little detail that they identify only her unusual rig and thus her identity.

A few contemporary watercolors of the *Barge* exist; some are in the prior chapter. But by far the best of these is a painting executed in August 1818 by deaf-mute artist George Ropes Jr. (1788–1819) of Salem, Massachusetts (fig. 3.2). It shows the elegant yacht from off the port quarter at the height of her

fame and beauty in August 1818, the same month she was put up for auction by her deceased owner's estate. Nearest to the viewer is the yacht's jaunty stern, with a bit of copper sheathing peeking out from under her waterline. Over the top of the rudder is the stern, dominated by five mullioned windows filling the beam of the brig. Next is the black hull, surmounted by the unique herringbone pattern painted onto the port side (the starboard had more traditional horizontal stripes), the differing patterns giving the vessel a striking and most eccentric appearance. Above two yellow wales are a line of seven gunports, through which the mouths of guns menacingly point. Although *Cleopatra's Barge* was by no means a warship, she still had a full complement of fourteen cannon to defend herself. Nearly all seagoing merchant ships of the period, in the aftermath of the War of 1812, continued to carry armament for defensive

reasons, not only relating to renewed warfare but also to defend from pirates or privateers worldwide. Also painted yellow, the gunwale displays remarkably little sheer for such a stylish vessel that by her fourth year would not have had much of an opportunity to hog, or sag at both ends.

As is common in nineteenth-century ship portraits, Ropes painted *Cleopatra's Barge* wearing a full suit of sails. These are driving the vessel at a high speed, as shown by a high bow wave and a wake at her stern. Two headsails, or flying and outer jibs, are set on the bowsprit, abaft which is the square-rigged foremast. This spar bears four traditional loose-footed squaresails stacked in decreasing size: the foresail, fore-topsail, -topgallant, and -royal. Two staysails bridge the gap to the mainmast, which is fore-and-aft rigged with a mainsail and main-topsail. The ship is completed by a US flag flying off the main gaff,[2]

Figure 3.2. *Deaf-mute artist George Ropes Jr. of Salem, Massachusetts, painted this elegant portrait of the Barge in 1818. Since her original owner, George Crowninshield Jr., was dead by this date, the painting was probably commissioned by George's brother Richard, who purchased the ship at the 1818 auction. Courtesy of the Peabody Essex Museum.*

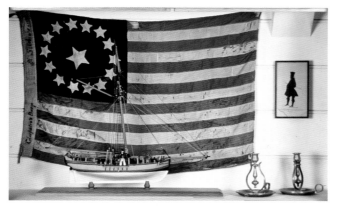

Figure 3.3. *The Barge's silk boat flag sported fifteen red and white stripes and a circle of fourteen stars around a fifteenth. The fifteen-star flag was in use from May 1795 until July 1818. The model is of the 22-ton sloop* Jefferson, *George Crowninshield Jr.'s first yacht (coastal) and War of 1812 privateer. The silhouette is of George Crowninshield Jr. Courtesy of the Peabody Essex Museum.*

and a starred-and-striped homeward-bound pennant fluttering at the forepeak (fig. 3.3).

Cleopatra's Barge was variously described as either a "brig" or a "hermaphrodite brig." The former is a two-masted square-rigged vessel. A hermaphrodite is square-rigged on the foremast and schooner-rigged (fore-and-aft rigged) on the mainmast. It differs from a brigantine, in that the latter carries some squaresails over the mainsail while the hermaphrodite carries no spars or squaresails on the mainmast. The schooner-rigged mainsail was easier and quicker to operate and thus made a hermaphrodite brig more maneuverable and efficient.

Other contemporary portraits variously depict the *Barge*'s starboard side, another (inner) jib, and other minor details. The 1820 ship's log for her voyage out to the Sandwich Islands records the usage of other, archaic sails such as the ring(tail) and water sails, at least when the *Barge* was owned by New Englanders.[3] It's reasonable to assume that these old-fashioned sails were first used on the vessel by her builder, who picked up his sailing knowledge and preferences from many oceanic voyages on his family's trading ships. A pair of watercolors executed by Italian artist Antoine Pittaluga when the *Barge* was in Genoa in 1817 adds the yacht's figurehead—a blue-jacketed sailor in white pants, brandishing a light sword out over the water. Considering the brig's name and the popularity of female figureheads, this male figurehead is enigmatic.

Unfortunately, only one contemporary picture of the ship is preserved from her Hawaiian period (1820–1824). This is a print published by the famous maritime historian Samuel Eliot Morison in early editions of his book *The Maritime History of Massachusetts 1783–1860*.[4] The image, probably produced around 1823, shows the *Barge* anchored with bare poles in the roads at Lahaina, Maui, where the royal family kept a favorite residence (see fig. 2.22). The ship's overall proportions and general details are accurate, right down to the Hawaiian national flag flying from the main gaff. However, the royal yacht has lost her herringbone pattern and seems to have sprouted an extra gunport on her port side, thus calling into question the accuracy of the image. She has also been converted from a hermaphrodite brig to a common brig, square-rigged on both masts.

Contemporary written descriptions add a few tantalizing details, but most of them describe the richness of the interior furniture and furnishings, understandably without much attention to construction details. One exception is a reference to "the figure of an Indian, with his arrows on his back, to stand on deck," but this and the others are mostly crumbs from a missing cake.[5] From them a rough layout of the yacht's interior can be derived, but there are contradictions, written by interested journal-keepers or tourists ignorant of ships, that are irreconcilable and confusing (see fig. 1.16).

There are no contemporary technical descriptions—such as a builder's con-

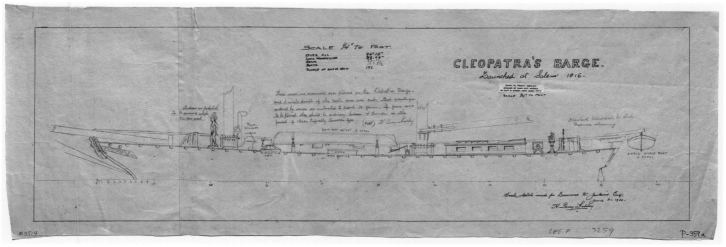

Figure 3.4. *Captain H. Percy Ashley modeled the* Barge *in the 1930s for the Peabody Museum of Salem. While researching the layout, he produced this waterline elevation (P-359a/M-3814) and deck plan (P-359b). Ashley mistakenly thought that no guns were ever placed on the* Barge *and that the gun ports were probably never cut, but that the contemporary painters were commissioned to show twelve brass four-pounder cannon anyway. He further says that the forward-facing, life-size Indian up forward was removed when the ship was under way, as was the custom when ships with figureheads sailed out of sight of land. Courtesy of the Peabody Essex Museum.*

tract—of the *Barge*'s hull, rig, or what made her unique beyond her fancy furnishings, although owner George Crowninshield was said to have put several innovations of his own design into her, based upon his decades of building and fitting out his family's fleet for the international blue-water trade. In the absence of any evidence to the contrary, the famous ship historian and naval architect Howard I. Chapelle, writing about the nation's earliest yachts, stated, "Though a number of yachts, including the famous Salem brigantine *Cleopatra's Barge* (1816) had been built earlier in the century, all of them were constructed on either the Baltimore Clipper or the pilot-boat model." In the basement of the Peabody Essex Museum lies an unfinished spar plan of the *Barge* by Chapelle drawn in late 1954, in which he was beginning to work out the topside details of the ship's rigging. Unfortunately, it is the first drawing he did of her and it does not attempt the underwater part of the hull. As reconstructed, the spars clearly lack the characteristic rake of the Baltimore clipper and thus display the evolution of his thought two decades after he wrote on the origins of the yacht (see fig. 2.8).[6]

In June 1930 the well-known model shipbuilder H. Percy Ashley developed a deck plan and elevation for Peabody Museum curator Lawrence Jenkins in association with a model he was commissioned to build (figs. 3.4 and 3.5). However, although their execution is quite detailed, his drawings clearly did not display access to all of the pictorial materials since assembled by the Peabody Museum, and some inaccuracies are obvious (see fig. 2.7). Another model was built in the 1950s by Richard Orr (fig. 3.6). Similarly, the Boston architectural firm Perry Shaw & Hepburn, Kehoe & Deen prepared a drawing of the ship's lines and other features in an effort to recreate the grand salon when they were commissioned to design the *Barge* exhibit by Louise Dupont Crowninshield in the early 1950s (fig. 3.7). While they were well led by contemporary descriptions of the latter in their replica of the salon, they did not cite any sources for their rendering of the underwater portion of the ship's hull, and it appears to be largely speculative.[7]

SHIP STRUCTURE AND EQUIPMENT **97**

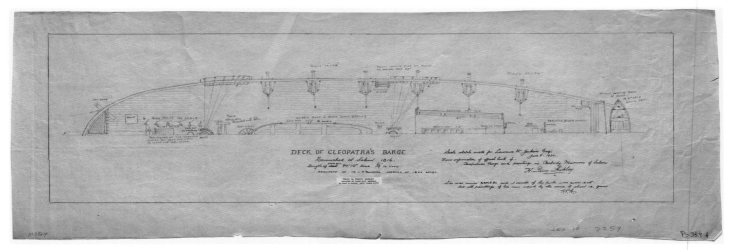

Figure 3.5. *Captain Percy Ashley's deck plan for the* Barge *was developed from contemporary graphic representations and verbal descriptions. Courtesy of the Peabody Essex Museum.*

Figure 3.6 Richard Orr's model of Cleopatra's Barge. *Courtesy of the Peabody Essex Museum.*

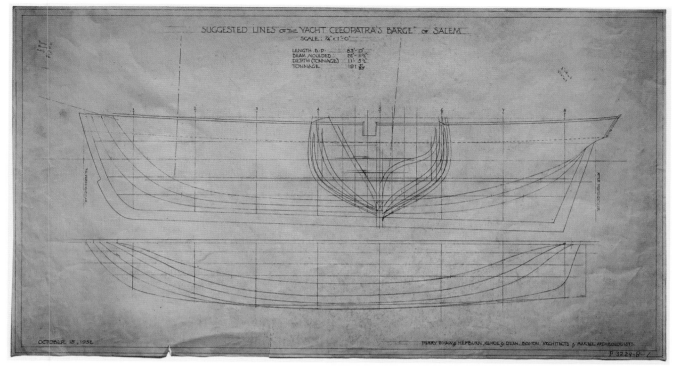

In 1888, some sixty-four years after the sinking of *Cleopatra's Barge,* Benjamin W. Crowninshield wrote that she was modeled after George Crowninshield Jr.'s favorite family vessel, the Salem ship *America IV* (fig. 3.8). Built as a 473-ton merchantman in 1804, *America* was razeed, or cut down by a deck, and converted to a privateer during the War of 1812. She took no fewer than forty-one prizes during that conflict, only six of which were retaken, and she made a fortune for her owners and crews. B. W. Crowninshield asserted confusingly that the *Barge*'s "prototype came from among commercial vessels, but particularly from vessels of war and privateers." He went on to say that her fittings, rigging, wheel, and capstan were all patterned after George Jr.'s "own ideas" and that her standing rigging was especially unusual, but he does not specify how it was different from standard contemporary New England rigs.[8] One known difference was that the ship was fitted with ring sails and water sails, which, like studdingsails, were used for light airs but were archaic by the 1880s when Crowninshield wrote. These sails are mentioned in the ship's logs for her 1820 voyage to Hawai'i. She probably would have been built a bit heavier than an unarmed merchantman in order to accommodate fourteen guns on deck, but how much closer in construction she was to an armed merchant vessel than a small warship—if there even were any significant differences in that time—is unknown.

Unfortunately, these tantalizing clues are the extent of modern knowledge concerning the construction and structural history of this famous yacht. Salem shipbuilder Retire Becket left no known business or personal records of his shipyard activities, and no builder's contract or specifications are preserved

Figure 3.7. *In the early 1950s, the architectural firm of Perry Shaw & Hepburn, Kehoe & Deen was commissioned by the Peabody Museum of Salem to build a reconstruction of the main salon of* Cleopatra's Barge *off East India Marine Hall. This hypothetical lines drawing of the vessel was part of the exercise, but it presents a rather portly vision of the brig's shape. Courtesy of the Peabody Essex Museum.*

Figure 3.8. *Painted by George Ropes Jr. in 1806, this portrait of Crowninshield Wharf in Salem depicts* America *with her upper deck still in place. Despite its presence, the ship still looks swift even when tied up at the wharf. The upper deck was removed to lighten the ship and increase her speed as a privateer during the War of 1812. Courtesy of the Peabody Essex Museum.*

for the *Barge*'s construction among any of the generation-spanning and voluminous Crowninshield papers preserved in various repositories. And the remains of the ship held out little promise for amplifying the record, considering where they had lain for 170 years. Contemporary shipwrecks add little to the record, as the only two known wrecks from the period are naval vessels from the War of 1812, both built on the freshwater Lake Champlain between Vermont and New York.[9] As they were warships built for shallow inland fresh waters and not oceangoing yachts designed for the open seas, the knowledge to be gained from a comparison is limited in scope.

The Environment of the Shipwreck

Mile-wide Hanalei Bay cuts into the north side of Kaua'i, the oldest and northernmost of the volcanic Hawaiian Islands, off to the west of the rest of the group (fig. 3.9). Nine months of the year, the little bay is pounded by heavy surf that originates in the Arctic and traverses deep Pacific waters before reaching the bay's shallow waters and dashing itself against Hanalei's sandy shore. Just off the bay's southwestern corner, right where the little Waioli River empties into the bay, there is a vertical reef in five feet of water depth,

Figure 3.9. *This aerial photograph of Hanalei Bay shows how small the bay and harbor are relative to the North Shore of Kauaʻi. Photograph by Smithsonian National Museum of American History.*

which drops off to fifteen or so feet deep (depending upon the relative strength of the previous winter's storms) (fig. 3.10).

It is this shallow reef that the *Barge* struck, onto which she could not be drawn for temporary repairs and against which she was abandoned in April 1824. So the wreck site is right at the littoral where the waves break over the reef, and it is not a kind or gentle place most of the year. To this seasonal surf may be added the three recorded tsunamis that struck Kauaʻi's North Shore in the 1940s and 1950s, and possibly other earlier, unrecorded such events as well. Add the 1991 Hurricane Iniki, the eye of which stalled over Hanalei before moving on its destructive course (fig. 3.11). Top it all off with a contemporary 1824 salvage, followed by another one—possibly even more destructive—thirty years later, magnified by the voracious teredo worm. Combined, these natural and manmade forces did not argue strongly for the preservation of much hull structure, as proposed in the original research hypothesis. That

Figure 3.10. *After a heavy rain,
the last bend of the Waioli River is
frequently blown out by the swollen
river water; the sand and silt from
upriver are carried out to the site
and deposited on it. Photograph by
Smithsonian National Museum of
American History.*

theory of no preserved hull structure lasted through the first season of survey and excavation and well into the second as well. However, during the last few days of the 1996 season, some few ship timbers were found lodged against and under the reef that the *Barge* struck.

Ship Remains

The 1996 structural finds included what appear to be a portion of one of the ship's ends, partial floors and first futtocks, runs of strakes (some with copper sheathing attached), and a possible deck beam with decking attached. All the major bow timbers found against the reef in 1996 were disarticulated and redeposited in disassociated positions; moreover, many were degraded and missing their edges and ends, rendering detailed measurement and interpretation difficult (figs. 3.12 and 3.13). Recording was further exacerbated by heavy rains and consequent flooding of the Waioli River, which cut through a sandbar blocking the river mouth and dumped heavily-silted flood water directly onto the site.

One visible section of timber measured 11 ft. in length; pieced together from two timbers, its sided and molded dimensions are $9\frac{1}{2}$ in. and 11 in. respectively. Along its molded face were several 1 in. treenails and two shallow, rectilinear notches where other timbers originally intersected it, along with

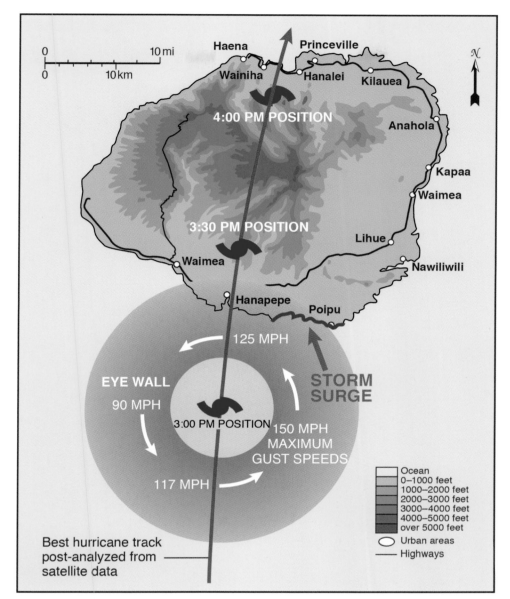

Figure 3.11. *A category 4 hurricane, Iniki was the strongest storm ever to hit the Hawaiian Islands. Its eye tracked from the southwest corner of Kaua'i northerly across the island, exiting on the western side of Hanalei Bay. It killed six people and destroyed thousands of homes. Illustration created and provided by Steven Businger, University of Hawai'i.*

several heavily concreted iron fasteners (fig. 3.14). The timber's eastern end continued into the trench baulk; the western end extended beneath another frame piece into the baulk on the other side of the trench. It appears to be a section of the keelson, its measured angle of 28 degrees on the basal surface indicating a relatively flat deadrise. However, some of its other features present interpretive challenges. From its basal surface, a heavily concreted 1 in. iron drift fastened it to a floor. This member's molded dimension tapered from a maximum of 9 in. (at the 28-degree angle directly below the keelson) to 6 in. at the eastern end; the western end was eroded off. Its preserved length measured 6 ft. $6\frac{1}{2}$ in., and several 1 in. treenails protrude from its basal surface at ca. 6 in. intervals (fig. 3.15). However, there was no evidence for a flat on the bottom surface of the floor, which should be present for fastening to the keel.

Figure 3.12. *The jumble of disarticulated ship timbers from the area of the ship's bow, when viewed against the other large section of hull in trench 37 and environs, suggests that this end of the ship struck the reef first with considerable force. These were the first heavy framing timbers we found, in trench E12 against the reef face. Drawing by Thomas Ormsby for the Smithsonian National Museum of American History.*

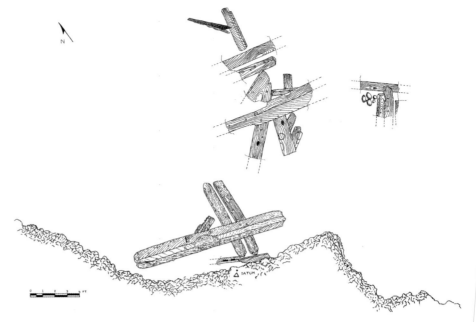

Figure 3.13. *Divers Rick Rogers and Tom Ormsby recording hull timbers in trench E12. Photograph by Smithsonian National Museum of American History.*

One of the disarticulated futtocks/floors (with sided and molded dimensions of $4\frac{1}{2}$ in. and $9\frac{1}{2}$ in.) had three fragmentary strakes still attached to its basal surface; these planks measured $3\frac{1}{2}$ in. thick and 7 to $7\frac{1}{2}$ in. wide. One of them is fashioned of two thicknesses of wood, indicating either a patch or a pieced member (fig. 3.16). Other fragmentary framing timbers varied widely in their sided and molded dimensions.

On the western edge of trench E12, a 6 ft. 3 in. straight timber with one cut and one eroded end was observed lodged beneath the coral reef. Measuring 5 by $5\frac{1}{2}$ in. in width and thickness, it had five 6 in. × 3 in. timbers butted together and fastened at its cut end. Since these dimensions differ significantly

Figure 3.14. *The southwest end of the ship's keelson, hard against the reef face. Photograph by Smithsonian National Museum of American History.*

Figure 3.15. *A floor timber with several treenails sticking up where another timber intersected this one. Photograph by Smithsonian National Museum of American History.*

from the other timbers, it is believed that this assemblage represents portions of a deck beam and decking (fig. 3.17). A fragmentary bevel-ended frame containing a concreted fastener through the bevel perpendicular to the frame side appears to be a hawse piece; however, the edges and end are too eroded and worm-eaten to derive useful measurements.

The above timbers represented the sum total of ship's structure found well into the final season in 2000. That year, trenches were set in all of the previously unexcavated spaces between earlier trenches in an effort to cover the rest of the debris zone on the bay bottom. Midway through the final 2000 campaign, the numbers of small finds diminished to almost none, indicating

Figure 3.16. *Floor with three strakes, or outer hull planks, still attached. The floor of a frame is the lowermost piece of it, attached to the keel at the bottom of the ship's structure. Photograph by Smithsonian National Museum of American History.*

Figure 3.17. *Deck beam and decking (inverted). Photograph by Smithsonian National Museum of American History.*

that the prior seasons' work had been thorough. Once a couple of dry trenches were excavated, it made sense to set a trench quite far from the main wreck deposit, against the reef on the south side of the notch where the ship had hit and sunk. Almost immediately, a series of vertical frame tips began to emerge from the sand against the reef (fig. 3.18), and excavations a bit further out revealed a flat section of the ship's structure that appeared to be decking. When the two trenches were joined, expanded, and augmented, they revealed a 40-foot section of the stern lying on its starboard side and listing at a 35-degree angle. The portside frames were vertical in the sand, while the starboard side

Figure 3.18. *Opening trench E37 during the 2000 season; the top ends of the ship's frames are just beginning to appear in the deep sand, hard against the reef face. Photograph by Smithsonian National Museum of American History.*

Figure 3.19. *This plan of the hull remains of Ha'aheo was stitched together from dozens of small 2 ft. × 2 ft. grid drawings, since that was all that the slumping sand at the bottom of the trenches would allow us to see at any one time. Drawing by Thomas Ormsby for the Smithsonian National Museum of American History.*

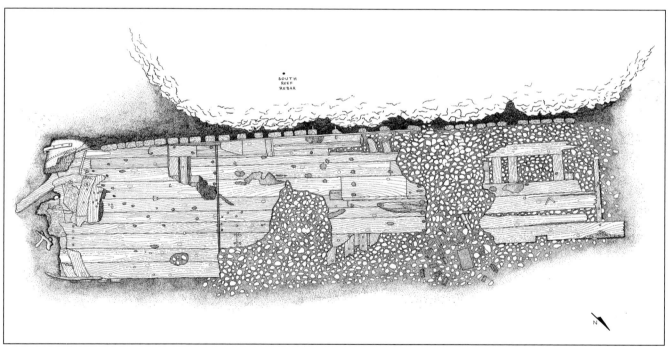

SOUTH
REEF
REBAR

of the preserved portion of the hull had split away and was virtually flat; this gave it the initial appearance of a section of the deck (fig. 3.19).

Observation and interpretation of this section of the hull were severely hampered by the depth to which it was buried in the sand. This depth varied from around two feet of overburden against the reef to around ten feet off the reef at the sternpost. The propwash deflector used to expose features created a cone-shaped trench, the bottom of which might only be three feet across. As soon as the deflector was turned off, the sand would begin to slump back

down into the bottom, obscuring the contents (fig. 3.20). Aggressive small fish feeding on the slanted sides of the trenches also undermined them and hastened the trickle of the sand. Getting any sense of the overall picture under these conditions was impossible, as we had to uncover a section or feature, map it, and then move on a few feet to expose the next section. As we did this, the previously exposed trenching would be almost completely backfilled by the sand from the new trench. Only when we returned to the lab and put all of the underwater drawings and measurements onto a fresh sheet of drafting film did the information begin to make overall sense.

An 11-foot lead draft mark (fig. 3.21) on the starboard side of the sternpost preserved below a few more inches of that member indicated that the stern of the yacht was preserved to a height of 11 ft. 6 in.—just a half inch over her registered depth (fig. 3.22). This was below the level of the ship's transom, none of which was found. Along with the Roman numeral draft marks at the copper-sheathed stern, the most characteristic feature was a perfectly preserved iron rudder gudgeon. Measuring 30 in. long, $2\frac{1}{2}$ in. high, and $\frac{3}{4}$ in. thick, at its aft end it had a vertical $2\frac{1}{2}$ in. diameter hole to receive the rudder pintle (fig. 3.23). Spaced along its length at $2\frac{1}{2}$, $7\frac{1}{2}$, and $14\frac{1}{4}$ in. intervals are three 1 in. bolt holes for securely fastening the gudgeon to the stern timbers over the copper hull sheathing (fig. 3.24). At this level, the sternpost,

made of white oak (*Quercus* sp. [Leucobalanus]) was shaped like the keystone of an arch, molded 24 in. (fore-and-aft) and sided 9 in. at the after end and 14 in. at the forward end (fig. 3.25). Undoubtedly it was pieced together from more than one timber (post and apron), but its heavily eroded surfaces made it impossible to determine precisely where one timber began and another ended or how they were fastened together. Ten inches forward of its aftermost surface, $2\frac{1}{2}$ in. thick strakes meet it on both sides at a 22-degree rabbet. Like the sternpost itself, these strakes were covered with heavily encrusted copper hull sheathing, obscuring any fastening details.

Forward of the sternpost, thirty-one portside frames are preserved, aligned almost vertically along the face of the reef (fig. 3.26). Despite an unbroken run of ceiling fastened along the interior, they are irregularly spaced, due either to their historic salvage or movement in the shallow and very dynamic surf zone

Figure 3.23. *Photo of rudder gudgeon on the ship's sternpost, into which the rudder pin would have been set to secure it. The rudder was not found; it probably floated off or was salvaged during the wrecking sequence. Photograph by Smithsonian National Museum of American History.*

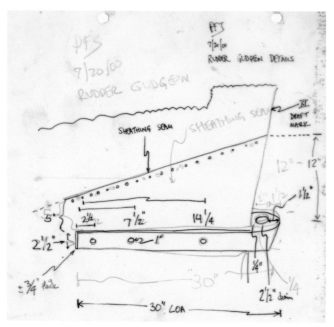

Figure 3.24. *Underwater sketch of rudder gudgeon. Important underwater sketches were cleaned up and copied after the day's fieldwork was completed. Since pencil marks could be rubbed off by contact with a diver's neoprene wetsuit, important sketches were overdrawn in permanent ink. Photograph by Smithsonian National Museum of American History.*

Figure 3.25. *A plan of the sternpost. Drawing by Thomas Ormsby for the Smithsonian National Museum of American History.*

on the shores of the bay. This spacing varies from 5 in. between frames, to runs of up to four frames with no space between them, with no visible pattern. Like the sternpost, the frames were made of white oak; their molded dimension was consistent at 7 in., while their sided dimension varied from $5\frac{1}{2}$ in. to a maximum of $9\frac{1}{2}$ in. In one or two spots along the outside of the hull, short pieces of copper-clad strakes are attached to the frames, $2\frac{1}{2}$ in. thick where measurable. Efforts to excavate deeper along the hull's exterior were hampered by slumping sands or, in the case of the forward end, proximity to the reef face.

Like the strakes, the preserved ceiling measured $2\frac{1}{2}$ in. in thickness, but plank widths varied from a minimum of 4 in. to a maximum of 9 in., with a single patch measuring 12 in. wide. Some of this variation is undoubtedly due to the extensive 1822 repairs by Captain Meek in the after half of the ship (as outlined in chapter 2), which certainly required some ceiling replacement and patching. Other evidence for repairs is found in the ceiling between frames 10 and 11 (counting from the sternpost), where there is a line of five planks all cut off at the same frame (see fig. 3.19). It would have seriously weakened the internal ceiling strength to cut a series of contiguous planks at the same place, and this is evidence for very hasty and poor-quality repairs by Captain Meek's band of carpenters. There was a distinct color difference between some of the frames observed under missing sections of the ceiling, which appeared to represent old (darker) and new (lighter, green) timbering. One of them exhibits signs of reuse in the form of a hook scarf at its end that is not met by a corresponding scarf on the timber it butts against (fig. 3.27). Unfortunately, the cellular structure of the samples taken from this area was so degraded that the wood types could not be identified.[10] Additional evidence of hasty repair work is seen in a straight-butt joint in at least one spot in the stern framing (fig. 3.28), with the frame timbers separated by inches and held together only by the inner and outer hull planks. Essentially, two sections of the same frame were unconnected by this joint and would have been very weak, allowing the two ends to rub or work against one another. This likely would not have been permitted by either the ship's original owner or its builder, so it appears that this must be later repairs. However, it is hard to imagine why Captain Meek would have permitted such shoddy repairs over his name, and what this said for his relationship with his employer Liholiho and his navy. He expected either that his repairs—hidden under other heavy ship timbers and sheathing—would never be seen or that anyone who might ever see them would not know any better, or he simply did not care.

The ceiling in this area (low down in the ship's structure) was fastened to the framing with iron spikes; their heads were too concreted to derive more specific information for these in situ elements of construction. Of course, iron fasteners and copper sheathing below the waterline would have been subject to galvanic action. Fortunately, enough are preserved in other contexts to allow some idea of their range of measurements. A few treenails also appeared as well, but in no discernible pattern. No limber boards were observed, unlike contemporary ships built in the Lake Champlain region.[11]

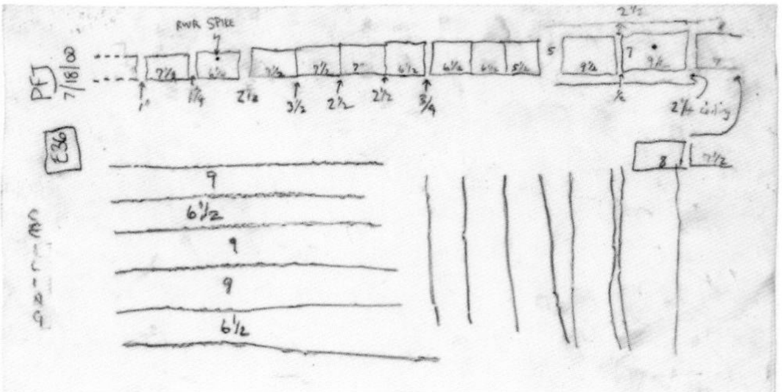

Figure 3.26. *Underwater sketch of the early emergence of ship frames against the reef face. Photograph by Smithsonian National Museum of American History.*

Hull Fasteners

Nearly all of the 509 iron-based concretions recovered during excavations of the royal yacht contained degraded iron fasteners of various shapes and sizes. They were found throughout the site, with no visible placement pattern. X-rays, casts of voids where the iron had dissolved, and a few original iron examples revealed that the vast majority of these iron spikes were square-sided, square-headed, and tapered iron spikes. The dimensions for the well-preserved spikes (both the artifacts themselves as well as x-rays) displayed a remarkably wide range of sizes, with a clear clustering around 6 in. long and $\frac{1}{2}$ in. wide measured just below the head. Some of this variety may be attributed to the variable preservation of the iron artifacts; for example, a spike

Figure 3.27. *Photo of different colored frames showing the 1822 repairs and an unmet hook scarf, demonstrating that the repairs to the royal yacht by Captain Meek were hasty, shoddy, or both. Photograph by Smithsonian National Museum of American History.*

Figure 3.28. *All wooden shipwrecks shift, settle, flatten, and deteriorate over time. Even taking this into account, the open seams of the futtocks making up the frames in* Haʻaheo'*s lower hull in the stern seem excessively wide for anything but hasty or shoddy repairs by Captain Meek. Photograph by Smithsonian National Museum of American History.*

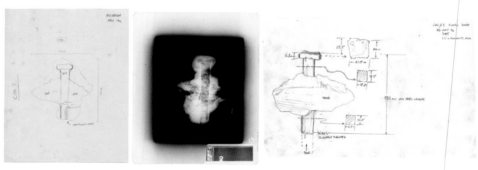

Figure 3.29. *This composite image shows different stages of work on an artifact in the conservation lab — the x-ray of the concretion, a sketch from the x-ray, and the reduction of the concretion into its original artifact. CON3 is a heavy iron fastener still piercing the piece of wood it originally fastened to another feature. Photograph by Smithsonian National Museum of American History.*

that originally measured 6 in. long when new might decay into a spike now only $5\frac{1}{2}$ in. in length. However, this would not account for the clearly intact half-inch spikes recovered that measured 6, $6\frac{1}{8}$, $6\frac{1}{4}$, $6\frac{1}{2}$, and $6\frac{5}{8}$ in. long (fig. 3.29). One example, broken off at both ends, even measured 13 in. $\times \frac{1}{2}$ in. There were other, smaller clusters of headed iron spikes sided $\frac{1}{4}$, $\frac{3}{8}$, and $\frac{5}{8}$ in. as well. Larger iron fasteners also measured $\frac{3}{4}$, $\frac{7}{8}$, and 1 in. on a side, and some of these were round. These larger fasteners, especially the round examples, were probably drifts, used to attach the framing timbers (keel, floors, and futtocks) together (possibly above the waterline). Some of these larger-dimension iron fasteners were over a foot long, ranging from $12\frac{1}{2}$ in. to one intact example measuring 22 in. $\times \frac{3}{4}$ in. (CON 243). Some of this group have peened, or flattened, heads from where they were hammered home.

Numerous types and sizes of copper fasteners were found scattered throughout the wreck site, ranging in size from heavy drifts to small hull sheathing nails. Copper fasteners were generally used below the waterline to prevent galvanic action corrosion and at plank ends for extra strength and durability. Iron fasteners used below the waterline under copper hull sheathing caused an electrical reaction between the two metals, resulting in the loss of the iron.

The heaviest of the copper fasteners is a massive 11 in. long upper end of a 1 in. drift (C8) (fig. 3.30), which would have fastened such members as keel, frame, and keelson together. Its tip is slightly peened where it was driven into the heavy timbers, and its lower end curves around before it is broken off. The broken end is rough and appears to have been snapped off, possibly emblematic of the forces at work as the ship's bottom was torn open by the reef. Next in size is C9, a $\frac{7}{8}$ in. curved bottom of a drift; the upper end is broken off, and the lower end is slightly tapered and dished, as though it had been rolled in a mill. C55 represents the top of a $\frac{3}{4}$ in. drift with heavily peened tip and sheared-off lower end; from the nature of the break, it appears that it was snapped off very quickly. The longest and best-preserved of the copper drifts is C59, a $\frac{3}{4}$ in. example with both ends preserved and measuring 24 in. long (fig. 3.31). Its head is heavily peened, and its lower end—slightly convex—shows no evidence of peening or widening as for riveting.

Two of the bolts have riveted or rove tips with washers attached to the lower end; one (C80) is $11\frac{1}{4}$ in. long and $\frac{5}{8}$ in. in diameter (fig. 3.32), and the other (C87) is $10\frac{1}{2}$ in. long with a $\frac{1}{2}$ in. diameter. These were found loose in trenches E36 and E37, the area of the stern section, but what they originally fastened is unknown (possibly plank ends or sister frames?). Another bolt (C16) is identical to C87 but lacks the washer at the lower end. It was found in trench E12, the bow area up against the reef. All three have heavily mushroomed upper ends where they were driven into the timbers. Another intact example measuring $12\frac{5}{8} \times \frac{5}{8}$ (C79) has a peened top and slightly tapered and dished bottom end, where it appears to have been rolled in the manufacturing process.

Six shorter $\frac{5}{8}$ in. copper bolts also were recovered from several trenches in the forward area of the ship. All are intact and range in length from $6\frac{3}{4}$ to 8 in. long. They all have slightly tapered and dished lower ends, and all have peened upper ends (C5, C14, C27, C32, C45, and C55). What wooden ship members this uniform group might have fastened is a mystery, given their relative shortness (fig. 3.33). A fragmentary example of this type (C11) was converted into an awl or pick by sharpening the lower end into a long, smooth, slightly flattened point (fig. 3.34). This example, clearly fashioned into a hand tool prior to the wrecking of the royal yacht, was found in E12 against the reef.

The largest group of copper fasteners consisted of square $\frac{1}{2}$ in. copper spikes with square heads and chisel points. Used for securing hull planks to the

Figure 3.30. *A selection of the heavy copper drifts or through bolts (C5–9) that originally fastened together the ship's frames and other heavy structural timbers. Photograph by Smithsonian National Museum of American History.*

Figure 3.31. *The longest copper drift was 24 in. long and would have likely fastened the keel and keelson together at some point (C59). Photograph by Richard Strauss, Smithsonian National Museum of American History.*

Figure 3.32. *Both ends of this copper bolt (C80) are peened or flattened from the force of driving it through heavy timber. At the left end the swelling on the shaft indicates where the wood was originally; the other end has a heavy washer to fix it in place. Photograph by Harold Dorwin, Smithsonian National Museum of American History.*

Figure 3.33. *These copper bolts (C45) are a common size (8 in. × 1¼ in.) found on the wreck. One end is peened where it was driven into the timber, and the other is slightly dished rather than sharp or pointed. Photograph by Smithsonian National Museum of American History.*

Figure 3.34. *C11 is a reworked sharpened copper spike, indicating secondary use after removal from the ship's structure. This may have been one of the fasteners pulled out of the rotten stern area. Photograph by Harold Dorwin, Smithsonian National Museum of American History.*

Figure 3.35. *C52 is a large, intact, chisel-pointed copper spike measuring 6½ in. long with a square head measuring ¹¹⁄₁₆ in. on a side. Photograph by Richard Strauss, Smithsonian National Museum of American History.*

frames below the waterline, these are much more uniform in size, with a common length of $6\frac{1}{2}$ in. and a head width of $\frac{7}{16}$ in. (fig. 3.35). Several are twisted and/or broken off cleanly at one or both ends, indicating that they may have hit a knot when originally driven. Alternately, they may be a dramatic display of the shearing force produced by the ship striking the reef and subsequent reduction of the hull into small pieces. Two were clearly larger originally, but how much larger is not known since their upper ends are broken off and the shafts are heavily twisted and bent as much as 90 degrees (C53 and C56).

In addition to these copper fasteners, common 1 in. treenails were found on portions of the hull planking (where it could be seen); all but one spruce example were oak. These were used to fasten the hull timbers to the frames, and they were in two forms: the most common type, where the wedge bisects the wooden head to spread it and make it more secure (W48), and an unusual type with a short square wedge centered in the head of the fastener (W36)

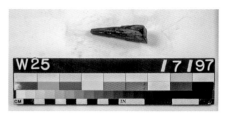

Figure 3.36. *A variety of treenails, most commonly used for fastening hull strakes to frames: common wedged example (W48); square wedged (W36); and an example of square wedge (W25). The variety may be due to the 1822 repairs. Photographs by Hugh Talman, Smithsonian National Museum of American History.*

(fig. 3.36). The reason for the difference in the two wedge types and species is unknown, and in the absence of further information it may be proposed that perhaps the square wedges were part of the 1822–1823 repairs to the ship.

Copper Hull Sheathing

One of the largest recovered components of the *Barge*'s construction was the copper hull sheathing that covered the bottom of the hull up to the waterline. Various hull coatings date back as far as the ancient Mediterranean in order to retard biological growth, prevent shipworms from penetrating the hull timbers, and extend a ship's life and speed. However, it was not until the later eighteenth century that British experiments proved that a thin sheet of copper nailed onto wooden ship bottoms prevented seaweed or grass from attaching themselves and also stopped the voracious teredo worms from tunneling into their wooden hulls. By 1816, approximately 18 percent of British-built merchant vessels were copper-sheathed, and coppering may have been one of first owner George Crowninshield's forward-looking innovations on his *Barge*.[12]

First found during the 1995 survey, a section of copper sheet turned out to be a diagnostic artifact for the shipwreck as a whole, in that one of the samples recovered bore the two-line stamp "W & G/G 24" in the lower right-hand corner of the exterior surface (HS4) (fig. 3.37). Tracing this stamp back to its source as the Liverpool, England, copper merchants Owen Williams and Pascoe Grenfell proved that the ship under investigation was a late eighteenth- or early nineteenth-century vessel, not one of the several later wrecks known to have been lost in or around Hanalei Bay.[13] The "G 24" designated 24-gauge

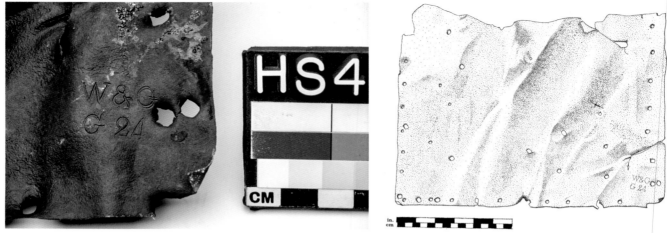

Figure 3.37. *The stamped piece of copper hull sheathing (HS4) was a diagnostic artifact which helped to identify the wreck as that of the royal yacht. The "W&G" mark turned out to signify the early nineteenth-century Liverpool copper dealer Williams & Grenfell. Photograph by Eric Long, Smithsonian National Museum of American History; drawing by Thomas Ormsby, Smithsonian National Museum of American History.*

copper, which measured at 24 ounces per square foot.[14] When combined with other diagnostic artifacts, it indicated with little doubt that the wreck was *Cleopatra's Barge.*

Between 1995 and 2000, 100 pieces of copper sheathing were recovered and cataloged. These range in size from two full sheets measuring the standard 14 in. × 48 in. (HS075 and HS098) (fig. 3.38) to groups of tiny fragments cataloged together. There are also two intact triangular gore end pieces that originally covered the gores or seams where two runs of larger sheets met at the ends of the ship (HS010 and HS092) (fig. 3.39). Regardless of size, all of the buckled, crumpled, and pleated sheets display some violent treatment, either at the hands of the yacht's crew while she was afloat or, more likely, encountered by the ship at the reef's edge, as the sheets were scraped off the side of the ship at the point of impact. Some, with intact nail holes, indicate that they fell off the wooden hull, probably once it reached a certain state of degradation caused by storms or by the teredo worm, and were subsequently buffeted by the heavy winter or storm surf to which Hanalei Bay is regularly subjected. Unfortunately, all the larger pieces are so twisted and crumpled that it is virtually impossible to determine a fastening pattern, although the ship almost certainly was coppered and repaired to a standard diagonal nailing pattern.[15]

The samples recovered were of several different thicknesses, ranging from the full "G 24" weight of 24 ounces per square foot to almost paper-thin. The thinner samples would be older, as copper sheathing works on the principle that nothing grows on its surface since the metal slowly dissolves in saltwater over a period of four to six years.[16] Some sources suggest that heavier weight of copper would be used at the bow, since the early British experiments indicated that this area of the ship was subject to the most frictional wear as the bow plunged into and out of the water. According to this theory, the main run of the hull and stern did not require sheathing as heavy. However, other evidence can indicate that the same weight of copper was used throughout a particular vessel, as was the case with the *Barge*'s near-contemporary, the 1810 Baltimore pilot schooner *Comet*. Nearly the same size as the *Barge*, the eighteen-gun *Comet* had 26-ounce copper covering her bottom.[17] The three pieces marked "G 24" from the *Barge* were found in both the bow and stern areas (HS004, HS098, and HS099 from trenches RT1A and E38 respectively), providing some limited evidence that the ship may have been sheathed with the same weight of copper throughout.

Historical references indicate that the yacht was at least partially resheathed after the 1822–1823 repairs, although the sources do not clarify whether the old copper was reused or new copper applied. At the time, used ship's copper in the Sandwich Islands cost $10 to $11 per 100 pounds, so reuse of the old sheathing wherever possible might have been preferred over more expensive new copper.[18] The Smithsonian's Conservation Analytical Laboratory performed x-ray fluorescence and scanning electronic microscopy of seven of the 1995 samples, which indicated two different sources or batches for the sheathing, both almost pure copper (±97.5 and ±98.5 percent).[19]

Limited evidence for graving (tarring) was documented on *Ha'aheo* in the form of small amounts of black tar occasionally found in tight folds and nooks of crumpled pieces of copper sheathing. No other preparation of the hull between the wooden strakes and copper sheathing (tar paper, sacrificial wood, etc.) was observed. Later in the nineteenth century, it became common to avoid any hull preparation prior to coppering for economy's sake;[20] could this have been considered an innovation by Crowninshield's contemporaries? Early British experiments in coppering vessels indicated that iron hull fasteners degraded badly under copper sheathing due to the galvanic reaction between the two metals. In some ships, this reaction was so pronounced that the structural integrity of the ship was threatened. Could the relative absence of any lining on the *Barge*'s hull between the hull strakes and copper sheathing, combined with the presence of large quantities of iron hull fasteners, have caused severe enough deterioration of the ship's hull to have appeared as—or at least contributed to—the dry rot discovered during the April 1822 survey?

Dozens of copper hull sheathing nails were recovered throughout the wreck site. They fall into two broad categories. The first group of "boat tacks" is small and square-shanked, tapering into points. Lengths range from 1 to $1\frac{1}{2}$ in., with most in the 1 to $1\frac{1}{4}$ in. range (fig. 3.40). Their irregular round heads are com-

Figure 3.38. *HS 075 is a full sheet of copper hull sheathing, flattened and folded. The presence of so many intact nail holes probably indicates that it fell off the rotting hull as it deteriorated, rather than having been scraped off from the wrecking event. Note the light concretion on the surface. Photograph by Richard Strauss, Smithsonian National Museum of American History.*

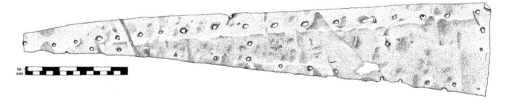

Figure 3.39. *This section of copper hull sheathing is trapezoidal in shape, but it is intact since there are nail holes on all four sides (HS10). It covered a gore, or area where two straight runs of sheathing met at a rounded portion of the ship's hull. Drawing by Thomas Ormsby for the Smithsonian National Museum of American History.*

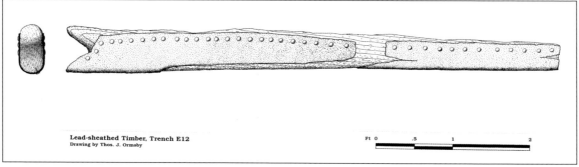

Lead-sheathed Timber, Trench E12
Drawing by Thos. J. Ormsby

Ft 0   .5   1   2

Figure 3.44. *The weight of the lead sheathing on this wooden cutwater at the ship's bow probably helped it fall off the ship in one piece and bury itself in the sand, preserving it. It was measured, documented, and photographed prior to onsite reburial in an empty trench. Drawing by Thomas Ormsby for the Smithsonian National Museum of American History.*

on ship stems to supplement the copper hull sheathing and prevent anchor cable from chafing through the stiffer and more expensive copper. The lead cut through the waves, and its softness and malleability made it bend easily around the sharp contours of a ship's bow. The piece was measured, drawn, and photographed, and then left in situ.[21] Exactly how it would have fit into the rest of the stem and how it joined with the remainder of the hull sheathing is not clear, and its relative lightness and form may indicate use as a shoe rather than a structural timber.

Three metal draft marks cut from thin sheets of lead also were recovered from widely separated trenches—E14, E16, and E23—on the western side of the wreck site; they represent respectively the depths of 6, 9, and 11 feet in Roman numerals (L15, L18, L30) (fig. 3.45). Still in use today on large vessels, these marks indicate the depth of water over the bottom of the keel, and they were used not only to gauge how deep a vessel was in the water but also the fore-and-aft trim (for best sailing qualities). Despite their distant findspots, all must have been originally nailed vertically to the bow of the ship, since the corresponding draft marks on the stern are still in place on the sternpost up to the 11-foot mark. The three recovered examples originally measured 6 in. high by $\frac{3}{32}$ in. thick, before being detached from the stem, twisted into almost unrecognizable form, and strewn over a wide area by the dynamic environment.

Also of lead were four large patches, three found in the general bow area (in trenches BB and E19) and one located in E22, 65 feet northwest of the main wreck area. L1 measures $10\frac{1}{4} \times 8\frac{1}{2} \times \frac{3}{32}$ in. L2, measuring $9\frac{1}{2}$ in. $\times$ 7 in. $\times 1\frac{3}{4}$ in. (H) $\times \frac{3}{32}$ in., originally measured $16\frac{3}{4}$ in. $\times$ 7 in. (fig. 3.46). L23 is too bent and crumpled to determine its original size, but it appears to have been square

Figure 3.45. *Lead draft marks, originally all from the bow of the ship, were recovered from three different and widely scattered trenches (from left, L30; L15, L18). Too delicate to physically straighten out due to the thinness of the lead, they were "visually" flattened for this measured drawing. Drawing by Thomas Ormsby for the Smithsonian National Museum of American History.*

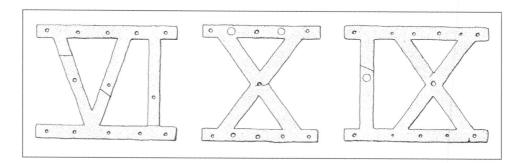

or rectangular with straight sides. All three were unused, in that they have no fastener holes. X-ray fluorescence indicates that L1 and L2 were from two distinctly different batches of lead, with L1 being more than 99 percent pure and L2 containing ±95 percent lead and ±1–3 percent copper. L23 was not tested.

By contrast, the much larger and heavier lead patch L29 from trench E22, originally measuring 16 in. × 10 in. × $\frac{1}{4}$ in., is characterized by a uniform thickness and large square fastener holes of three sizes along three edges with an even larger square fastener hole in the approximate center (fig. 3.47). Its fourth edge is straight, but lacks any holes along its length. This latter feature may indicate that it was not finished or applied prior to the loss of the ship, or that it may actually have been used during the yacht's wrecking to patch a hole but was abandoned before it could be nailed on its fourth edge when the ship's mast broke and the ship fell back in to the water adjacent to the reef. While this sort of speculation is tempting, it is equally possible that the patch may have been scrap, stored aboard the yacht as raw material for musket balls (see below). Several other smaller, thinner strips of lead that appeared to have been cut from larger sheets also were recovered from various findspots around the site (L27, L31, L38) (fig. 3.48). These may have been carried for patching or on-deck flashing around masts or other spots where the deck was penetrated and its watertight integrity needed to be reinforced. Alternately, these strips also may have served simply as future gunball stock.

Also of lead were eight sections of $1\frac{3}{8}$ in. (outside diameter) pipe, for a total length of 9.98 ft. (L8, L17, L20–22, L24, L35, L36). These must have been a significant fraction of the ship's three plumbing pipes mentioned in a contemporary account of the ship's features (see chapter 2, note 3). The longest piece measures $43\frac{1}{2}$ in. long; the wall thickness is $\frac{3}{32}$ in., with an original inside diameter of $1\frac{1}{4}$ in. (fig. 3.49). All eight were fashioned of long, narrow sheets rolled over a mandrel into a tube, with the overlapped joint then soldered with a darker substance, probably tin or a lead/tin amalgam, in use as solder for centuries. In fact, tin is one of the few metals with a lower melting point than lead. The long sections were then soldered at the ends into longer sections, with one end flared to fit over the end of the next piece. Then the soldered joint was strengthened with a single small rivet. The original length of the sections is unknown, as only two of the fragments have the transverse joins and the other ends are broken off. Both the longitudinal and transverse

Figure 3.46. L2 is a large 9 in. × 7 in. rectangle of 3/32 in. thick lead sheet, folded in half. It has no marks of usage or wear and probably would have served as a deck or hull patch when needed. Photograph by Eric Long, drawing by Thomas Ormsby for the Smithsonian National Museum of American History.

Figure 3.47. *This large, heavy lead patch (L29) measures 15¾ × 6¾ in. and ¼ in. thick. Fastener holes are preserved along three edges; the fourth edge is straight but has no nail holes. Photograph by Richard Strauss, Smithsonian National Museum of American History.*

Figure 3.49. *One of the wonders of George Crowninshield Jr.'s fancy new yacht mentioned by visitors was plumbing. Several samples of lead pipe were found in the wreck site, but all were short, cut sections instead of long pieces. Perhaps the pipes were not used by the Hawaiians and were cut up for scrap and reuse. This image of shows how the seams were sealed with some sort of mastic or tar. Photograph by Harold Dorwin, Smithsonian National Museum of American History.*

Figure 3.48. *This triangular strip of lead, crumpled and bent, tapers to a point (L27). Lacking any fastener holes, it's probably a scrap piece left over from cutting a larger sheet to patch a leaky spot on the ship's deck or hull. Photograph by Richard Strauss, Smithsonian National Museum of American History.*

seams protrude a bit from the surface of the piping, but all seam welds are smooth without any lumps, indicating a professional's hand. All eight pieces were heavily bent, crushed, and twisted when recovered, with both ends pinched together, indicating that they may not have been in use as ship's plumbing at the time the ship wrecked. Their findspots, scattered in three trenches, two far from the reef (E 15 and E 19) and one against the reef (E38), bear this out. Alternatively, they may have been cut out during the salvage and then lost overboard, or possibly they were removed earlier and stored below with other lead scraps for recycling into patch material or musket balls and the like. The ends of one of the pieces (L21) were carefully opened to inspect the two types of seams from the inside and obtain accurate measurements of the pipe's original size.

Another piece of lead tubing was discovered near the E38 lead pipes, but it is significantly different from the others (L39). Measuring $8\frac{1}{4}$ in. in length, it has much thicker walls ($\frac{5}{8}$ in.) and is flared at both ends (fig. 3.50). No seams are visible, and it was found with a wooden plug closing off the smaller of the flared ends. The lack of seams indicates that it was cast, and in the absence of further information or features it may be interpreted as either a scupper or overboard discharge pipe. The lack of wear prevents interpretation of this heavy, 6.88-pound tube as a hawsehole or hawsepipe, as an anchor cable running through it would have left evidence of rubbing against the soft lead. A

Figure 3.50. *In the shape of a heavy cast lead tube, L39 appears to be a lead scupper or overboard discharge pipe. Photographs by Harold Dorwin, Smithsonian National Museum of American History.*

lead flanged connector (originally circular) was found against the reef nearby in E36, but it is so badly battered and crushed that it is difficult to derive much useful information from it (L33). Its $\frac{3}{4}$ in. flange has fastener holes spaced at $1\frac{1}{4}$ to $1\frac{1}{2}$ in. intervals (where measurable) around the circumference; the collared section is quite high relative to the general size of the piece, but now it is folded over and inward, and it is not possible to derive adequate measurements without unfolding the sides (and thus risk its destruction in the process).

One of the most unusual hull-related finds discovered in the entire excavation was the intact upper valve of the ship's copper or brass bilge pump (MISC56), measuring 12 in. long and with a head diameter of $4\frac{1}{2}$ in. and containing a two-part flapper or claque. When first located in E17, it was lightly concreted on all surfaces and looked very much like a large piston from a truck engine, complete with its connecting rod, which was presumed to have found its way into the center of the wreck site in Hanalei Bay via a heavy storm or tidal wave (fig. 3.51). Although neither the lower valve nor the pump tube/ sleeve was located, what was preserved, when combined with the historical record, conveyed a considerable amount of information about one of the most important systems aboard any ship.

Figure 3.51. *Before conservation, the ship's pump (MISC56) looked like a rusty, encrusted piston from a truck or tractor engine. Photograph by Richard Strauss, Smithsonian National Museum of American History.*

Essentially, it was the moving part in a vertical hollow tube that ran from the bilge at the bottom of the ship's keel up the deck level, where it would exhaust and empty the bilgewater over the side. The tube might be either a hollowed-out tree trunk or a metal pipe. As the valve lowered down the metal or wooden pump tube on the end of a chain, the flappers or claques on either side would open to allow water to flow freely through the device. At the bottom of its stroke, the pump would then be raised, at which point the leather-surfaced claques would close, seal-

Figure 3.52. *Views of the ship's pump (MISC 56) after conservation; note that the leathers were restored on the wrong side of the flappers to show the stamped lettering. Photographs by Harold Dorwin, Smithsonian National Museum of American History.*

ing against the opening. Whatever was in the water column would be drawn upward to vent on deck and run over the side. The ovoid leathers were fastened onto their metal backings by four nuts and bolts and a thin copper sheet gasket, and it is a certainty that the pumps were frequently checked and maintained due to their importance for the ship's flotation (fig. 3.52). As indicated in chapter 2, some unspecified pump parts (perhaps the leathers?) were replaced on 4 March 1823 when the ship's rebuilding was nearly complete.

The lifting frame was fastened to the piston by means of a threaded nut on each side, and its upper end terminates in a ring through which the clevised lifting arm was fastened by square nuts on both sides. Interestingly, around the hole on one side of the ring is stamped: "J.BAKER'S/PATENT/I." This is echoed and amplified on the underside of one of the clappers (where it would have been invisible): "J.BAKER'S/PATENT/J.DAVIS/MAKER/ BOSTON."

A search through the Boston city directory for the period reveals that J. Davis operated a brass and copper foundry in that New England city,[22] but no amount of hunting will provide more detail about the Baker pump patent, for it does not exist. An exhaustive search in the contemporary patent records for the United States, Britain, and France revealed no patent in J. Baker's name for anything, much less a ship's pump or associated mechanisms. Instead, he may have had a patent pending, or perhaps he was bluffing in order to keep any competitors at bay.

Moving upward in the ship's wooden structure, a number of decorative wooden moldings were recovered from scattered points around the wreck site. Two examples were attached to the hull parallel to the ceiling planking and separated by 1 in. over their 6 ft. length in E36. Their position indicates that they hid the bottom edge of a light bulkhead or partition in the stern

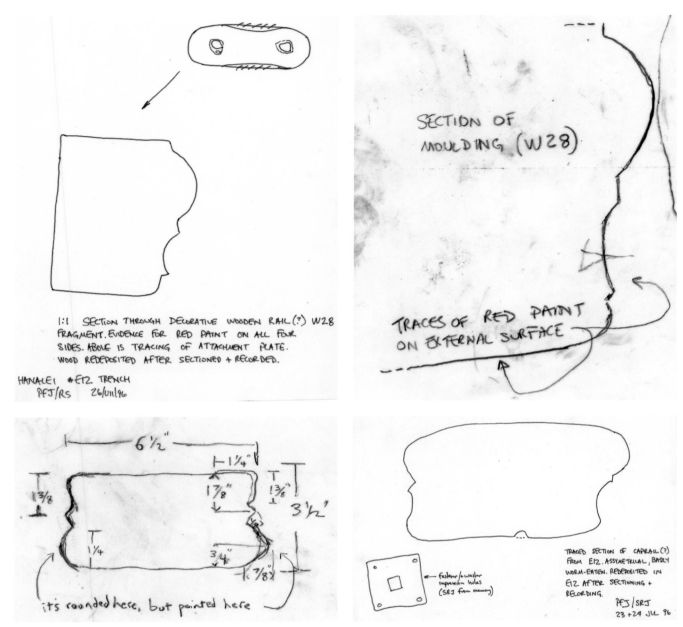

1:1 SECTION THROUGH DECORATIVE WOODEN RAIL (?) W28 FRAGMENT. EVIDENCE FOR RED PAINT ON ALL FOUR SIDES. ABOVE IS TRACING OF ATTACHMENT PLATE. WOOD REDEPOSITED AFTER SECTIONED + RECORDED.

HANALEI #E12 TRENCH
PFJ/RS 26/JUN/96

SECTION OF MOULDING (W28)

TRACES OF RED PAINT ON EXTERNAL SURFACE

6½"
1¼"
1⅜
1⅞"
1⅜"
3½"
1¼
3/4"
7/8"

it's rounded here, but pointed here

Fastener/washer impression holes (SRJ from memory)

TRACED SECTION OF CAPRAIL (?) FROM E12. ASSYMETRICAL, BADLY WORM-EATEN. REDEPOSITED IN E12 AFTER SECTIONING + RECORDING.

PFJ/SRJ
23 + 24 JUL 96

Figure 3.53. *Sections of decorative moldings from various findspots around the wreck site demonstrate the rich variety of surface treatments in the yacht. Most of these were sectioned, profiled, and reburied in the empty trench designated for reburial. Photographs by Hugh Talman, Smithsonian National Museum of American History.*

area down by the bilges. These were the only examples found fastened to the ship's structure; the remainder were all found free-floating, making attribution to a specific area of the ship difficult (fig. 3.53). For the most part they were teredo-ridden and in poor condition. Consequently, most of them were recorded, sectioned, and redeposited in an empty excavation trench (E13).

Two examples discovered during the 1996 and 1998 seasons were clearly sections of a large rail cap. They were finished on both sides with a torus, or large bead molding, atop a fillet and reverse bead. Interestingly, the sections were asymmetrical, with sides that echoed but did not mirror each other. The bottom surface of the example located in E12 contained the impression of a square base plate with a square central hole and a round fastener hole at

Figure 3.54. *Made of white oak, this section of decorative molding was heavily damaged by the teredo, whose channels are visible throughout the entire piece (W28). Photograph by Hugh Talman, Smithsonian National Museum of American History.*

Figure 3.55. *This tapered copper pin has an eye at the top for passing a line through. The 3½ in. shouldered shaft shows how deeply it would have been set into a gunwale or rail. Photograph by Richard Strauss, Smithsonian National Museum of American History.*

each of the four corners. A stanchion or post of some sort would have connected the base plate to the wood below.

A couple of days later, another wooden molding fragment emerged from a lower level in the same trench. This one was squared on three sides; only one side was molded with an astragal, reverse bead, and fillet (fig. 3.54). Surprisingly, all four sides displayed traces of bright red paint. It also had a fastening plate impression on one side in the form of an elongated figure eight. Where this white oak molding was used and why all four sides were painted—when only one or two could have been seen—is a mystery. That same trench up against the reef yielded even another sample of molding at a deeper level. Flat on one side and unfinished on the back, it has a half bead at either end separated by a scotia and other complex curves. With two unfinished sides, this white oak molding clearly decorated the top or bottom of some larger piece of furniture or ship feature. Traces of bright red paint were found on its face and one side.

Three of the recovered wooden moldings are much finer than the thick, heavy ones described above. One, found in E12 concreted to a fragmentary iron eyebolt (CON121), has a complex profile and a 45-degree miter at one end with a nail hole through it. W34, from the same trench along the reef, is a much longer section of the same type of molding, and it too has a 45-degree miter at one end with a nail hole through it. It is $25\frac{3}{8}$ in. long and has nail holes (with nail stubs in them) along its length, showing how it was fastened to the wood behind; they also indicate that they were architectural (or furniture) moldings rather than picture frame fragments. Both pieces are made of mahogany—obviously distasteful to the otherwise voracious teredo worms that infested the wreck, as they are still solid. The last piece of molding also is well preserved, but it is made of spruce (W29). Wider, flatter, and with a more complex worked surface than any of the other examples, it too has a hole in the middle with a bit of iron nail showing how it was fastened.

Several artifacts relate to the construction of the royal yacht at the deck level. One is a cast copper pin with an eye at one end and a shaft end $3\frac{1}{2}$ in. long at the other for setting into some sort of rail or gunwale (fig. 3.55). The object is 9 in. long and was designed to stick out of its socket $5\frac{1}{2}$ in. The eye has a hammered flat on its upper surface and contains a 1 in. hole, through which a rope would have passed, to serve as some sort of stanchion. It was found in E19, roughly the amidships spill area on the site.

Figure 3.56. *The clear glass deck light (G186) was one of the innovations incorporated into the* Barge's *structure by Crowninshield. It admitted light through the main deck into the spaces below. Photographs by Harold Dorwin, Smithsonian National Museum of American History.*

The rarest and most beautiful deck-level find is a disk of light green glass, convex on one side and flat on the other (G186) (fig. 3.56); it was found lying on the ceiling planking in E37, in the ship's stern. A beveled edge connects the two sides, and the piece measures $6\frac{5}{8}$ in. in diameter and $1\frac{3}{8}$ in. thick at the thickest point. The flat side has swirls in the surface, which is otherwise quite shiny; one large and one small chip mar its otherwise smooth finish. The rounded side is uniformly roughened and looks almost sandblasted. Its surface is pocked and chipped by many circular gouges, leaving some very sharp edges. This unusual object is a deck light, originally set into the upper deck, convex side up, to admit light into the lower areas of the ship. Presumably, the reason that the round side was up was to gather and focus the light downward; otherwise it would only have presented a hazard to stubbed toes. That is why the rounded surface is so scarred and chipped—from contact with harder things.

Deck lights "for admitting Light into the internal Parts of Ships, Vessels, Buildings and other Places" were first patented by British glass manufacturer Apsley Pellatt in London in 1807, just eight years before *Cleopatra's Barge* began to take shape. Pellatt's "illuminator is a piece of solid glass, of a circular . . . form at the base . . . convex on the side to be presented outwards, to receive and condense the rays of light, and has a flat or plane surface on the inside of the room or apartment which it is intended to light . . . One side should be ground or roughed."[23] In other words, the deck light is nothing more than a simple glass lens that gathers ambient light and focuses it downward belowdecks.

The earliest known American examples were two found on the wreck of the US Navy's twenty-gun brig *Jefferson,* built on Lake Ontario in 1814;[24] others from the War of 1812 are known through historical references. The wear pattern on the *Jefferson*'s lights, as well as the *Cleopatra's Barge* example, proves that the rounded surface indeed faced upward. This would seem to close the topic, but a simple experiment testing the lens's utility indicated that its presence aboard the fabled yacht may have been little more than a conversational curiosity—a novelty displaying the latest technology.

A 6 in. hole was cut into an oversized 31 in. × 41½ in. piece of cardboard to simulate a ship's deck. The glass deck light was set into the hole, and a flashlight with low batteries was held over it at varying distances to simulate ambient light. Both sides were tested upward, and the one with the flat side up provided more light and diffused it more widely. Why then would Pellatt recommend that the convex side point upward, thereby not only providing less light but also presenting a tripping hazard to people on deck? As a glass manufacturer, he certainly would have had knowledge of the basic light-bending properties of simple lenses, worked out hundreds of years earlier by Galileo and his successors.

All this points to the possibility that Pellatt's idea may have taken a few years to find its way across the Atlantic and then was picked up earlier by the brig *Jefferson*'s builder Henry Eckford in 1814, a few other War of 1812 ships, and perhaps a bit later by George Crowninshield Jr. as a "new" idea to incorporate aboard his luxury yacht—an "artificial curiosity" for visitors to marvel at and admire. This certainly fits what we know of Crowninshield's tastes, and the historical record does say that he tried out some new ideas on the *Barge*. To continue the hypothesis, the round-side-up application may have proven over time to work better as a conversation piece and toe-stubber, so builders soon after inverted it for better light. For example, an 1818 British description of a combination deck light and ventilator unit included an 1817 testimonial that praised them with the words "they not only give as much light as the patent illuminator, but are also more convenient in walking the deck, by not having the rise,"[25] so the convex side did not last long in the top position. By the mid-nineteenth century, deck lights were mainly placed with the flat side up, as evidenced by the eight prismatic examples aboard the 1841 whaler *Charles W. Morgan* at Mystic Seaport, Connecticut, and the dozens aboard the Civil War ironclad USS *Monitor* and later *Monitor*-class gunboats.

Rigging

Missionary Hiram Bingham, as he observed the salvage attempt by the Hawaiians at Hanalei Bay in early May 1824, mentioned the recovery and removal to the shore of the "spars, rigging, and other articles" from the wreck of the royal yacht.[26] However, about fifty items related to the vessel's rigging were dropped, missed, or otherwise left behind on the wreck.

Iron

Most of the iron rigging artifacts were lodged deep inside concretions, clumps of iron objects rusted together and bonded with the surrounding sand as they oxidized over time. They often grow into shapeless lumps, incorporating whatever happened to be next to them, and the outside of the lump looks like concrete (hence the name). Equally often, the actual iron artifact has degraded completely, leaving only a perfectly shaped cavity denoting its original form. Commonly, the only way to tell what is inside an amorphous concretion is by x-raying it in the laboratory after returning from fieldwork. After the x-rays, a decision is made whether the concretions warrant further investigation. This is one of the more exciting points in archaeological research, as a concretion that appears to be a simple hull fastener might be something as exotic as a pistol, cutlass, or item of tableware.

What an individual concretion contains is not known until the x-ray emerges from the stop bath in the lead-lined laboratory. Most often, it contains only an iron spike, a piece of modern barbed wire, or the like. In these cases, the object(s) can be merely measured in the x-ray, and then the lump slowly desalinated, dehydrated, and set aside in long-term storage. This happens most often when the x-ray reveals that an object is a duplicate of one already in better condition (for example). If further investigation appears worthwhile, then the concretion is opened carefully and the object(s) removed. If only a void in the shape of the original artifact remains, then the cavity can be cleaned out and a resin mold of the object can be cast. In the hands of a good conservator, these castings are often remarkably accurate, sometimes visually indistinguishable copies of the original object.

All of the objects identified as rigging elements in the x-rays were set aside for further inquiry and conservation. The iron rigging fell mostly into a few broad categories, like thimbles, hooks, eyes, and eyebolts, with only an exception or two. Six thimbles were recovered altogether, mostly from up against the reef in trenches E12, E35, E19, and E41 (CON68, CON126, CON191, CON300, CON494, and CON509). These circular iron rings were (and are) used most commonly for linking rope ends to other objects, such as rings or hooks, by being wrapped around the concave outer surface and then spliced into itself (fig. 3.57). Most commonly associated with the standing rigging, thimbles are one of the most ubiquitous shipboard items. They also appear in the running rigging and as reinforcements in the corners of sails (where they are known as cringles). The examples from the yacht have an inside diameter ranging in size from $1\frac{1}{2}$ in. to as large as 3 in.; all of the thimbles are round except for one triangular example. One has a piece of $1\frac{1}{2}$ in. thick rope still preserved around its perimeter, while another has a fragment of $1\frac{3}{4}$ in. rope wound with heavy $\frac{1}{4}$ in. whipping at the thimble's peak. CON300, the triangular one, would have been used in a spot where the rope it terminated required a more stationary fastener than a round thimble would have been able to provide. It is more difficult to manufacture than a round example,

Figure 3.57. *Thimbles, after conservation, stabilization, and some casting of voids (from upper left: CON68, CON126, CON494; from lower left: CON509, CON191, CON300). Thimbles are metal rings, concave on the outer surface, around which lines are bent to prevent chafing on board ships. The two examples in the middle still have rope wrapped around them. Photograph by Harold Dorwin, Smithsonian National Museum of American History.*

THIMBLES

and the fact that the weld is not easily visible attests to the high quality of its workmanship. A small iron ring also is preserved with two pieces of thin rope around its circumference, which is then whipped all the way around; this is oval in section and appears to be a cringle. W17, a perfectly preserved lignum vitae bulls-eye, also fits into this category; these items were used most commonly as fairleads through which ropes passed to prevent binding or chafing. This example, found in the bow area against the reef in trench E12, has an outside diameter of $2\frac{3}{4}$ in. and is 1 in. thick; it has a $1\frac{1}{4}$ in. hole in the middle for the rope to pass through (fig. 3.58).[27]

One of the significant objects that emerged from a shapeless concretion was a cast iron mast band or partner. CON368 is a $\frac{1}{2}$ in. thick band, $1\frac{7}{8}$ in. high, that belted a rectangular timber $6\frac{3}{4}$ in. × $7\frac{3}{4}$ in.—probably a bowsprit or jibboom-size spar at the head of the ship (fig. 3.59). It was strapped around the timber and fastened through holes in three sides. One of the shorter sides has a reinforced eye on its outer surface for attaching another piece of rigging. Another unique object is CON483—a long, slender, well-preserved iron rod with a delicate hook at one end and an eye at the other. The shaft and eye are covered with an underlayer of canvas wrapped in an outer layer of leather, or "hide," as it was called in the early rigging manuals (fig. 3.60). The rod has an overall length of $24\frac{1}{2}$ in. and a diameter of $\frac{1}{2}$ in. The hook is $2\frac{1}{2}$ in. long (measured from the inside), and the inside diameter of the eye at the other end measures $1\frac{1}{4}$ in. A glance at any of the standard volumes on historic rigging confirmed what I was told by ship blacksmith Kelly Smyth—

Figure 3.58. *It's exceedingly rare to find an artifact with an exact duplicate in a reference book, complete with picture and definition. Here an unused wooden thimble (W17) from* Haʻaheo *is photographed with Clifford Ashley's 1944 volume* The Ashley Book of Knots, *where the "lignum vitae truck, thimble or bull's-eye" (no. 3281 on page 534) is a mirror image of the artifact. Photograph by Harold Dorwin, Smithsonian National Museum of American History.*

that this was an intact futtock shroud, a rigid part of the standing rigging used to support upper mast steps, deadeye rails, crosstrees, and mast tops.[28] The lack of wear on either end, but especially the wrapped eye, indicates that it must have been an unused spare at the time of the ship's loss.

The twelve concreted hooks recovered from the wreck site present another side of the ship's rigging; several were extracted from their concretions and cast for study, and the remainder were x-rayed and left intact (fig. 3.61). Shipboard uses for these ubiquitous articles range from holding parts of the standing and running rigging to hoisting cargo or other heavy objects around the vessel. Seven were found in a nearly straight line 33 feet long and ca. 50 feet off the reef where the stern section was discovered (CON204 from E16; CON214

Figure 3.59. *CON368 is a well-preserved iron spar partner, possibly for a bowsprit or jibboom. These were used to attach elements of a vessel's standing rigging to the various spars. Photograph by Smithsonian National Museum of American History.*

Figure 3.60. *With the assistance of ship blacksmith Kelly Smyth, this nearly intact iron artifact (CON483) was identified as a futtock shroud, which was used on sailing ships to link and stabilize a mast top with the mast below. The shroud's stitched leather sheath, which prevented chafing with lines and other rigging elements, is remarkably well preserved. Photograph by Harold Dorwin, Smithsonian National Museum of American History.*

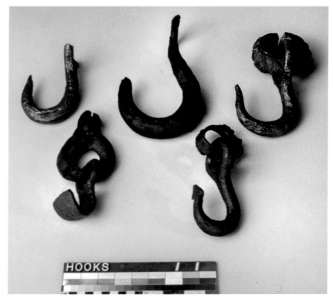

Figure 3.61. *Various types of forged iron shipboard hooks, from rigging to cargo examples (from upper left: CON250, CON158, CON204, CON126, CON481). Photograph by Harold Dorwin, Smithsonian National Museum of American History.*

from E17; CON230, CON244, and CON250 from E18; CON278 and CON290 from E19). Interestingly, several of them pair up, in that they are quite similar in size and general aspect. It is hard not to speculate that these might represent symmetrical port and starboard remains of the main mast and upper spar rigging, which snapped off during the attempted salvage, plunging the hull of the royal yacht back into deeper water and causing her total loss.

For example, CON204 and CON250 are virtually identical; their large size (respectively 7 and $7\frac{1}{8}$ in. high × 3 and $3\frac{1}{2}$ in. wide at the bill) may indicate they were "rigging hooks" attached to blocks. Similarly, CON244 and CON290 are close matches; their size may indicate they were cargo hooks. CON244's hook is more open and likely was bent at some point. Likewise, CON158 and CON278 are very similar, differing only in the beautifully preserved "arrowhead" bill on the former, so designed to prevent anything from slipping off the point of the hook (fig. 3.62). That bill also would have allowed for better mousing, or tying a line across the hook's mouth to keep the contents in place. An intact round iron thimble with rope fragments still attached is preserved through its eye; this may be a futtock shroud hook or strop hook. Several others of the group also have thimbles through their eyes, with or without rope fragments preserved (CON126, CON204, CON214, CON230, CON250,

Figure 3.62. *The arrowhead at the tip of this iron hook prevented a line from slipping off easily (CON158); the original line around the iron eye is partially preserved. Photograph by Harold Dorwin, Smithsonian National Museum of American History.*

CON278, CON290). Obviously, these represented the ends of ropes, but further speculation as to their shipboard placement and usages is difficult, as they are pretty much uniform in size and shape. One hook, CON481, is flattened from its ring to its bill; normally, this might be some sort of hook for light lifting. However, its eye is attached in turn to the eye of a leather-covered $\frac{7}{8}$ in. bolt or pin rather than a thimble. The degree of preservation of the leather indicates some type of static application that prevented the wearing of its cover prior to the ship's loss—possibly as part of a hook block, wherein the hook is strapped to one end of a block.

Another category of iron fasteners is represented by iron eyebolts, of which five examples are preserved from the wreck site. One is at the end of flat hook CON481, as described above. CON64 consists of a $\frac{5}{8}$ in. eyebolt 6 in. long (fig. 3.63). Its eye contains a $\frac{1}{2}$ in. iron ring with an inside diameter of $2\frac{1}{2}$ in.; the other end of the shank is peened over a $\frac{7}{8}$ in. washer. The shank is covered by a wormy wood plank fragment originally 4 in. thick. Since deck eyebolts would pass through both deck and beam, this may be a lighter bulwarks eyebolt, or possibly even a gun carriage bolt. Another $\frac{5}{8}$ in. fragmentary eyebolt has a large $\frac{1}{2}$ in. ring with an inside diameter of $2\frac{1}{2}$ in. through its eye (CON121); unfortunately, the shank is broken less than an inch below the eye (fig. 3.63), obscuring its original length and purpose. Eyebolts with rings through their eyes were also called ringbolts.[29] CON87a, also a $\frac{5}{8}$ in. eyebolt, has a slightly smaller $1\frac{3}{4}$ in. eye; it too is broken off at the start of the shank. Lastly, the upper shank and eye of a small $\frac{3}{8}$ in. eyebolt is preserved with an inside diameter of $1\frac{1}{4}$ in. Laid through it is the leather-wrapped eye of another, much heavier $\frac{3}{4}$ in. eyebolt (CON65). The leather wrap is missing from the inside of the eye, indicating swiveling of the little eye within the larger eye's interior.

Blocks

Certainly some of the hooks, thimbles, and rings would have ended at blocks, and there is a small assortment of single blocks and their parts from the wreck as well (fig. 3.64). Captain George Biddlecombe of the Royal British Navy, at the end of his 1848 revision of David Steel's seminal 1794 book on masting and rigging, included a table of rigging elements listing no fewer than 294 blocks of various sorts and sizes for a standard 200-ton merchant brig (very close to the 191-ton hermaphrodite brig *Cleopatra's Barge*). Of these, 205 were plain single blocks of different sizes, like those recovered. The largest recovered from the wreck is MISC49, a nearly intact example that was covered with red-orange paint when discovered in E12, the bow area up against the reef.

Figure 3.63. *Eyes of various types and placements were found all over the wreck site (from left: CON121, CON64, CON87A, CON65). Photograph by Harold Dorwin, Smithsonian National Museum of American History.*

It is a large "made" strap-bound block, so called because it is "made" or fashioned of several pieces, with a deep groove along the long dimension of its one preserved cheek or side to carry a strap. The other end of the strap would have carried a hook, loop, or thimble, depending on the block's placement and use. Measuring 13 in. high × 8½ in. wide, the shell and chocks are ash; the sheave, or inner wheel around which rope was bent, is lignum vitae. The pin and sheave bushing were originally metal; both are missing, as is one side of the block itself. Originally, the head of the pin was square, as shown by the square hole in the center of the cheek. The sheave has an 8 in. diameter and is 1 in. thick, with a keyhole-shaped aperture for the missing metal bushing, and it would have rove a rope no larger than 1 in. A block of this size from the bow area could have been used in the lower rigging on fairly light duty, but exactly what cannot be known.

Figure 3.64. *Wooden blocks and block parts (from left: MISC86, W51 (upper), CON151 (lower), MISC49 (center), MISC5 (upper), CON306 (lower). Photograph by Harold Dorwin, Smithsonian National Museum of American History.*

Next in size is a fragmentary sheave with a 5½ in. diameter and 1 in. thick (CON175). It is pierced by two ½ in. holes to either side of a central hole that would have secured the circular shouldered bushing (which was not preserved). It was found amidships in E14, concreted together with two copper spikes, so its findspot and associated artifacts do not reveal its use. MISC5 is a "mortised" block, with its shell carved from a single piece of wood. Originally, it was the most intact and best preserved of all of the blocks recovered, with an intact leather-covered rope strap, but it did not survive its conservation treatment well and is now in several pieces (fig. 3.65). What survived was originally 7 in. high × 4½ in. wide; the surrounding strap is 1¼ in. in diameter, and the leather-wrapped rope inside is 1 in. in diameter. The 4 in. lignum vitae sheave is ⅞ in. thick and is very well preserved. The metal bushing is triangular in shape on one side, with fasteners at each on the three angles, and a significant portion of its hollow ½ in. metal pin also is preserved.

Figure 3.65. *Shown before conservation and stabilization, this single block (MISC5) still has its rope around the sheave and a leather-wrapped strap around the exterior. Photograph by Ricardo Vargas, Smithsonian National Museum of American History.*

Breaking up concretion CON306 yielded one of the best-preserved elements of rigging recovered—a lignum vitae sheave with a diameter of 3¾ in. measuring 1 in. thick (fig. 3.66). There is no sign of wear on any surface, and the pin axle was well preserved. The axle is triangular and has squared corners; the sides measure 2¼ in. The axle is held in place by a ¼ in. fastener at each angle, the heads of which are countersunk to allow smooth rolling of the sheave. The diameter of the hole for the pin is ¾ in., which seems quite heavy for the ¾ in. (or smaller) rope rove through the original block.

Last is W51, the intact shell of a small fashioned

Figure 3.66. *The hardest parts of blocks getting the most wear were the sheaves (CON306), the circular wheels in the middle around which the line was wrapped. They were often made of lignum vitae, a very dense hardwood with little appeal to the teredo worm. Photograph by Harold Dorwin, Smithsonian National Museum of American History.*

Figure 3.67. *W51 is the shell of a one-piece block that would have been used for smaller rigging. The triangular iron axle casting was not in good shape, so a silicon casting was made to replace it. Photograph by Hugh Talman, Smithsonian National Museum of American History.*

block, apparently carved from a piece of the South American hardwood peroba rosa (fig. 3.67). Measuring only $5\frac{1}{8}$ in. high × $2\frac{3}{4}$ in. wide × 2 in. thick, the block's sheave opening measures only $\frac{5}{8}$ in. wide; its rough outer surface may indicate that it was hand-carved. Only a small line could have been rove through such a little block—perhaps something for a little pennant or flag or a very light line. Its findspot in E12 against the reef sheds little light on its original deployment within the bow area of the yacht.

Rope and Leathering

Considering the wreck site's dynamic environment on a reef in the Hanalei surf zone, it was surprising to find any rope on the site. Nevertheless, several fragments were recovered, ranging in diameter from 1 in. down to $\frac{1}{2}$ in. Despite their obvious bulk, not enough cellular structure was preserved in any of the rope samples to determine their composition (almost certainly hemp). Of the two types of rope (cable- and hawser-laid), all *Ha'aheo* samples are of the cheaper, lighter, and less durable hawser-laid variety, consisting of three strands wound counterclockwise. Two of the shortest pieces are whipped, or wrapped to prevent fraying, indicating the ends of the line (MISC33). Six of the rope fragments were wormed, wherein another thin line is wound around the seams or contlines of the central three strands for strength. However, only three of the samples of worming survived conservation, indicating that the worming was made of more fragile stuff than the heavier strands it supported (fig. 3.68).

Several other pieces of rope were wrapped in leather (cowhide), including one example identified as an intact block strap loop (fig. 3.69). A few of these wrapped pieces are curved, indicating they were thimbles or other forms of rope terminals. Some originally had vermilion color on their outer surfaces;

at first it was thought that they were covered with red lead as a preservative, but later analysis indicated that the vermilion was a pigment and not a preservative. These red-painted pieces of leather rigging must have made the yacht quite colorful.

One section of leather measuring $33\frac{1}{2}$ in. × 6 in. × $\frac{1}{8}$ in. thick has finished edges on all four sides, indicating it is intact; the two long sides are bordered by holes punched through for stitching around the rope (fig. 3.70). Several of the pieces have the stitch holes and sometimes even the impressions left in the leather's surface by the stitches; none of the stitching that bound the hide around the rope was preserved or recovered. Leathering the rigging was quite common in the Age of Sail; it prevented rope from wearing prematurely and chafing against sails, lines, or any other surfaces it might touch. One recent source states that leathering was limited to naval ships on account of the expense; since *Ha'aheo* was a royal yacht, the use of leather chafing gear aboard her does not contradict this.[30]

Ballast and the Anchor

Several items were found and documented that were not part of the ship's construction or rigging, yet they are associated with those elements of the wreck site. For example, we recovered a representative sample of sixty-seven stones ostensibly foreign to the Hawaiian Islands from the 1995 survey trenches, ranging in size from 0.7 to 15 ounces. Included were granite, tonatite gneiss, quartzite, quartz-bearing breccia, gabbro, limestone, mafic gneiss, granite gneiss, mylonite gneiss, blue schist, basalt or tolonite, and basalt. With the possible exception of the last two, all are non-Hawaiian, according to limited analysis by the Geology Department at the University of Hawai'i, indicating that they were ballast from the wreck site.[31] The blue schist is of particular interest; it is known to originate from only a few places globally, one of which is in the area of Rio de Janeiro, Brazil. Since the *Barge*

Figure 3.68. *Different types of rope end treatments from the ship. MISC33 is whipped with a spiral wrap, which prevented the rope end from unraveling. MISC52 is wormed, with a thinner line between the thicker main strands or contlines. This strengthened the line and kept more water out. Photographs by Hugh Talman, Smithsonian National Museum of American History.*

Figure 3.69. *This leather-wrapped block strap (MISC86) was part of a larger concretion, which is probably what preserved it. The leather sheath served as chafing gear to prevent the rope from wearing through and breaking. Several pieces of leather chafing gear aboard the yacht were painted bright red. Photograph by Harold Dorwin, Smithsonian National Museum of American History.*

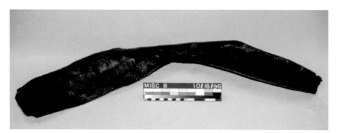

Figure 3.70. *The largest piece of intact leather was this 35 in. long piece of heavy cowhide, with stitch holes along the two long sides (MISC8). The inner surface is rough and the outer surface is finished smooth, with a bevel on one end. Patches of red mercuric oxide (vermilion) are visible on the outside surface. Photograph by Ricardo Vargas, Smithsonian National Museum of American History.*

made a coffee voyage to Rio in late 1818, it is possible that this stone may be a souvenir of that voyage. Further examples of ballast were noted and recorded but not recovered.

A reconnaissance trip to Hanalei Bay in early 1994 resulted in a couple of dives in the bay with marine biology graduate students Alan Friedlander and Ralph DeFelice of the University of Hawai'i, who were kind enough to take me along on their fish counts. They spun a tale of a big old anchor, lost over on the northeast side of the mouth of Hanalei Bay, and offered to take me to it. Since the historical record included the statement by Kaua'i missionary Samuel Wilcox that one of the reasons that the *Barge* wrecked was because she parted her (anchor) cables in a gale, it seemed worthwhile to groundtruth the story. After dropping anchor in 60 feet of water over a low-lying patch reef, we descended to the reef edge, where it met the sandy bay bottom. Sure enough, there lay a large $9\frac{1}{2}$ ft. high stockless iron anchor with its ring broken off and lying beside the eye. One of the flukes lay wedged beneath a coral edge, indicating how this particular anchor had fouled and been cut away. Did it belong to the royal yacht? Was this where the ship would have anchored, standing off out at the mouth of the bay, if she arrived at night? There is no way to tell, as anchors are notoriously difficult to date and any potential diagnostic marks on this one were covered by coral growth or concreted iron.

Salvaged at the time of her loss and slowly ground down by subsequent seas, seasons, teredo worms and storms, enough of the structure of the royal yacht was preserved to derive some limited but significant information about her construction, possible innovations, and subsequent repairs. Other questions were unanswered by the remains of the ship, which were backfilled and reburied at the end of each excavation season.

The Finds

Over the course of the five seasons from 1995 to 2000, 1,257 artifact lots were recovered, identified by the primary materials they were made from, and cataloged. Where an artifact contained more than one material, or when the artifact material was unidentified in the field, an artifact was assigned to the miscellaneous category (MISC). Most of the catalog numbers were assigned to individual artifacts; some were given to small lots of objects, so a group of copper fasteners or lead musket balls found together were given the same number. While a majority of the artifacts found and recovered are part of the artifact assemblage specifically associated with the actual wreck of the royal yacht, many are later, and some were quite recent (fig. 4.1). For example, discarding chicken bones over the side of the research vessel after lunch stopped abruptly when the crew had to catalog several of them.

The artifact catalog and associated materials outside the scope of this book are available at this Smithsonian website: americanhistory.si.edu/cleopatras barge.

"Modern" Finds

For most of the year, strong northerly winds hit Hanalei Bay, which faces north. Starting in the Arctic, these prevailing northerlies blow over deep water for thousands of miles and then shoal abruptly when they reach Hanalei, driving into the bay's southern shore. During the summer months, the winds shift around and blow much more gently from the east; these gentle, warm breezes are known locally as the trade winds or trades.

Over time, these northerly and easterly winds tend to drive everything that has ever fallen into the bay into its southwestern corner, where the shallow reef struck by the shipwreck serves as a natural barrier to further movement. Consequently, a considerable amount of intrusive, or nonwreck, material ended up mixed into the wreck artifacts, producing an odd and sometimes even bizarre snapshot of Hanalei's history from the early nineteenth century to the present.

For the purpose of this discussion, "modern" is very broadly defined as post-1824, or in the jargon, postdepositional (after the shipwreck was deposited). A lot of the material found within the wreck site is quite a bit later than the wreck itself. What follows is a discussion of that material, beginning with the more recent. Where known, suspected, or hypothesized, it is so indicated. Otherwise, the finds are treated as part of the wreck assemblage.

One of the first things we found during the 1995 search for the royal yacht

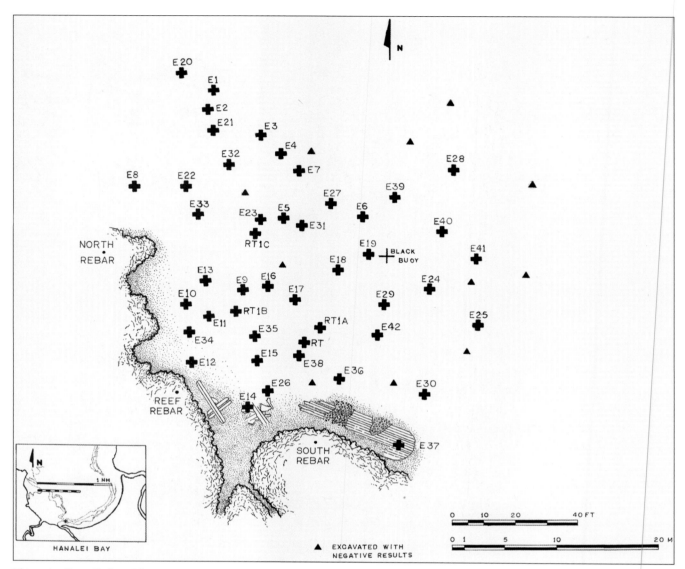

Figure 4.1. *Overall plan of the wreck site. The trenches and artifacts were trilaterated into the site plan using rebar datum points in the reef. The 1995 survey trenches were given names; in the following seasons the trenches were numbered. The unnumbered triangles represent trenches that were excavated but contained no cultural material. Drawing by Thomas Ormsby for the Smithsonian National Museum of American History.*

was the fiberglass mast from a windsurfing board floating freely on the sandy bay bottom around the reef, headed for destruction against the underwater coral heads. This was rescued and promptly pressed into service aboard RV *Pilialoha* as the small boat boom, which duty it served admirably for the duration of the excavations. It also introduced the crew to one of the more entertaining categories of modern finds, and one to which we actively contributed steadily throughout the project—watersports equipment parts. A dive watch (broken) and dive watch bezel, a surfboard skeg, a stainless steel band from an old-fashioned 1960s dive mask, and a lead fishing weight reflect today's principal use of Hanalei Bay as a recreational spot, with surfing, snorkeling, scuba, body surfing, swimming, fishing, sailing, kayaking, and canoeing all about equally popular among the area's local users and tourists (fig. 4.2). One of our visitors snorkeling over from the beach lost an expensive mask en route to a tour of the shipwreck, and we never found it. Luckily, one of *Pilialoha*'s

The foremost evidence was W13, a gun carriage truck or wheel, on which the gun would have rolled forward and backward for loading and maintenance. This was found in trench E12, the bow section up against the reef. It was intact when it was recovered, but when raised out of the water, half of it collapsed of its own weight because it was so riddled with teredo worm tunnels (fig. 4.4). The conservation process lost another small segment, so around half remains of the original circle. The wheel is cut across the wood grain; one side has an incised line $\frac{1}{2}$ in. inside the outer rim. The edge opposite the incised line is beveled to prevent wear. The outside diameter measures $7\frac{1}{4}$ in., and the axle originally supporting the carriage was $3\frac{1}{2}$ in. in diameter. The wheel measures 2 in. thick. These features and dimensions resemble those of the hind or rear truck of contemporary four-pounder gun carriages, or slightly smaller.[5]

Figure 4.4. *Fragmentary wooden gun carriage or truck wheel (W13); its size doesn't distinguish between a military or signal gun truck. Photograph by Richard Strauss, Smithsonian National Museum of American History.*

Some of the eyebolts and rings, such as CON64, CON87a, or CON121, discussed in chapter 3, also may actually have served as gun carriage breeching rings, bed bolts, or eyebolts as easily as deck rings. Similar examples were found on a gun carriage from the wreck of the Revolutionary War gunboat *Spitfire*, recently discovered on the bottom of Lake Champlain.[6]

A beautiful and well-preserved cannon apron also was recovered from E18, roughly in the center of the wreck site (L19) (fig. 4.5). Made of two pieces of lead sheet, it has a pair of holes on either side for lashing a lanyard through and around the circumference of the cannon to keep the vent or touch hole covered, dry, spark-free, and ready for action. The back edge still has the impression of the square touch hole plate, and the leading edge is decorated with chisel-cut scalloping along its entire width. Like the lead pipe found aboard the yacht, the apron is fashioned from two sections of lead welded together. Although it is not possible to reconstruct the apron's original curvature and thus the approximate size and shape of the cannon due to its fragility and crushed form, its size and general aspect argue for a sizeable gun (not a small signal cannon). A nearly identical example was recovered from an area containing

Figure 4.5. *The cannon apron (L19) was designed to keep a gun's vent and powder dry and at the ready. The shape of the vent field is visible in the curve of the apron, and the two holes on each side were for tying it down to the gun barrel. The scalloped edge is decorative. Photographs by Richard Strauss, Smithsonian National Museum of American History; drawing by Thomas Ormsby for the Smithsonian National Museum of American History.*

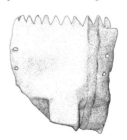

Figure 4.6. *Exploding shell (MISC89b), after conservation. Note the fuse hole, into which gunpowder was poured and then sealed in with a fuse. Photograph by Smithsonian National Museum of American History.*

Figure 4.7. *Made of heavy, durable lignum vitae, this cannon tompion (W52) was used to seal the bore of a cannon at the muzzle against moisture. The hole through the end was for a lanyard so it could be dropped but not lost. The 2½ in. diameter of the tompion indicates a small gun, perhaps a two-pounder used more for signaling than warfare. Photograph by Richard Strauss, Smithsonian National Museum of American History.*

a group of cannon from the wreck of HMS *Carysfort,* which sank in 1770 on what is now known as Carysfort Reef in the Florida Keys National Marine Sanctuary; other, simpler examples are known from earlier shipwrecks in Florida and Britain.[7]

Also suggesting the presence of a large gun on the royal yacht was what first appeared to be a large iron cannonball found concreted to a large, flat Hawaiian sharpening stone located in E38, the midships region of the vessel. With its concreted iron crust, the ball's diameter originally measured nearly 7 in., but when it came back from the Texas A&M Conservation Lab, it measured only $4\frac{1}{4}$ in. in diameter (fig. 4.6). Other new details emerged after conservation as well, in particular that it was round and hollow, weighed 8.762 pounds, and had a $\frac{5}{16}$ in. hole on one side. These features combined to indicate that it was not in fact a cannon ball, but a spherical exploding shell, which would have been packed with gunpowder and then plugged with a wooden timer fuse ignited by the cannon's firing. Upon ignition, the shell was intended to burst into smaller pieces of shrapnel like a modern grenade and level any enemies in its path. A $4\frac{1}{2}$ in. ball diameter corresponds with a nine-pounder. This weight dovetails nicely with the measured weight of the shell, subtracting a bit for the hollowness and material loss during a lengthy seawater submersion. Was this a significant weapon in the yacht's arsenal, aboard to threaten or kill Kauaians on the verge of a revolt from Liholiho's kingdom? Might there have been several of them aboard, most of which were recovered during the 1824 salvage and this one simply overlooked down in a recess in the shipwreck's hull? Perhaps it was used as a threat, or it may even have been aboard as merely a deadly curiosity from a *haole* arms maker.

The final bit of evidence for cannon aboard *Ha'aheo* is presented by a nearly foot-long cylinder of hardwood from nearby trench E16 (W52). The cylinder shaft's diameter is $2\frac{1}{2}$ in., and its head's diameter is larger than the shaft by an inch and is pierced by a $\frac{1}{2}$ in. transverse hole. Made of lignum vitae, the object is identified as a cannon tompion, part of a gunner's tool kit that was stuck into the mouth of a cannon when it was not in use to keep the bore and any contents dry and at the ready for use (fig. 4.7). A line or lanyard would have gone through the hole to prevent the item's loss if dropped. The $2\frac{1}{2}$ in. size indicates that the gun it plugged was a two-pounder or so, with a diameter of 2.2 in. This is slightly smaller than the more common sizes of weapon-size cannon balls and slightly larger than canister or grape or verso shot, perhaps suggesting that this particular tompion plugged the bore of something the size of a signal or swiveling yacht gun.[8]

Bridging the gap between big and small guns aboard the yacht is an incomplete keg or cask of gunpowder from trench E17, whose discovery and identification are described in chapter 1 (MISC58). All that was found was the roughly cylindrical contents of the container ($6\frac{1}{4}$ in. wide × $5\frac{1}{2}$ in. high), which slumped from its original form once liberated from the seawater, and the head or top of the keg with a diameter of $5\frac{3}{4}$ in. and thickness of $\frac{3}{8}$ in. (fig. 4.8). This would have been an example of dry-tight coopering, in which dry but valuable contents were contained. These containers were generally intended for single use, and their component parts were consequently a bit lighter than those required for heavy liquids, where water-tightness was required.[9] The relative lightness of the parts for this type of container might account for the

Figure 4.8. *Keg of gunpowder (MISC58). Bryant & Sturgis's Hawaiian business agent Charles H. Hammat's journal entry for 24 March 1824 records that a keg of gunpowder costs $6.00 in Honolulu. Photograph by Richard Strauss, Smithsonian National Museum of American History.*

loss of the staves and other head. Barrels appear relatively often on shipwreck sites, although only a limited number of examples containing gunpowder have come to light aboard other ships (both earlier): HMS *Invincible,* lost in 1781 off Portsmouth, England, and *La Belle,* lost off the Texas coast in 1686.[10]

Some evidence for a shoulder weapon also is preserved on the yacht in the form of a wooden forestock from trench E38. Made of white oak and measuring $27\frac{1}{4}$ in. long × 2 in. wide, both ends of this dished length of wood are filleted for barrel bands or ramrod fasteners (W63) (fig. 4.9). Projecting the sides into a circle indicates that the original diameter of the weapon was quite large, as would be found on a contemporary boat gun, British Sea Service musket, or blunderbuss. Such arms were deck guns that shot pistol balls or lead pellets, most commonly for antipersonnel operations.[11] Curiously, none of the hard metal parts of this weapon (firing mechanism, barrel, trigger guard)—those most commonly found on archaeological sites—were found, only the wooden barrel component.

To accompany the shoulder arm, a very well-preserved musket (or pocket) powder flask also was recovered from E37, lying on the stern's ceiling planking (C94) (fig. 4.10). When raised, it had a heavy smell of sulphur, indicating that some of the contents were preserved. Made of two copper halves welded together with no visible seam, the 7 in. high teardrop-shaped flask is missing

Figure 4.9. *The projected diameter of this wooden gunstock (W63) would indicate that it came from a boat gun or blunderbuss. The filleted parts are for barrel bands, which would have held the forestock to the barrel. Aboard ships, these guns were deck arms used as antipersonnel scatter guns, firing pistol balls or big lead pellets. Photograph by Harold Dorwin, Smithsonian National Museum of American History.*

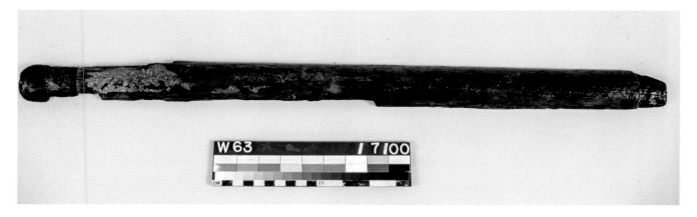

Figure 4.10. *Nearly intact copper powder flask (C94). The bottom (not shown) is slightly flatter than the top to keep it from rolling around. It may be an American copy of an 1818 patented British flask. Photographs by Harold Dorwin, Smithsonian National Museum of American History.*

only its cap. Its cutter, which separated a measured amount of powder from the rest of the contents, fell inside—probably when the steel blade and spring rusted away. Measuring 3 in. wide and $1\frac{3}{4}$ in. thick, the flask has a knurled ring at the start of the taper; the neck, with a four-step spring-activated adjustable charger for measuring different amounts of powder, is stamped "PATENT" and screws into the neck. It most closely resembles a type first patented in 1814 by Englishman Thomas Sykes; a lack of more patent information on the piece may indicate that it is a copy of a Sykes flask by the company Peter Frith & Sons, which was sued by Sykes in 1818 for patent infringement.[12]

Thirty-nine lead shot complete *Ha'aheo*'s arsenal of Western arms. All but six of this number were found at varying levels of trench E12, the broken-up section of the ship's bow hard against the reef. The remainder were found in E34, just ten feet away to the north. Each was measured at more than one spot on its circumference due to irregularities in surface and shape, and they break down into three sizes (fig. 4.11). Seven measure in the range of 0.5 in. in diameter, from a low of 0.512 in. to 0.59 in. Sixteen are in the 0.6 in. range, from 0.629 to 0.689 in. Twelve cluster in the 0.7 range, from 0.71 to 0.79 in. Generally, the first group, the ones measuring around 0.525 in., fall into the .54 caliber range; these would have been used with pistols or smaller shoulder arms. They could also have served as grapeshot, to be fired out of a cannon in quantity as an antipersonnel weapon. Those balls with diameters around 0.640 in. are consistent with a .64 or .69 caliber weapon (allowing for windage)—most likely a musket or the longer carbine. Examples with a diameter of 0.695 in. or larger would fit a .75 caliber weapon, or larger shoulder piece.[13]

Less certain in use are some of the amorphous pieces of lead scrap and a little sand-cast lead "bun" ingot (L25) (fig. 4.12). The smaller, thinner scraps are probably the best candidates for melting down into shot, keeping the larger, thicker pieces for patches or any of the many other shipboard applications. Certainly the $3\frac{1}{2}$ in. diameter ingot was intended for melting down and reuse, but whether that use was military or for ship repair is of course unknow-

Figure 4.11. *Different sizes of lead shot found on the wreck site (L11 and L12). Photographs by Hugh Talman, Smithsonian National Museum of American History.*

Figure 4.12. *Top and bottom surfaces of a small cast lead ingot (L25). Photographs by Richard Strauss, Smithsonian National Museum of American History.*

able without a shot mold or some other archaeological find that could suggest an answer. A fragmentary chipped flint cobble, $3\frac{1}{4}$ in. long, may have served as a source of gun flints, and indeed one side does appear to have a gun flint emerging from its surface (MISC59).

Western Tools and Instruments

During the 1995 season a small amorphous concretion was recovered from trench BB or "Black Buoy," a trench away from the reef in the center of the wreck site used as a site benchmark. Several organic and inorganic artifacts were spotted in the x-ray of the concretion, one of which looked like a turkey

Figure 4.13. *Although both delicate glass bulbs of this sandglass were found on the wreck site, only one survived conservation (CON44). The leather caps and fragments of the posts also survived. Photograph by Richard Strauss, Smithsonian National Museum of American History.*

baster—one of those large kitchen syringes used to keep baked and roasted foods moist while cooking. The object was carefully removed from its surrounding matrix at the Conservation Lab at Texas A&M and turned out to be a small sandglass, complete with one of its glass bulbs, two of the wooden side supports, and two small pieces of leather to buffer the glass from shock (fig. 4.13). Its relatively small size indicates that it was used for determining hull speed, in conjunction with a chip log, rather than any sort of watchkeeping; it probably measured only 14–30 seconds (at most).[14] Interestingly, two seasons later the other glass ball was found inside another concretion discovered in trench E12, against the reef and some 70 feet away from its other half (CON151). Unfortunately the delicate, thin glass part of this bulb did not survive the conservation process, so it is preserved only through a sample of its contents and in the concretion x-ray.

One large concretion yielded a trove of several tools cemented together, both Western and Hawaiian. CON36 was found in 1995 in trench RT, just a few feet to the north of what we would discover five years later was the port-side section of the ship's hull at the stern, in the last excavation season when we were test-trenching in the spaces between the trenches we had already dug to ensure that we didn't miss anything. One of the tools uncovered was a flat, thick wrought iron strap, bent in the middle and terminating in an open hook; it measured 10 in. long × 1 in. wide × $\frac{1}{4}$ in. thick, with a $\frac{3}{4}$ in. inside width of the hook (fig. 4.14). The likeliest candidate is a fragmentary doubletree, used for hanging pots over a hearth.[15] In the same concretion was an incomplete leather holster containing a fragmentary wrought iron tool. The holster comprises a single piece of heavy leather, folded over with stitch holes preserved along one edge (CON36). The fragmentary tool, measuring $3\frac{1}{2}$ in. long × $4\frac{3}{4}$ in. wide, is a round rod of $\frac{1}{2}$ in. thick iron, looped into the form of a "T" at the top and degraded away at the bottom end (fig. 4.15). The closest parallel for this tool appears to be the handle of a sailmaker's heaver or stitch mallet.[16] In E27, a trench adjacent to RT, a curved sailmaker's needle, triangular in section, was found (CON419). Measuring $3\frac{3}{16}$ in. long, missing its eye, and apparently made of steel, it may be part of the same sailmakers' kit as the holstered tool.

Figure 4.14. *This heavy wrought iron strap with a hook at one end is believed to be a doubletree, for hanging a pot over a fire (CON36). Photograph by Richard Strauss, Smithsonian National Museum of American History.*

Toward the northern side of the wreck site, CON445 was found, containing a hafted tool. Unfortunately the iron content had corroded away, but a cast of the cavity was made that emulates the original implement (fig. 4.16). It consists of a thick blade, with a curved section behind it leading into a truncated

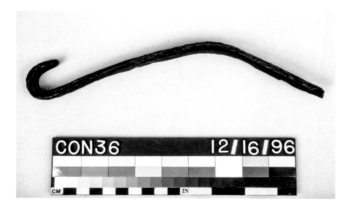

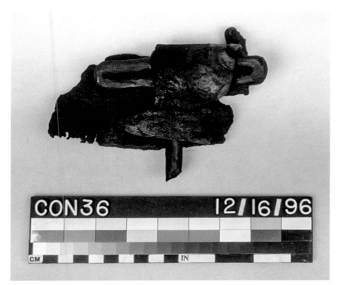

Figure 4.15. *In this photo the handle of the tool is secured in the leather holster by the leather strap (CON36). Photograph by Richard Strauss, Smithsonian National Museum of American History.*

Figure 4.16. *The iron of the blade in this knife or tool oxidized, leaving a cavity of its shape in the concretion. The void was cast with resin, forming a perfect duplicate of the original artifact (CON445). Photograph by Smithsonian National Museum of American History.*

Figure 4.17. *The different sizes of holes in this flat copper artifact, together with the stamped numbers "5" and "6" on one side, might indicate a wire gauge (C88). Some of the holes on one side are countersunk, adding to the uncertainty. Photograph by Harold Dorwin, Smithsonian National Museum of American History.*

haft. It resembles most closely a small wood saw or chopper, missing only a sharp edge (which might have eroded or not survived the casting process). A short section of copper wire (C3) and a pierced copper plate (C88), possibly a wire gauge, may or may not be contemporary with the wreck assemblage. Measuring $1\frac{1}{8}$ square, C88 has the numbers "5" and "6" stamped on one side (fig. 4.17).

Personal Items

Relatively few personal items—nearly all of Western manufacture—were found on the wreck site. This is not surprising, as personal possessions are the sort of thing that certainly would be salvaged quickly and easily from a relatively intact wreck so close to shore, leaving little or no hint of their presence aboard the vessel. Three possible exceptions within this class of finds are carved ivory objects found in E12–13. At least two are presumed to be Native Hawaiian in origin and are in the form of two squarely sawn pieces of sperm whale teeth. One is a long, thin section of tooth with two long sides and one end cut. The fourth surface contains part of the tooth's root (B20) (fig. 4.18). The second is a squared section cut from the upper tip of a whale's tooth (B19) (fig. 4.19). These pieces of

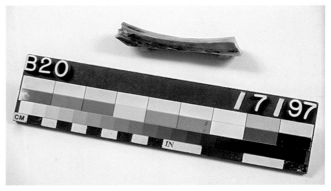

Figure 4.18. *Two of the long sides and one end are cut on this section of sperm whale tooth (B20). A fourth surface appears to be the root of the tooth. This may be debitage, or a leftover piece, from the carving of an ivory fish hook,* lei niho palaoa *(hair and ivory necklace), or other form of pendant. Photograph by Hugh Talman, Smithsonian National Museum of American History.*

Figure 4.19. *This sawn piece from the tip of an ivory sperm whale tooth (B19) has an unfinished secondary cut and is probably a leftover piece from a larger carving. Photographs by Hugh Talman, Smithsonian National Museum of American History.*

ivory would appear to be the result of someone carving some sort of personal item for a high chief (possibly a *lei niho palaoa* or *aliʻi*'s whale tooth necklace), as *kapu* dictated that only chiefs could own whale ivory.[17] However, it is not clear whether these were the pieces being carved or whether they were waste product from something larger being whittled out of the raw tooth.

The third ivory object recovered is less uncertain, as it is a small, intact ivory finger ring (B21) with a plain, rounded outer surface measuring only $\frac{13}{16}$ in. in outer diameter (fig. 4.20). However, unlike the two other pieces, the ring is made of palm (vegetal) ivory rather than animal ivory—whose closest parallel is the *Phytelephas* seed found in South America and Panama.[18] A tiny, almost invisible sample was removed for materials analysis; in order not to alter the appearance unduly, it was taken from the interior surface. Unfortunately, the sample was returned in the US mail just a few short weeks after the events of September 11, 2001, and the anthrax discovered at the US Post Office's Brentwood mail sorting facility in Washington, DC. It was irradiated at extremely high temperatures—like the rest of the government's mail after the events in Washington—while being returned after source materials identification, and further, more detailed identification became impossible. About all that can be further said is that with an inside diameter of only $\frac{11}{16}$ in., it would fit only the finger of a child or young adolescent, and not an adult's.

Figure 4.20. *The only piece of identifiable jewelry on the royal yacht was this little ivory ring (B21), made from vegetal rather than animal ivory. Photograph by Hugh Talman, Smithsonian National Museum of American History.*

Two of the personal items might also be classified under the category of tools. One is a small ($3\frac{1}{2}$ in. long) pair of scissors with slightly curved blades, blunted tips, and delicate finger holes (CON441), found about 40 feet off the reef at the stern section of the hull in E29 (fig. 4.21). The curved blades and blunt tips argue against sewing scissors, which commonly have sharp points and flat blades; the closest parallels are found among the type of scissors for personal grooming (nail/cuticle or hair). The other is a $4\frac{1}{16}$ in. long closed, single-blade folding knife or penknife (CON52), found in trench BB, adjacent to E29. It has a smooth, dark wood or bone handle, slightly curved to fit the hand; brass end caps; case inlays; and a decomposed steel or iron blade,

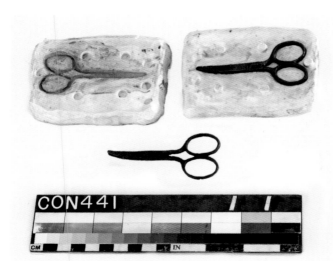

Figure 4.21. *The size and shape of personal or nail scissors have changed so little over time that it is not possible to determine the age of this concreted pair from the wreck site (CON441). Photograph by Smithsonian National Museum of American History.*

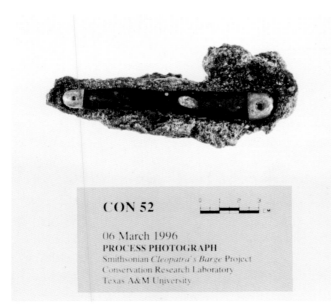

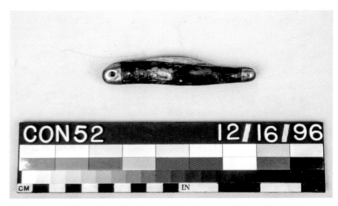

Figure 4.22. *Like the nail scissors, the shape and size of penknives have changed very little over the past two hundred years. However, the thickness of the concretion over the body of this knife (CON52) would argue for some age. Photographs by TAMU Conservation Lab and Smithsonian National Museum of American History.*

which was reconstituted in the conservation process (fig. 4.22). Pocketknives have changed little over time, and this particular example would be just as much at home in colonial times as today.

A small intact bone button in good condition was found in trench BB, the very first test trench sunk on the site in 1995. The thread, or hole area, contains four holes and is slightly countersunk into the surface; the reverse is slightly convex (B1) (fig. 4.23). Measuring only $\frac{1}{2}$ in. in diameter and $\frac{1}{8}$ in. thick, the button was judged too small to warrant sampling for its animal source; it probably fastened a Western-style garment of some sort.

Slightly more than half of an orange glass bead, neatly split in two along the long axis, was recovered from trench E36, the stern section against the reef (MISC87). The wound oval shape is not uncommon for the early nineteenth century, although the color is quite rare. At the time, most glass beads

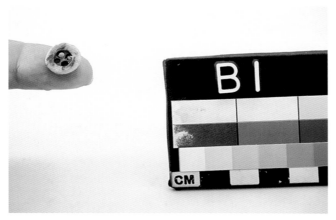

Figure 4.23. *This intact four-hole button (B1) has an inset thread (hole area), and the back side is slightly convex. The size and condition of the button were too good to risk sampling the bone for the source material. Photograph by Eric Long, Smithsonian National Museum of American History.*

Figure 4.24. *The original iron in this buckle was so thin that it oxidized in the salt water, but the void was clean enough for casting (CON452). Here the cast is shown with the casting to illustrate the process. Photograph by Smithsonian National Museum of American History.*

Figure 4.25. *Only a single wooden checker was recovered from the wreck site (W56); the bright red paint is still preserved after 172 years in the salt waters of Hanalei Bay. The turned game piece measures 1 1/16 in. in diameter × 1/2 in. thick. Photograph by Harold Dorwin, Smithsonian National Museum of American History.*

Figure 4.26. *These glass fragments from several different Dutch gin bottles of the early nineteenth century attest to the presence of spirits aboard the royal yacht at the time of her encounter with the shallow reef on the southwest side of Hanalei Bay. They also lend weight to the missionary account for one of the reasons for the ship's loss. Photograph by Harold Dorwin, Smithsonian National Museum of American History.*

were produced in Venice, and a bead of this sort was likelier part of a brace-let or necklace than stitched onto a textile.[19] A small iron buckle that turned up fully oxidized in a concretion (CON452) was of a fairly common type with a tongue that could have fastened a light leather belt, or possibly served as an accessory clasp for a shoe, pair of breeches, or a bag (fig. 4.24). A bright red wooden game checker turned up in E36, measuring $1\frac{1}{16}$ in. in diameter × $\frac{1}{2}$ in. thick (W56) (fig. 4.25). Its wood was not sourced, as it was very fragile due to teredo damage, but it appears turned, with concentric rings around a central boss.

Spanning the gap between personal items and tableware, the next category of finds is the group of approximately eighteen case gin bottle fragments (G13–15, G20, G70, G79, G88, G105–107, G111, G128, G131–132, G155, G167, G171, G178–180) (fig. 4.26).[20] Developed by a Dutch scientist seeking a diuretic in the mid-seventeenth century, gin was first dispensed as a medicine in square bottles for ease of packing in crates or cases. It was easy to produce and inexpensive and quickly became popular among British consumers. Its containers showed its apothecary roots, and the shape was retained for ease of packing in cases.[21]

Collectively, these dark green bottle fragments represent the fundamental reason for the royal yacht's loss and offer material evidence in support of Reverend Samuel Whitney's April 1824 account from Waimea, Kaua'i, of the drunken crew (see chapter 2 for fuller discussion). Since most of the fragments are from the bodies of the bottles and are therefore nondiagnostic, it is not possible to know how many individual containers they represent. A few mouth, neck, shoulder, and base fragments are preserved as well. Of course, any intact bottles—alone or in cases—would have been retrieved during the initial 1824 salvage of the vessel right after she sank, so they would not have left behind any evidence of their existence in any quantity.

Western Food Preparation and Consumption

When conserved, a long, intact forked concretion yielded a $20\frac{1}{2}$ in. long iron two-pronged fork, with a shaft rectangular for the first $2\frac{1}{2}$ in. and then round for the remainder (CON482) (fig. 4.27). It was found in E33, in the outer region of the wreck site. This is probably a meat or "flesh" fork, long-handled to

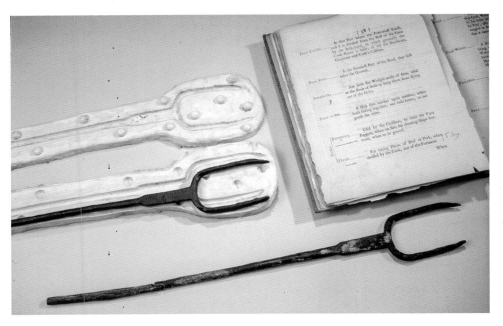

Figure 4.27. *Breaming or flesh fork, with an early nineteenth-century marine dictionary showing a picture and definition of the artifact (CON482). Breaming a vessel is burning off the growth on a ship bottom before graving, or dry-docking, the vessel. Although ship crews probably did not use the two forks interchangeably, they do appear identical in the illustrated dictionary. Photograph by Harold Dorwin, Smithsonian National Museum of American History.*

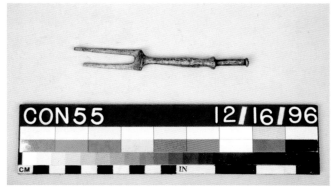

Figure 4.28. *Fork and knives found on the wreck site (CON55 and CON197). Cutlery was still rare enough in the early nineteenth century that many members of the fashionable classes carried and used their own knives, forks, and spoons. These examples may have been on the yacht to serve foreign guests or may have been simple curiosities. Photographs by Richard Strauss and Harold Dorwin, Smithsonian National Museum of American History.*

Figure 4.29. *The original iron in this little cutlery handle oxidized, but it left a castable void (CON122). The amorphous background is not part of the object. Photograph by Richard Strauss, Smithsonian National Museum of American History.*

prevent the user from getting burned when barbecuing and/or "taking Pieces of Beef or Pork, when dressed by the Cook, out of the Furnaces."[22]

A few items of Western tableware also turned up on the *Haʻaheo ʻo Hawaiʻi* wreck site: a fork, a knife, and a piece of glassware. Until the later eighteenth century, table forks were quite rare and generally were items personally owned for individual use, but whether the same circumstance applied to the Hawaiians or not at this point in time is unknown.[23] Certainly they may have been aboard for use by *haole* visitors, guests, or passengers, and a case could be made that a full set might have been aboard and removed during the earliest salvage attempt. In the absence of further information, it is impossible to know.

Found in trench BB, the fork is a two-tine example, probably originally steel, now in the form of a casting of the void it left behind as it oxidized in a concretion (CON55). A ball terminal on a round shaft held in place the original wood or bone handle, now missing. Although no marks were preserved, the form is an English type dating from the 1770s to 1835; Sheffield, England, was the main production center during the period. The knife, found lodged in the reef during a survey of the wreck environs, is a fairly common sort for the period; it was likewise too degraded to preserve intact, so the void it left as it oxidized was flushed and cast (CON197) (fig. 4.28). Both blade and handle were steel, with the tang overhang and straight upper edge arguing for an earlier rather than a more recent date.[24] At the time of the wrecking, these two pieces of flatware might have been considered old-fashioned by Western standards. Less certain is a small concretion casting in the form of an elongated teardrop $2\frac{1}{4}$ in. long (CON122) (fig. 4.29). It has two rivets along its center line and appears to have been the handle of a small piece of tableware, but not enough is preserved to be more certain. And last in this section is G134, found in E27 on the stern hull section. It is a small, clear glass fragment of the rim of a punchbowl or open dish with an everted lip. The glass is relatively thick for this sort of dish, and the original diameter of the fragment, which is nearly

Figure 4.30. *Amid a jumble of concreted ballast and bricks against the ceiling planking was this wooden box, with its top intact but collapsed into the box. Photograph by Smithsonian National Museum of American History.*

flat, would have been quite large. Its closest parallel is mid-1820s Massachusetts shallow glass bowls.[25]

Furniture and Furnishings

Bits and pieces of the furniture and furnishings of the royal yacht reveal tantalizing glimpses of her outfit and appearance at the time of her sinking, and perhaps even offer a few clues to her earlier existence as George Crowninshield Jr.'s plaything. One of the most intriguing features of the ship's contents was the inverted box found in the concreted ballast rubble in trench E36 (fig. 4.30). Measuring 18 in. long × 10 in. wide × 6 in. deep, with sides $\frac{5}{8}$ in. thick, the box was made of white pine; the piece of charcoal found inside derived from the branch of an unidentified species of tropical hardwood. The green glass sherd found inside also was undiagnostic, offering no clues to the box's original contents or purpose.

Clearly on the ship's list of furnishings is a heavy, rectilinear, lipped iron tray of some sort, complete with lugs at regular intervals (CON178) (fig. 4.31). When discovered, it was concreted to a hand-formed brick, which was removed for shipment back to the Smithsonian. Although the purpose of this object is unknown, the nearest equivalent would appear to be a grill or ash tray for the ship's oven or cookstove or perhaps a portable brazier.

Another heat-related artifact is a small, polygonal cast iron door (CON102) with wrought iron fittings (bar stock hinges, rat's-tail lift, stop), which was found in E8, the easternmost trench on the site and one of the farthest trenches from the main hull section

Figure 4.31. *One of the largest recovered concretions was this heavy, thick iron tray, with a raised lip and lugs spaced along its perimeter (CON178). The lugs may represent some sort of suspension system, possibly for cooking. Photograph by Hugh Talman, Smithsonian National Museum of American History.*

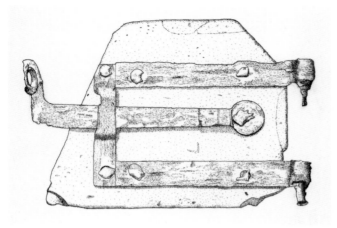
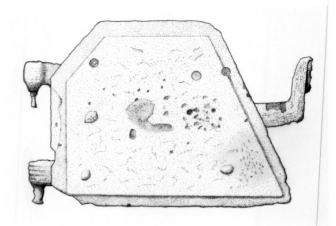

Figure 4.32. *One of the more unusual artifacts emerged from an amorphous concretion and turned out to be the door of a small Shaker stove (CON102). Its odd shape may indicate it was a custom built-in feature of Crowninshield's original yacht. Drawings by Thomas Ormsby for the Smithsonian National Museum of American History.*

Figure 4.33. *Not everything was fancy, gaudy, or gilded aboard the storied yacht. This plain iron doorknob would have been used in some behind-the-scenes spot not intended for public viewing (CON1). Photograph by Richard Strauss, Smithsonian National Museum of American History.*

(fig. 4.32). The composition of this piece, which measures $7\frac{1}{2}$ in. × $10\frac{1}{2}$ in. × $\frac{1}{4}$ in. thick, indicates that it served as the door of a small box or Shaker stove. In terrestrial applications, these were relatively simple rectangular boxes placed in the middle of rooms for keeping warm, and the *Barge* example, almost certainly an original Crowninshield installation, probably served a similar purpose on the yacht. Since even the Shaker examples tended to have simple decorations and this one does not, it may be assumed that this stove was built into an irregular space somewhere aboard the ship and was not intended for public view. It may even be the very stove mentioned by John Dodge on 6 December 1817 as associated with George Crowninshield Jr.'s death: "When I first went into his after cabin he had a small open stove of coals & was seated near it, his head resting on his hands directly over the coals."[26] Obviously, there would have been little need for such a device in Hawai'i, but it may have been kept aboard by the king as a symbol of status or simply not removed if custom-built into a confined or irregularly shaped space.

Several door fittings also were recovered from various spots around the wreck site. The very first concretion recovered during the initial 1995 survey searching for the wreck was a small but heavy solid iron doorknob, with tapered top and bottom leading to a rectangular shaft (CON1) (fig. 4.33). This utilitarian device was probably not designed for public view, judging from a far more decorative example that was recovered with its escutcheon plate from E37 in the stern section against the reef. Both pieces are copper, and both are decorated with a running meander border—fine examples of the Greek Revival style so popular in the early nineteenth century (C90 and C91) (fig. 4.34). Unfortunately, the paste or glass interior of the knob, which measures $2\frac{1}{8}$ in. wide, was not preserved. The plate, with a 2 in. diameter, is intact with two small tack holes flanking a $\frac{3}{8}$ in. square central aperture for the knob shaft. Considering the findspot in the stern

Figure 4.34. *Found in the same trench, this doorknob (C91) and escutcheon plate (C90) share a Greek meander pattern popular in the early nineteenth-century Greek Revival period. Unfortunately, the paste or glass knob was not found. Photograph by Harold Dorwin, Smithsonian National Museum of American History.*

Figure 4.35. *Measuring 2 in. in diameter, this embossed copper boss or finial (C73) would have decorated a lamp or piece of furniture. Photograph by Harold Dorwin, Smithsonian National Museum of American History.*

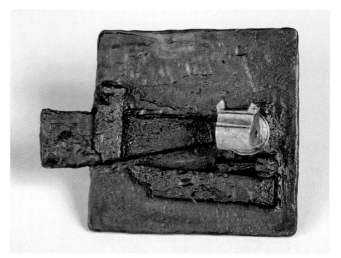

Figure 4.36. *The original iron in this door or cabinet latch oxidized, so the void it left behind was cast with epoxy resin (CON240). Photograph by Harold Dorwin, Smithsonian National Museum of American History.*

of the yacht, it is tempting to attribute this hardware to the owner's cabin. Found nearby in E36 was a round dished copper boss with a 2 in. diameter and a $\frac{1}{2}$ in. height (C73). At the $\frac{1}{4}$ in. height is a circular border of perforations, while the rim is decorated with a running laurel leaf pattern (fig. 4.35). This motif also appears in the Greek Revival repertoire, and it and its near-coincident diameter to the meandered knob may link the piece to the door hardware. There is no visible means of fastening this boss to another object, indicating that it may have had something like thin posts, which have disappeared, or that it was fastened to another piece with an adhesive.[27] CON240 represents more modest hardware, in the form of a "spring" latch; rather than fastening an outside or closet door, it more likely secured the door of a smaller cabinet, cupboard, or lazarette (CON240) (fig. 4.36). Measuring $3\frac{1}{4}$ in. square, its drop is raised with a knuckle hinge, of which the axle is missing, and it is almost identical to colonial-period English examples.[28] Only slightly more decorative is a solid round copper knob, $\frac{7}{8}$ in. in diameter, on a flared base with a square shank: some remnants of plating that originally were visible on its upper surface did not survive the conservation process (C89) (fig. 4.37). This probably served as a small drawer pull or the like. At the other end of the spectrum is a large, heavy iron handle with pear-shaped, pierced cusps for attachment to a flat surface (CON444) (fig. 4.38). This resembles

Figure 4.37. *This copper knob shows signs of gold plating and probably was a small drawer pull or cabinet door knob (C89). Photograph by Harold Dorwin, Smithsonian National Museum of American History.*

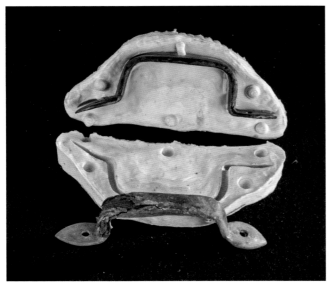

Figure 4.38. *This heavy iron handle may have been a utility or tool drawer pull (CON444). Photograph by Smithsonian National Museum of American History.*

Figure 4.39. *In a 1904 article,* Rudder *magazine published a photograph of a bull's-eye mirror from* Cleopatra's Barge. *One of the Russian visitors to the ship in March 1821 also mentioned gilt mirrors (see chapter 2). The two gilded beads (W41) discussed in chapter 1 may have decorated one of these mirrors or a gilded picture frame. Photograph by Hugh Talman, Smithsonian National Museum of American History.*

piercings, indicating use as sharpening stones. The two smaller examples are small, flat squarish pebbles (fig. 4.56); one (MISC 90) has multiple, slightly converging incised grooves on its convex surface. The other (MISC64) is flat, thin, and almost square, with two short grooves cut into either side; were the grooves carried through, they would have joined to form a notch through the stone. The two larger examples (fig. 4.57) are pierced lava stone; one is the size and shape of a large egg with five longitudinal piercings, of which two penetrate all the way through the stone (MISC83). It also has four longitudinal grooves in its various surfaces—two deep and two shallow—in sum total, an unusual stone sharpener, heavily modified on every surface. The other (MISC36) is pierced longitudinally and is almost square in section, with five of its six sides flattened as though used as a smoother or burnisher.

A larger, flattened triangular lava stone also was a smoother or polisher

Figure 4.55. *This piece of flat slate was reworked into a scraper, burnisher, or polisher (MISC84). Photograph by Harold Dorwin, Smithsonian National Museum of American History.*

Figure 4.56. *Small, flat stones reworked into hand tools (MISC90, MISC64). Photographs by Harold Dorwin and Richard Strauss, Smithsonian National Museum of American History.*

Figure 4.57. *Although MISC36 and MISC83 look like beads, they are probably too large at 2 in. and 2⅝ in. in length respectively. Other options might be sharpeners for hand tools. Photographs by Harold Dorwin and Hugh Talman, Smithsonian National Museum of American History.*

Figure 4.58. *This piece of local lava stone (MISC27) was reworked into a hand-size burnisher or polisher. Photograph by Hugh Talman, Smithsonian National Museum of American History.*

Figure 4.59. *A large, flattened sharpening stone or pounder anvil with three worked surfaces and three grooves on one side; the other side has a large, worked surface trough or platform (MISC89A). The blackened area is where the explosive shell (MISC89B) was concreted to the stone. Photograph by Smithsonian National Museum of American History.*

(MISC27), as evidenced by its multiple smoothed surfaces with several small flats or working surfaces ground onto them (fig. 4.58). Measuring $6\frac{1}{2}$ in. long × $5\frac{1}{4}$ in. wide × 2 in. at its thickest point, this implement clearly saw service on larger jobs. But two even larger grindstones or sharpening stones were recovered from the wreck site from the area of concreted ballast stones in trenches E36 and E38, just north of the stern section against the reef. MISC 89 is a large, 33-pound flat stone (gray limestone?), roughly triangular in shape; when found, it had a large circular iron object concreted to its surface that turned out to be an explosive shell (discussed earlier in this chapter). On one of its flat sides is a shallow trough centered on the long axis, with three converging deep grooves cut into its surface. The central trough is flanked by another shallower one to either side (fig. 4.59). The other side of the stone is characterized by a centrally oriented shallow groove running the length of the stone. On one of the long sides is a stepped flattish platform with another shallow trough on its outer perimeter. The other one is a large 60-pound oblong slab of fine, smooth basalt (MISC88). One side has a single wide, shallow trough ground into the center of its long axis; the other side has two troughs along the same axis (fig. 4.60). All edges are smoothed, and the elegant simplicity of this object is striking.

Far rougher and more utilitarian are two large pounders from E12, made of coarse, porous lava (MISC66–67) (fig. 4.61). Both are in the form of slightly lopsided truncated cones with incurved sides and convex bases; both are 6 in. high, with MISC66 measuring 5 in. wide and MISC 67 an inch smaller. Made from an almost identical coarse lava is a kukui nut oil lamp (MISC30); it has a small flat on the bottom upon which it sits (fig. 4.62). In Old Hawai'i small,

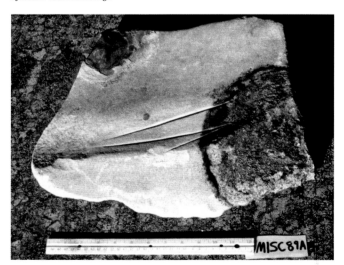

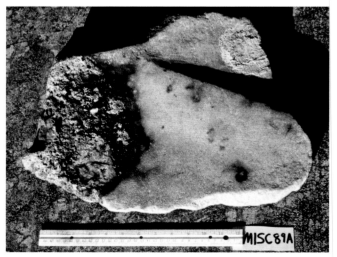

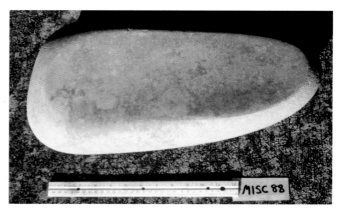

Figure 4.60. *Measuring 19 1/2 in. long, this large, heavy two-sided grindstone is one of the most elegant artifacts from the wreck site (MISC88). Uses for these stones ranged from such diverse purposes as adze sharpeners to platforms for poi pounding. Photograph by Smithsonian National Museum of American History.*

Figure 4.61. *Made of coarse lava, these crude poi pounders or mullers (MISC66 and MISC67) are not the expected quality of artifact from the royal yacht; perhaps they belonged to a crew member instead of Liholiho. Photograph by Richard Strauss, Smithsonian National Museum of American History.*

Figure 4.62. *This little flat-bottom lava cup is a kukui nut lamp (MISC30); the oily nut was stripped of its outer husk, dropped into the bowl, and set on fire for illumination. The kukui nut, which resembles a chestnut, is also known as a candlenut. Photograph by Hugh Talman, Smithsonian National Museum of American History.*

oily kukui nuts, which resemble small chestnuts, were baked, then stripped of their outer shells and burned intact, strung out in a candle. Alternatively, the oil could be extracted by pressing and then burned in these little lamps. Two kukui nuts also were recovered (MISC73) in E24, nearly 80 feet away from the lamp's findspot.[45]

Foodways
Although too few artifacts were recovered from the wreck to develop any broad observations about the foodways aboard the royal yacht, the preparation and consumption of food was the second-largest category of Hawai-

Figure 4.63. *Archaeologist Steve James holding a thin-walled gourd bowl (MISC6). Unfortunately, this artifact only survived conservation in pieces. Photograph by Smithsonian National Museum of American History.*

ian finds aboard *Ha'aheo 'o Hawai'i*. Unfortunately, the rarest and most delicate organic find in this category did not survive the fieldwork intact. This was a large, thin-walled gourd bowl that originally measured at least 20 in. wide (MISC6) (fig. 4.63). Unfortunately, shortly after the field photograph was taken and the measurements were made, the fragment separated into three pieces. During the conservation process, these three pieces fragmented into even smaller pieces, so nothing remains of the earlier shape of what was probably a large, shallow communal poi bowl, outside of the photograph of the artifact with archaeologist Steve James. More than a dozen smaller pieces of broken gourd were recovered (MISC28, MISC39, and MISC50) from the reef's edge in E12 and E14, but none of these had diagnostic finished edges that might have helped to identify their original purpose.

Maritime (Weapons, Fishing, Tools)

Three Hawaiian naval weapons were found in the wreck site in the form of canoe breakers (*pohaku ku'i wa'a*). These were large, coarse ovoid lava stones with grooves cut around the short side (MISC63, MISC69, and MISC77) (fig. 4.64). The grooves were for ropes to encircle the big rocks, which were slung at enemy canoes or their crews and then hauled back for another broadside. One author quoted missionary Hiram Bingham on the use of these bludgeons, which were "swung in the powerful grasp of the Hawaiian chief much like the 'morning stars' of medieval warfare."[46] However, the size and weight of the largest example (MISC77), at $15\frac{3}{4}$ in. × $10\frac{1}{4}$ in. × 6 in. and 46 lbs, would argue against this particular delivery method. In any event, it is hard to believe that these weapons aboard *Ha'aheo 'o Hawai'i* at this late date were anything but anachronisms—or perhaps a nod to tradition—especially with evidence on board for the contrasting presence of Western firearms, powder, and ammunition.

Two medium-size cowrie shells (*Cypraea* spp.) were found in trenches E29 and E30, slightly to the north of the stern hull section (MISC79–80). Both were pierced with two aligned holes on the ventral (upper) surface (fig. 4.65), indicating usage as squid or octopus lures (*leho he'e*). In this application, a stick was threaded through the holes and then adorned at either end with a bright feather or similar attraction. These were then dangled in the water outside the den of a cephalopod, which would then grab onto the enticing lure, only to be hauled quickly to the surface. Oil of the kukui nut could be spat on the water to smooth the waves to see through them.[47] Alternately, the holes could be used for attaching a line to the lure for hauling the catch to the surface.

Figure 4.64. *Different sizes of canoe breakers (MISC63, MISC69, MISC77). A line was tied around the groove bisecting the middle of the stone, and then the stone was slung or thrown at an enemy canoe as an antipersonnel weapon. The line allowed retrieval of the stone weapon for another shot. Photographs by Richard Strauss, Smithsonian National Museum of American History.*

Figure 4.65. *Cowrie shell octopus and/or squid lures (MISC79–80). These were pierced by little sticks with feathered ends and then dangled in front of cephalopod lairs, presenting an irresistible attraction to the curious creatures. Photograph by Harold Dorwin, Smithsonian National Museum of American History.*

Figure 4.66. *Five inches on a side, this pierced lava stone is either a big fishing net sinker or a reef anchor for a small canoe (MISC4b). Photograph by Ricardo Vargas, Smithsonian National Museum of American History.*

Some stone tools also were found, with apparent maritime connections. One is a flattish triangular stone of coarse lava, with a hole worked through both sides of one end (MISC4b) (fig. 4.66). This is identical in shape and size to a stone object identified by Bennett as a fishing net sinker, although it appears to be large enough, at 5 in. × $5\frac{1}{2}$ in. × 2 in., to be a small reef anchor for a canoe.[48] MISC18, an oblong piece of lava, has a worked channel around one edge; one side of this channel is deeper. Above the channel the side of the stone is flattened, and in the middle of the flat side is a protuberance (fig. 4.67). Although clearly worked, the purpose of this stone object is not known; the clearest parallels are a larger stone in the Bishop Museum, rather dubiously identified as a canoe anchor, and what Buck termed a "bread-loaf" sinker, used for the Hawaiian dip net.[49] MISC75 is a perfectly hemispherical stone of coarse, porous lava measuring 2 in. across the bottom (fig. 4.68); similar examples

Figure 4.67. *Smoothed on all sides, this shouldered and knobbed tool may be a canoe rubber, polisher, or other surface finishing tool for canoe making (MISC18). Photograph by Hugh Talman, Smithsonian National Museum of American History.*

Figure 4.68. *This 2 in. diameter lava canoe rubber or bowl smoother (MISC75) is virtually identical to a published example in Peter Buck,* Arts and Crafts of Hawaii, *fig. 182d. Photograph by Richard Strauss, Smithsonian National Museum of American History.*

Figure 4.69. *This Old Hawaiian lava ʻulu maika game stone (MISC65) is shaped like a hockey puck and was rolled some distance down a beach between two upright sticks, like croquet wickets. Photograph by Richard Strauss, Smithsonian National Museum of American History.*

Figure 4.70. *Rounded basalt game or rubbing stone (MISC81). The* ulu maika *game stones almost always had a flat edge, but sometimes they could have a rounded edge like this stone. Photograph by Harold Dorwin, Smithsonian National Museum of American History.*

are most commonly identified as canoe rubbers (*pohaku ʻanai*), or possibly for use on wooden bowls.[50]

At least one object aboard the ship relates to a leisure-time activity. MISC65, found in E29 just off the stern hull section, is a coarse, round lava stone measuring $2\frac{3}{4}$ in. in diameter × $1\frac{1}{2}$ in. thick, with flattened sides and edge, like a small stone hockey puck (fig. 4.69). This is from the game ʻulu maika (or *maika*), in which the disk is rolled on edge along a prepared ground or beach either for distance, or to send it at stakes a few inches apart, 30–40 yards away. Another, slightly larger disk of far finer-grained basalt (MISC81) differs from the *maika* stone only in that its edge is rounded; it may be some other sort of game stone—perhaps for a pitching game or quoits variant (fig. 4.70).[51]

Ceremonial

One of the most unusual Hawaiian finds from *Ha'aheo* was a shell horn or trumpet (*pu*), found in E22 at the northwestern side of the debris field. It comprised a 6 in. tall conch shell (*Strombidae* spp.?), with the crown or apex ground off for the mouth hole and a tonal hole knocked into the body (MISC70) (fig. 4.71). In Old Hawai'i, these were used more for ceremony and signaling than music, with a range of up to two miles. In the last Cook expedition, Captain James King mentioned hearing conch horns after the loss of Captain Cook, in association with the movements of large parties of armed warriors. They were also used for congregational assemblage by the missionaries in the early 1820s.[52] Aboard *Ha'aheo,* the *pu* likely was used to announce the arrival and/or departure of the royal yacht, along with a multigun salute. They may also have marked other ceremonial events of various sorts or perhaps were used to pipe aboard important personages. Authentic Old Hawaiian examples are rare, with only a few at the Bishop Museum in Honolulu.

Figure 4.71. *The royal* pu, *or conch horn (MISC70). In Old Hawai'i conch horns were used for signaling rather than music. Photograph by Richard Strauss, Smithsonian National Museum of American History.*

Personal

The only personal items recovered that could reasonably be interpreted as Hawaiian are the *maika* stone (MISC65) and the three ivory artifacts discussed above—the two unfinished pieces of carved sperm whale's teeth (B19, B20) and the ivory ring (B21). Of course, Western things aboard could fit into the personal category, such as the knives, fork, possibly the furniture mount, and some of the hand tools, but otherwise the wreck is curiously lacking in Hawaiian objects that may be clearly identified as having belonged to the crew or owner. Perhaps since the ship's inter-island voyages were commonly so short, the crew had no need to take personal possessions aboard. Any personal items aboard at the wrecking might have been either organic, in which case they might not have survived the postdepositional period, or they might have been salvaged shortly after the wreck.

Miscellaneous

Some of the artifacts recovered do not fall into easily defined typologies. One of the most intriguing finds was an amorphous hard, flattened, rock-like concretion (CON21) found during the 1995 season in one of the first offshore trenches (BB) that we excavated away from the reef face. It contains a thin lens or band of a white substance through it (fig. 4.72). That white layer in the concretion was found to be smithsonite, the mineral named posthumously in 1832 after James Smithson (1765–1829), the eponymous namesake of the

Figure 4.72. *Sample of smithsonite, represented by the white lens running through the middle of the upper left concretion (CON21). Photograph by Eric Long, Smithsonian National Museum of American History.*

Figure 4.73. *This thin grooved copper band (C96), measuring 3¼ in. in outside diameter and just over 1 in. wide, may be a small part of the ship's rigging. Photograph by Harold Dorwin, Smithsonian National Museum of American History.*

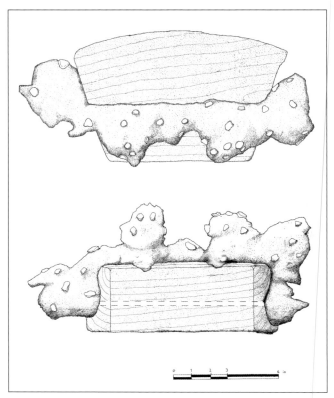

Figure 4.74. *Every archaeological site has its share of mystery objects; Haʻaheo ʻo Hawaiʻi was no exception. This massive block of hardwood, unconsumed by the teredo, is pierced through the center and girdled by a heavily concreted metal band on three sides. Some sort of chock or keystone? Ship construction or cargo? Drawing by Thomas Ormsby for the Smithsonian National Museum of American History.*

Smithsonian Institution. In the early nineteenth century, Smithson had undertaken mineralogical studies and proved that zinc carbonates were carbonate rather than zinc oxides. It was on account of this advance that a mineral was named after him.[53] The coincidence of the presence of the smithsonite and the modern Smithsonian investigation was quite remarkable, but the reason for the presence of this mineral aboard a shipwreck in a remote bay in the middle of the Pacific Ocean is still a mystery.

Some of the finds are of unknown origin and purpose. An example is a pair of small concretions composed mainly of matted organic material, held together with hydrocarbons, hair, fats, and other contents—"an organic garden" according to Smithsonian chemist Walter Hopgood (CON58–59). A tipoff might be the presence of pine tar, which would indicate that the likeliest purpose of this substance was as a waterproofing, with the hair and degraded fibrous plant stalk serving as binding agents to

from another culture, comfortably using the best-adapted implement for the particular job at hand, wherever it was from.

Among Liholiho's first acts after succeeding his father in 1819 was to abolish the *kapu* (taboo) system that November. Just a few months later, in April 1820, he allowed the Boston Christian missionaries into the islands. He had inherited a fleet of Western watercraft from his father, Kamehameha I, and added to it rather prodigiously as well and as long as he could. The jewel of his fleet immediately became *Cleopatra's Barge* as soon as he acquired the alluring vessel in January 1821, and he paid for her with the local currency — sandalwood — in an equivalent dollar amount unmatched by any other purchase during his reign.

Kamehameha I had recognized early on the advantages of Western ships over the local watercraft for simple travel, as troop transports, weapon platforms, and large-scale cargo carriers. He passed on that wisdom to his son Liholiho, who now had to sustain his father's far-flung kingdom. But this was not merely an invasion of foreign craft, for as early as the mid-1790s, the Hawaiians themselves had been building Western-type vessels, recognizing their superiority for certain tasks.[2] Western ships may also have contained symbolic value, not merely as status-enhancing objects but also as vehicles generally representative of improved inter-island trade, tribute collection, travel, and communications.

Far from hastening the dissolution of indigenous culture, *Ha'aheo* and other Western ships in the fleets of the Hawaiian chiefs may be perceived as helping to sustain it. For example, Liholiho used his yacht to cement his hereditary monarchy when he kidnapped Kaumuali'i from Kaua'i and transported him to O'ahu, thereby neutralizing that island's longstanding independence from the rest of the kingdom. He used his vessel to transport other chiefs, foreigners, and the Boston missionaries, which broadened his relationships with the region's power base and gained influence and granted favors among his chiefs. However, other aspects of foreign influence may not have had the same effect on the Hawaiian ways that may be argued for ships.

It may be worthwhile to make a few observations on the intersection between the archaeology and the history of the ship. For example, the wreck was found off the mouth of the Waioli River, precisely where Bingham said she lay in 1824 in his passage describing Kalanimoku's first stop on Kaua'i after the death of its chief Kaumuali'i. *Ha'aheo* lies in ten feet of water against the reef she struck, on her starboard side at a 30-degree list. The top of the reef, which extends a hundred yards or so into the water from the beach, is five feet deep, and well-informed visitors can walk out to its edge and step right into the water over the wrecked hull. Since *Ha'aheo,* at least in her original clothes, had a registered depth of hold of $11\frac{1}{2}$ ft., it does not take a mathematician to calculate the difference in depth that caused the wreck.

Fragments of several case gin bottles were recovered from the shipwreck. Their presence supports the contemporary missionaries' assertions that alcoholic beverages were a factor in the ship's loss, and perhaps justifies Hiram Bingham's strong words on the dire consequences of indulgence in spirits other than the Christian one. Along those same lines, it might be inferred from the presence of mid-nineteenth-century tiger whiskey jug fragments found on the site that the wreck salvor A. S. Nu'uanu was doing more than merely diving on the wreck. He may well have been emulating rather closely the activity of *Ha'aheo*'s crew on her last voyage so many years earlier.

Nothing is preserved today of the midships section of *Ha'aheo*'s hull, and little remains of her bow beyond a few disarticulated timbers lodged against and beneath the reef 80 feet away. However, the 40-foot stern section, with the copper-sheathed sternpost preserved to the 11-foot draft mark, was located against the reef in the final season of excavations. The timbers remaining from the ship are in exactly the same condition reported in the brief 1845 newspaper article on her: so teredo-ridden that a single finger easily penetrates even as heavy a timber as the solid oak sternpost.[3] Evidence of new (and not very good) construction was found in the stern area, as described by Bryant & Sturgis agent Charles Hammatt in May 1823. However, samples of this green wood were so degraded by teredo that the wood species could not even be positively identified, much less sourced from Norfolk Sound, Alaska.[4] Also paralleling the nineteenth-century accounts, large quantities of copper nails and spikes, iron spikes, and copper hull sheathing were found and have been recovered from the wreck site.

Secondly, it may be definitively stated that there were no cannon left after Nu'uanu's 1857 salvage—either within the wreck environs, which were thoroughly excavated, or the surrounding reef, which was fully surveyed. As built, *Cleopatra's Barge* had fourteen gun ports, seven on each side. If Liholiho kept all those gun ports active prior to the 1822 discovery of rot, then when he sold ten of her cannon in exchange for the *Wellington* hulk in October 1822, as many as four may have remained aboard. With two raised by Nu'uanu in 1857, this leaves a maximum of two that could possibly have been recovered by Kalanimoku, since none remain on the site today. Nor are the two guns recovered from the wreck in 1857 known to be on Kaua'i's North Shore, in any Hawaiian museum, or in the possession of anyone in the state of Hawai'i by the name of Nu'uanu. Thus far their whereabouts remain a mystery, perhaps lending credibility to the Wilcox story that a British warship carried them off.[5]

In the hopes that parts of the *Barge* that washed up or were salvaged might be found on shore in the modern village of Hanalei, a comprehensive survey of the local buildings was undertaken at the same time as the underwater excavations. The only nineteenth-century structure in the entire community is the upper portion of the original Waioli Mission Church bell tower, preserved on cinder blocks behind the modern church. This mission was founded in 1834, and the bell tower is believed to date to the 1840s. Unfortunately, none of its interior construction contains anything resembling ship timbers (fig. 5.2). Similarly, considerable effort over the several excavation seasons was devoted to "talking story" with the elders of the local Hawaiian community to see if there were any folktales or memories of the loss of the royal yacht, with disappointing results.

One of the most consistent categories of finds on the wreck site throughout the five seasons of excavations was bricks. Nearly every season yielded broken and intact examples. At first, it was hypothesized that they represented portions of the cookstove, scattered about the wreck site by winter seas, storms, and the multiple tsunamis known to have struck Kaua'i's North Shore since the 1824 wrecking. However, over time it became clear that very few of these bricks were the same size, color, mold quality, or matrix, which ruled out the cookstove hypothesis. It was not until archival research in 1999 that the source of these bricks was revealed: they were part of the missionary shipment that was lost in the wreck. The mismatching is explained by the dire financial straits detailed in the missionary accounts back to the American Board of Commissioners for Foreign Missions office in Boston: the Hawaiian missionaries had so little cash for everyday purchases that they had to borrow money from foreign traders and were forced to buy odd lots of all sorts of commodities for their houses, including bricks. Several sections of barrel hoop and nine beef bones also were found, verifying the mission's losses from the wreck; three of the beef bones (not a major part of the Hawaiian diet at this early date) displayed signs of butchery, and one cow rib had been fashioned into a long, slender Hawaiian shellfish meat pick or mat-maker's leaf-splitter (B11).[6]

As discussed in chapter 2, there were several contemporary sources for the original construction and fitting out of *Cleopatra's Barge* back in Salem in 1816. Some of these provide construction details, and at least one mentions that George Crowninshield incorporated several of his own innovative ideas into the brig's construction. Unfortunately, due to the poor degree of preservation; voracious teredo damage; multiple salvage operations; and natural forces at work on her wreck, comparatively little of her hull and fittings remains above the waterline to augment or amplify the historical accounts of Crowninshield invention or innovation. However, a bilge pump marked "J.BAKER'S/ PATENT/J.DAVIS/MAKER/BOSTON" was found, verifying two separate 1817 accounts of the installation and performance of Baker's patent—one in the *Barge*'s logbook and the other in a George Crowninshield letter from aboard the *Barge* to Commodore Isaac Hull (see figs. 3.46 and 3.47).[7] The plumbing noted by one Mediterranean visitor to the brig also appeared in the

Figure 5.2. *The bell tower of the Waioli Mission House church in Hanalei contains old timbers and reused timbers, but none that appear to be from wooden ship construction. Photograph by Captain Richard W. Rogers.*

Figure 5.3. *Aerial view of Hanalei Bay. Photograph by Peter Burroughs.*

archaeological record in the form of several sections of heavy, $1\frac{3}{8}$ in. diameter lead pipe scattered throughout the wreck site. They were made from short sections of rolled lead sheet, soldered along their length and then soldered at their ends to form longer runs. Oddly and without exception, all of the fragments found within the wreck site had both ends pinched off, as though they had been removed and altered manually to prevent them from rolling around in some form of storage (see fig. 3.49). The *Barge*'s lead plumbing might account for some of the owner George Crowninshield's eccentric behavior during his six-month Mediterranean cruise, since several of the effects of lead poisoning are neurological.[8]

The *Pride of Hawai'i* continues to show life. As of this writing, Hawai'i's State Historic Preservation Division has designated the Kaua'i Museum as the curation facility of record for the artifacts—something the state has never done before.[9] Two potential venues on the shores of Hanalei Bay—private and public—have expressed strong interest in long-term exhibitions, and a management group of volunteers was assembled to oversee various aspects of the future efforts to tell the Hawaiian chapter of the famous ship's short but intense life, through both the historical and archaeological records preserved today.

The site should prove useful to archaeologists working in Hawai'i, as it is very tightly dated, unlike many terrestrial sites where occupation may have been continual for centuries. In addition, much Hawai'iana discovered today at archaeological excavations is either from places with no real context, a disturbed one like a construction site, or a farmer's field, from which little information can be derived. Moreover, at many Hawaiian archaeological sites dates are provided only by an absolute dating technique (like C14 dating), which provides broad brackets most useful in the older sites, with an error factor of a hundred years or more. *Ha'aheo,* however, provides the Hawaiian archaeological finds with a finite *terminus ante quem* of early April 1824, thus providing a precise date against which other objects found elsewhere—for example, iron adzes—can be compared.

Around a quarter of *Ha'aheo*'s hull structure below the waterline remains buried in the shallow sands of Hanalei Bay, one of the most beautiful spots in Hawai'i (fig. 5.3). It and the artifacts recovered from five seasons of excavations are all that remain of the storied ship, one New Englander's dream, and a Hawaiian king's favorite, shipwrecked in paradise.

Notes

Chapter 1

1. See P. F. Johnston, "DOWN-BOUND: The History of the Early Great Lakes Propeller Indiana," *American Neptune* 55, no.4 (1995): 323–355 and bibliography.

2. See Whitehill, *George Crowninshield's Yacht,* 10; and "Boston Arrivals," *Charleston Courier,* 14 April 1819, 2: "BOSTON, April 3 . . . Also, brig Cleopatra's Barge, Williams, Rio Janerio [*sic*] 60 days. . . ."

3. See J. R. Harris, *The Copper King* (Liverpool: Liverpool University Press, 1964).

4. The missionaries were accustomed to having dogs as pets in their own culture; however, they were appalled by the affection lavished by the Hawaiian chiefs upon their pet pigs, and they never failed to mention it when they witnessed such behavior.

Chapter 2

1. Whitehill, *George Crowninshield's Yacht,* 7n10.

2. Crowninshield, *Story of George Crowninshield's Yacht,* 15–16. For a brief history of *America IV,* see Eastman, *Some Famous Privateers,* 32–38.

3. For a description of the *Barge* plumbing, see Crowninshield, "An Account of the Yacht," 112, citing *Diario di Roma,* published in Rome in August 1817 and reprinted in the *Essex Register,* 11 October 1817: "Near was another apartment, which admitted all the offices of a kitchen, and in it was a pump with three tubes, which passed through the vessel, to supply water from the sea, or discharge what they pleased, with the greatest ease."

4. See, for example, Crowninshield, *Story of George Crowninshield's Yacht,* 21–26.

5. Ferguson, Cleopatra's Barge, 99.

6. Verification of the presence of a black cook named W. Chapman who accompanied Captain Cook in 1772–1774 is found in Whitehill, "George Crowninshield's Yacht," 249n212: "The final detail, concerning the colored man's service as a cabin boy during Captain James Cook's last voyage, *sounds* unlikely. Nevertheless, George Crowninshield's cook was William Chapman, and, among the list of officers and men of Cook's *second* voyage of 1772–1774 [published in Arthur Kitson, *Captain James Cook* (London, 1907), 513–515] a W. Chapman appears as an able seaman in H.M.S. *Resolution.* He was subsequently transferred to be the cook in H.M.S. *Adventure!*" However, other sources indicate he is not among the crew listing for Cook's third and final voyage, in which *Adventure* did not participate. Crowninshield, "An Account of the Yacht," 103, tells the story as well.

7. Mary Boardman Crowninshield to Benjamin Williams Crowninshield (her husband), 2 April 1817, in Ferguson, Cleopatra's Barge, 100.

8. Crowninshield, *Story of George Crowninshield's Yacht,* 136–138.

9. Ferguson, Cleopatra's Barge, 102–103; not surprisingly, neither Whitehill nor F. B. Crowninshield recount this story.

10. Crowninshield, *Story of George Crowninshield's Yacht,* 213.

11. The most detailed accounts are ibid., 237; Whitehill, *George Crowninshield's Yacht,* 10–15; Ferguson, Cleopatra's Barge, 77–83; Crowninshield, "An Account of the Yacht," 106–107; Whitehill, "George Crowninshield's Yacht," 249–251.

12. I am grateful to the late Angie VanDereedt of the National Archives for locating *Cleopatra's Barge*'s three registration certificates in Record Group 41 (Records of the Bureau of Marine Inspection and Navigation).

13. For Bryant & Sturgis, see Morison, *Maritime History of Massachusetts,* 62–268. The Bryant & Sturgis papers are at the Baker Library, Bryant & Stugis Collection, Harvard University, Cambridge, MA; some of the corporate letters also are preserved in the John Suter Papers at the Massachusetts Historical Society, Boston.

14. The description of Suter's youth and early career is derived in part from the fifteen-page typescript "A Trader on the North-West Coast," read by John Wallace Suter at a meeting of the Club of Odd Volumes in Boston in 1920. The original is at the Boston Marine Society; I am grateful to Dr. Mary Malloy of the Sea Education Association, Wood's Hole, MA, for bringing it to my attention. See also Morison, *Maritime History of Massachusetts,* 70–78.

15. Captain Suter's fur trips on *Pearl* and *Atahualpa* netted $234,000 and ca. $120,000 respectively, making him one of the most successful Northwest traders. See Gibson, *Otter Skins,* 177, and Morison, *Maritime History of Massachusetts,* 70–72. *Bering,* lost on the south shore of Kaua'i in 1815 while loaded with furs, was the first documented Western shipwreck on Kaua'i and only the second in the Hawaiian Islands. Under the guise of recovering her cargo, the Russians tried to establish a toehold on Kaua'i and actually hatched an unsuccessful plan to make the island a Russian outpost.

16. The vessel was named after King Kamehameha; early writers in Hawai'i transcribed letters differently (especially Ks and Ts) before they were standardized later in the nineteenth century. Judd, *Voyages to Hawaii,* 90, offers a distillation of Suter's career with slightly different dates.

17. The cargo listing is from the *Barge*'s (undated) Bill of Health, published in Morison, *Maritime History of Massachusetts,* opp. 266. However, it is incomplete; letters from Bryant & Sturgis's Hawaiian agent, Charles B. Bullard, dated 22 December 1820 and 23 March 1821, add the articles outside of the quotations. A "pikel" (picul) is a Chinese measure of $133\frac{1}{3}$ pounds, frequently used in the China trade.

18. Bryant & Sturgis to Suter, 20 June 1820, John Suter Papers.

19. Both logs (in three volumes) are preserved at the Peabody Essex Museum in Salem, Massachusetts. One is the logbook of *Cleopatra's Barge* (June 1820–August 1821), no. 1820C3. Prob-

ably kept by the first mate, it will be cited hereafter as *Barge* log. The other (22 June–3 July 1820) is in the back of the logbook of *Mentor* (1816–1820), by Captain John Suter, no. 1820C3. Cited hereafter as Suter *Barge* log, this one is continued from 1 July 1820 to 19 December 1820 in a fresh logbook. Some of the sails' names were archaic even then, reflecting George Crowninshield's personal preferences.

20. The name Liholiho ("Shining" or "Glowing") was itself an abbreviation of Kalaninuikualiholihoikekapu ("Great Chief with the Burning Back Taboo"); see Judd, *Let Us Go,* foreword (unpaginated). Liholiho's "official" Hawaiian name was Iolani Lunalilo.

21. Suter *Barge* log, 10 November 1820.

22. Maria Loomis Journal, 11 November 1820, original and typescript at the Hawaiian Mission Children's Society (HMCS) Library, Honolulu. I am grateful to HMCS librarian Marilyn L. Reppun for her interest and tireless assistance in the acquisition of the original contemporary sources for the *Barge* and her period in Hawaii.

23. Naval-type cannon salutes were a relatively recent phenomenon in Hawaii; Kotzebue claims to have fired the first one (of seven guns) on 14 December 1816. See Barratt, *Russian View of Honolulu,* Narrative 12, 148.

24. *Barge* log and Suter *Barge* log, 16 November 1820. Since the Chinese picul measured $133\frac{1}{3}$ pounds, the value of the *Barge* was 1,066,640 pounds of sandalwood. The fragrant wood was a principal commodity of the American China traders, prized by the Chinese mainly for incense but also for furniture and craft objects.

25. In addition to the in-text citation for Bryant & Sturgis to Suter, see also Bryant & Sturgis to Bullard, 12 October 1820, in Cushing Letter Book, Bryant & Sturgis Collection, vol. 10, 161–162, Baker Library, Harvard University, Cambridge, MA.

26. See, for example, Byron, *Voyage of H.M.S.* Blonde, 38n, and 40–41; Daws, *Shoals of Time,* 45.

27. I'i, *Fragments of Hawaiian History,* 29–30, 53. Born in 1800, I'i was Liholiho's *kahu,* or personal companion/attendant,

from an early age. Racing pond models, sometimes with large wagers riding on the outcomes, was a game called "little ships" and lasted into manhood among the Hawaiian chiefs, according to Kotzebue, writing in mid-December 1824; see Barratt, *Russian View of Honolulu,* Narrative 114, 244. Pond model racing was a popular sport in the American Northeast up to the mid-twentieth century.

28. Virtually every history of Hawai'i discusses these seminal events in greater detail than is possible here; see, for example, Kame'eleihiwa, *Native Land and Foreign Desires,* 68 ff.

29. The ABCFM-Hawai'i Papers (1820–1900) are at Harvard University's Houghton Library, with typescript copies at the HMCS Library.

30. Elisha Loomis Journal, 21 December 1820, in original and typescript at the HMCS Library. Loomis was printer for the Pioneer Company (first missionary group); he remained in Hawai'i until 1827. See Gulick and Gulick, *Pilgrims of Hawaii,* 29.

31. Ka'ahumanu was the first to hold the title of *kuhina nui,* or powerful officer; it is most frequently translated as "prime minister." This information about Rives is derived from several Hawaiian and Western sources; see I'i, *Fragments of Hawaiian History,* 86–87; Kamakau, *Ruling Chiefs of Hawaii,* 330–331; Dibble, *History of the Sandwich Islands,* 317–319; and Cottez, "Jean-Baptiste Rives."

32. Suter *Barge* log, 15 and 18 December 1820; Suter to Bryant & Sturgis, 22 December 1820, John Suter Papers.

33. Gast and Conrad, *Don Francisco de Paula Marin,* 236. Marin was a local foreign merchant (Spanish), who frequently served as a business agent and translator for the Hawaiian chiefs. Later he was a farmer and plantation owner. The Gast and Conrad volume contains Marin's edited journal.

34. Journal of the Sandwich Islands Mission (JSIM), 7 January 1821, vol. 1, 101–102. The journal was "probably written by Hiram Bingham, Asa Thurston and Elisha Loomis in turn." The first volume is known as "The Thaddeus Journal," and it covers the voyage, arrival, and first

several months of the Pioneer Company (23 March 1819–15 November 1821). The original and typescript are at the HMCS Library. The remainder is in the ABCFM Papers, Houghton Library, Harvard University. All are in typescript photocopy at the HMCS Library; the first volume is paginated in the typescript; the remainder is paginated as in the original manuscript, so the citations may appear inconsistent.

35. Maria Loomis Journal II, 7 January 1821.

36. Bingham, *Residence,* 126. The entries for 4 February 1821 in the Maria Loomis Journal and Elisha Loomis Journal also provided some of the details in the description of this event.

37. Elisha Loomis Journal and Maria Loomis Journal, 14 February 1821.

38. See, for example, Kamakau, *Ruling Chiefs of Hawaii,* 251–255.

39. Maria Loomis Journal II, 10 March 1821, 313, and Marin's journal for the same date. According to I'i, *Fragments of Hawaiian History,* 128, Liholiho used his knowledge of the English language "to obtain bottles of rum from ships' captains. Apparently he wrote for rum, nothing else."

40. Captain Jack was commander of the king's vessels and was called this or "Admiral" by Westerners; his real name was Naihe-Kukui or Kapihe. Sandra Wagner-Wright, in Hammatt, *Ships, Furs, and Sandalwood,* 84, states that Captain Jack was a "third-rank chief who worked as the Honolulu harbor pilot." See JSIM, 18 March 1821, and Pleadwell, *Voyage to England,* 3. Captain Adams was probably Englishman Alexander Adams, who worked for Kamehameha I and II for several years as master of various vessels. According to Gast and Conrad, *Don Francisco de Paula Marin,* 80, in early 1820 Captain Alexander Adams was harbor master at Honolulu. According to Russian Karl Gillesem, the king's fleet was commanded by Englishmen, excepting only the royal yacht; see Barratt, *Russian View of Honolulu,* Narrative 52, 184.

41. The *Bordeaux Packet* was purchased by Kamehameha I from Captain Andrew Blanchard in 1817 for an undisclosed amount of sandalwood.

42. Maria Loomis Journal and Elisha Loomis Journal II, 3 April 1821; JSIM, 4 April 1821.

43. Karl Gillesem, as cited in Barratt, *Russian View of Honolulu,* Narrative 28, 163. Although he got the date and the number of guns for the brig wrong, Gillesem did provide the useful details of the gilt mirrors (confirmed elsewhere) and the presence of twelve-pounders for the deck guns.

44. A. P. Lazarev (1791–1862), as cited in ibid., Narrative 127, 260–263.

45. Jones to Marshall, 5 October 1821, in Morison, "Boston Traders in the Hawaiian Islands," 35–37. John Quincy Adams's letter of commission of 7 September 1820 appointed Jones "Agent of the United States for Commerce and Seamen at the Sandwich Islands," Record Group 59, Consular Despatches, Honolulu, vol. 1, M40/16, National Archives. According to Gast and Conrad, *Don Francisco de Paula Marin,* 97n10, "Jones erroneously called himself American Consul when signing documents, and even assumed powers generally reserved for ambassadors." Bradley, *American Frontier,* 89–91, supports and amplifies the view of Jones as a poseur insofar as his federal duties, but Gast, *Contentious Consul,* 32, quotes John Quincy Adams's extant State Department correspondence, "Your duties under the appointment herewith will be those ordinarily assigned to consuls," which, however, the Sandwich Islands lacked since their government was not quite ready for such recognition by the United States.

46. Charles B. Bullard, 1 November 1821, in "Type Script of Letterbook of Charles B. Bullard/Supercargo (or Trading Master) for Bryant & Sturgis at the Hawaiian Islands and at Canton March 20, 1821–July 11, 1823," edited by Francis B. Lothrop, with assistance from E. S. Dodge, December 1969, HMCS Library. All letters are to Bryant & Sturgis unless otherwise noted. *Tartar* was transporting 5,618 piculs of *Barge* sandalwood payments to Canton on this voyage, as per Bullard, "Type Script of Letterbook, " 25 October 1821.

47. This account of the Kaua'i episode has been compiled from several sources,

including the Suter *Barge* log, 14–17 July 1821; Bingham, *Residence,* 138–48; Hiram Bingham Journal, 22 July 1821, reprinted in the *Missionary Herald* 18, no. 8 (August 1822): 242–250; Mercy Partridge (Mrs. Samuel) Whitney Journal, 17 September 1821, HMCS Library (typescript copy from Kaua'i Museum, 1978); Elisha Loomis Journal II, 25 July 1821; Stewart, *Journal of a Residence,* 104; Sybil (Mrs. Hiram) Bingham, draft letter, n.d. (1821), Bingham Family Papers, box 3, folder 1: "1820–37 drafts, incomplete," HMSC Library; Gast and Conrad, *Don Francisco de Paula Marin,* 256 for 30 September 1821.

48. Bingham Family Papers, box 3, folder 1: "1820–37 drafts, incomplete."

49. Kame'eleihiwa, *Native Land and Foreign Desires,* 84–85, provides a radically different interpretation of the kidnapping from the one here. She calls this event a "small victory" for Liholiho and declares Ka'ahumanu the ultimate victor of the kidnapping, for by marrying Kaumuali'i she effectively deprived Liholiho of the tribute and obtained it for herself.

50. Suter, "A Trader on the North-West Coast," 14.

51. Mercy Partridge Whitney Journal, 26 March 1821; Asa Thurston to Rev. Samuel Worcester, 4 May 1821, Asa Thurston File, 1821–1844, HMCS Library (photocopies). Reverend Worcester in Salem was the corresponding secretary of the ABCFM at the time.

52. JSIM, 1 October 1821, 169.

53. Suter, "A Trader on the North-West Coast," 9.

54. JSIM, 15 October 1821, 171.

55. Ibid., 27 December 1821, 258.

56. Certificate of Registry, 16 March 1822, Record Group 41, National Archives.

57. Bullard, "Type Script of Letterbook," 3 July/5 August 1822.

58. Jones, 10 August 1822, in Morison, "Boston Traders in the Hawaiian Islands," 40–42.

59. Mathison, *Narrative of a Visit to Brazil,* 463.

60. JSIM, 3 May 1822, 291. I am grateful to Dr. Peter Mills of the Univer-

sity of Hawai'i, Hilo, for pointing out that *moku* also means "island" in Hawaiian. A chief so naming a vessel may have conferred metaphorical possession of an island upon himself; see Kame'eleihiwa, *Native Land and Foreign Desires,* 27.

61. Bullard, "Type Script of Letterbook," 8 October 1822.

62. JSIM, 10–11 October 1822, 338. Trader Stephen Reynolds offers a somewhat different sequence of events for *Wellington;* see King, *Journal of Stephen Reynolds,* 230–250. I have favored the missionary account of this episode, as they were more directly involved in the ship's transactions than Reynolds.

63. Bullard, "Type Script of Letterbook," 8 and 13 October 1822. Captain Meek, originally from Marblehead, Massachusetts, was at the time a ship's pilot in Liholiho's employ, according to Morison, "Boston Traders in the Hawaiian Islands," 35n2. Morison further notes that Meek had settled in Honolulu and married a Hawaiian. Prior to that, he had been a merchant trader in China and the Pacific Northwest.

64. Former Marbleheaders Captain Thomas Meek and his brother James were in the king's employ at the time, serving as everything from ship captains to general contractors for ship repair. Meek's 1821–1825 log for the *Arab* is in the H. H. Bancroft Collection, Bancroft Library, University of California, Berkeley; I am grateful to Dr. Peter Mills of the University of Hawai'i for bringing to my attention and sharing his voluminous notes from it.

65. Bullard, "Type Script of Letterbook," 8 November 1822. James Hunnewell was one of the earliest retail merchants in Hawai'i and had been supercargo of *Thaddeus* on the 1819–1820 voyage that brought the Pioneer Company of missionaries from Boston to Hawai'i. See Bradley, *American Frontier,* 84 and 88n195. Hunnewell later replaced Bullard's replacement, Charles H. Hammatt, as Bryant & Sturgis agent from 1826 to 1830.

66. Bullard, "Type Script of Letterbook," 10 December 1822 (at sea, bound for Canton aboard *Tartar*).

67. This reference to caulking so soon

after sealing indicates that the two activities were somehow different. Might sealing signify paying the seams or coating the hull with something before coppering? The archaeological evidence does not support the latter hypothesis, as nothing was found between the strakes' outer surface and the coppering on the wreck.

68. Work specifically mentioning the *Barge*'s name ended on 16 March 1823, although painting of an unnamed ship (that *may* have been the *Barge*) continued beyond that date in the *Arab* log.

69. Edited letter in Morison, "Boston Traders in the Hawaiian Islands," 46–47.

70. C. H. Hammatt Journal (1823–1825), Bryant & Sturgis Collection, vol. 15, Baker Library, Harvard University. Hammatt's journal is published in Hammatt, *Ships, Furs, and Sandalwood.*

71. Hammatt Journal, 10 May 1823.

72. JSIM, 11 May 1823, 394.

73. Hammatt Journal, 18 May 1823.

74. Ibid., 30 May 1823; Bingham, *Residence,* 190; Stewart, *Journal of a Residence,* 172–175.

75. Stewart, *Journal of a Residence,* 172–175.

76. Hammatt Journal.

77. Ibid., 17 June 1823. The *Barge* won three of her other four "races"—the first of which was an informal duel with the frigate *United States* between Cartagena and Port Mahone in the Mediterranean in May 1817. Crowninshield reveled in his victory, although it should be noted that it is not clear whether fleet Commodore John Shaw knew his flagship was engaged in a contest, and Shaw was in debt to Crowninshield in the amount of $1,500 as well! The second was against a French man-of-war keeping an eye on Napoleon's family in Italy, and the third was with the Baltimore clipper *General Jackson,* a few days after the contest with the Frenchman. See Crowninshield, "An Account of the Yacht," 100–105; Crowninshield, *Story of George Crowninshield's Yacht,* 95. The fourth, again with the frigate *United States* in the Mediterranean, was fought to a draw with Crowninshield giving ground in strong winds but easily overtaking in light airs; see Crowninshield, *Story of George Crowninshield's Yacht,* 113–114.

78. As secretary of state in 1816, James Monroe had signed two different passports for the first voyage of *Cleopatra's Barge* out of Salem; the first was when she was (briefly) named *Car of Concordia.* Both were obtained through George's brother Benjamin, then secretary of the navy. That same week, Monroe also wrote George Crowninshield Jr. a letter of reference to John Quincy Adams, then Envoy Extraordinary and Minister Plenipotentiary of the United States at London. See Crowninshield, *Story of George Crowninshield's Yacht,* 32–33. Bradley, *American Frontier,* 98, cites contemporary sources that say Liholiho had lost so much power and popularity by this time that he felt a "cooling off" period might be beneficial to his reign. Kamakau, *Ruling Chiefs of Hawaii,* 256, avers that Liholiho felt his power and wealth were so diminished he had to leave.

79. Bingham, *Residence,* 204; Pleadwell, *Voyage to England,* 1. See Corley, "British Press Greets the King," for a thorough discussion of Liholiho's motives for his visit and activities in England.

80. See Mills, *Hawai'i's Russian Adventure.*

81. Kamehameha I had nearly twenty wives. Kamamalu was the daughter of Kamehameha I and Kaniu (Kalakua). Bingham, *Residence,* 202, says that only eight went to England; Kamakau, *Ruling Chiefs of Hawaii,* 356, lists the entire party of twelve.

82. I am grateful to Dr. Stuart M. Frank of the Kendall Whaling Museum for furnishing extensive information on *L'Aigle*'s history. She was wrecked at Tonga in the South Pacific in 1830.

83. For Ellis's background in Polynesia with the London Missionary Society, see Hiney, *On the Missionary Trail,* chap. 4: "The Hawaiian Adventure."

84. William Ellis, "11 Letters," no. 8 (presumed to the Rev. G. Burder, Secretary, London Missionary Society), 20 November 1823, HMCS Library. Also found in W. Ellis to George Burder (LMS Secretary), 20 November 1823, transcribed by Donald Angus, "Letters Received from the Sandwich Islands," typescript, p. 49, London Missionary Society

Collection, Hawai'i Historical Society Library, Honolulu. Starbuck was born on Nantucket in 1791, the offspring of two famous local whaling families (the Folgers and Starbucks).

85. Bingham, *Residence,* 202.

86. Pleadwell, *Voyage to England,* 3–4, 8; Bingham to Everts, 12 January 1824, in Missionary Letters, 1:81, HMCS Library; Bingham, *Residence:,* 204.

87. JSIM, 26 December 1821, 257 (ms.).

88. Hammatt Journal, 5 June 1823 and 17 July 1823.

89. JSIM, 31 October 1823, 438 (ms.); Levi Chamberlain Journal II, 31 October and 1 November 1823, 35, original and typescript at the HMCS Library (page numbers refer to typescript). Chamberlain was business agent for the mission, arriving with the second company on 27 April 1823.

90. Levi Chamberlain Journal II, 2 December 1823, 45; King, *Journal of Stephen Reynolds,* 10. Stephen Pupuhi was a Tahitian youth affiliated with the Boston missionaries.

91. Stewart, *Journal of a Residence,* 279; Kuykendall, *The Hawaiian Kingdom,* Appendix B, 3:430–434.

92. Levi Chamberlain Journal III, 4 February 1824, 12; Joseph Goodrich and Samuel Ruggles, "Public Journal Kept at Waiakea, Hawaii," in Missionary Letters, 7 February 1824, 3:882–890; S. Ruggles to L. Chamberlain, 2 February 1824, in Samuel Ruggles to Depository, 1824–1836, Missionary Letters Collection, HMCS Library. Levi Chamberlain called Kouhou a "low chief;" his name is alternately spelled Kohou and Koakou by various correspondents.

93. Levi Chamberlain Journal III, 19 February 1824, 19; JSIM, 19 February 1824, 474 (ms.); King, *Journal of Stephen Reynolds,* 19. It was the same Captain Blanchard who had transported the Pioneer Company of missionaries from Boston in 1820.

94. A. Bishop to J. Evarts, Missionary Letters, 22–27 February 1824, 2:591–593; King, *Journal of Stephen Reynolds,* 20; JSIM, 26 February 1824, 474 (ms.).

95. A. Thurston and A. Bishop, "Kai-

lua Station Report," 10 March 1824, HMCS Library; A. Bishop to L. Chamberlain, 17–18 March 1824, Artemas Bishop Folder (1823–1827), Missionary Letters Collection, HMCS Library.

96. Samuel Whitney Journal, 8 April 1824, HMCS Library. Interestingly, in this entry Whitney says that the wreck occurred on 6 April, although virtually all later missionary (and other) sources date the event to the 5th. This journal entry also was published in Ethel M. Damon, ed. "The First Missionary Settlement on Kauai: Extracts from the Manuscript Journals of Rev. Samuel Whitney and Mrs. Mercy Partridge Whitney, 1819–1824," *The Friend,* October 1925, 230–231.

97. Today there is a large, stockless iron anchor of unknown date lodged beneath a coral head just off the northeastern corner of Hanalei Bay. See fig. 1.21.

98. Liholiho's co-regent Ka'ahumanu did not make it any easier for the new king to consolidate his inheritance and enforce his monarchy; see Kame'eleihawa, *Native Land and Foreign Desires,* 69 ff.

99. Bingham, *Residence,* 218.

100. Ibid., 221–223. Kaumuali'i died on 26 April at Honolulu, further destabilizing the situation on Kaua'i.

101. The hibiscus used was not the flowering shrub known as such on the mainland but *Hibiscus tiliaceous,* known in Hawaiian as *hau.*

102. Levi Chamberlain Journal III, 12–13 May 1824, 48.

103. A. Bishop (in Kailua) to L. Chamberlain, 5 June 1824, Artemas Bishop Folder, HMCS Library.

104. Bingham, *Residence,* 232.

105. James Young was the English name for Chief James Young Kanehoa, according to Ellis, *Journal of William Ellis,* 42, and Pleadwell, *Voyage to England,* 3. A *punahele* is a favorite (friend or trusted advisor). Young's father was a British citizen named John Young as well; he arrived in the Hawaiian islands in 1790 and rose as high as governor of Hawai'i and O'ahu for Kamehameha I. See Bradley, *American Frontier,* 37; Emmett Cahill, *The Life and Times of John Young: Confidant and Advisor to Kamehameha the Great* (Aiea, HI: Island Heritage Publishing, 1999). James

Young Kanehoa first left the Hawaiian Islands in 1806 aboard *Pearl,* under the command of a Captain Ebbets; John Suter was mate for this voyage. Kanehoa went to the United States and learned English there. For a description of the royal entourage of twelve to England, see Kamakau, *Ruling Chiefs of Hawaii,* 256.

106. See James Young Kanehoa, "Letter to R. C. Wyllie," *The Polynesian,* 11 October 1851, 90.

107. See Kamakau, *Ruling Chiefs of Hawaii,* 257; Kamakau attributed Young's failure to board *L'Aigle* at Rio to drunkenness—an opinion not shared by the Hawaiians actually on the voyage. For an account of the journey aboard *L'Aigle,* see Corley, "Kamehameha II's Ill-Starred Journey."

108. Pleadwell, *Voyage to England,* 8.

109. The trip of the royal Hawaiian party to England is worthy of a separate article; this brief account is derived from Pleadwell, *Voyage to England;* "The Late King of the Sandwich Islands," *Edinburgh Evening Courant,* 19 July and 6 September 1824; "The King and Queen of the Sandwich Islands," *John Bull,* 23 May, 13 and 28 June, and 11 and 18 July 1824; Dampier, *To the Sandwich Islands;* Byron, *Voyage of H.M.S.* Blonde, 53–75; Frankenstein, *Royal Visitors;* and Adrienne Kaeppler, "*L'Aigle* and HMS *Blonde:* The Use of History in the Study of Ethnography," *Hawaiian Journal of History* 12 (1978): 28–44; see also Corley, "British Press Greets the King." Gast, *Contentious Consul,* 71–72, offers an account of Rives after Lihiliho's death more favorable to the Frenchman.

110. *The Polynesian,* n.s., vol. 1, no. 40 (22 February 1845): 162.

111. "Ports of the Sandwich Islands," *Pacific Commercial Advertiser,* 19 February 1857, n.p. (no. 5 of a series). The same article appeared in *The Friend,* May 1857, 39.

112. John U. Kuapu'u, *Ka Hae Hawaii,* ca. 11 May 1857. This article was paraphrased in *The Polynesian,* 23 May 1857, n.p., which supplements the account by translating correspondent Kuapu'u's name as "Mr. Hunchback" and changed the date on the cannon to 1818. I am grateful to

Molly Ka'imi Summers of Kaua'i Community College for the translation of the original Hawaiian.

113. Lydgate, "The Story of Cleopatra's Barge," 7. This article is reprinted in Kaua'i Historical Society, *The Kauai Papers* (Kaua'i: Kauai Historical Society, 1991), 20–22. I am grateful to Kaua'i journalist and historian Chris Cook, who provided an 1893 Hanalei and Princeville map that shows Nu'uanu's property near the mouth of the Hanalei River. According to Bishop Museum, "Anthropology Report 10/1273" (Typescript Ms. 101273), HMS *Sulphur* was in Hanalei Bay in July 1837 to purchase cattle and rewater the ship, surveying the bay while there. See Belcher, *Narrative of a Voyage,* 1:160 and 166–167. Both *Sulphur* and *Starling* were at Hanalei, but there is no mention of cannon recovery. They revisited Hanalei in 1839 (Belcher, *Narrative of a Voyage,* 1:276–277), but there is no mention of cannon for that visit either.

114. Edward P. Wilcox to his nieces in Winsted, Connecticut, 19 December 1920, Grove Farm Homestead Museum, Lihue, Kaua'i. It is unfortunate that the capstan has not survived, for it was built according to George Crowninshield's "own ideas"; see Crowninshield, *Story of George Crowninshield's Yacht,* 22.

Chapter 3

1. See Whitehill, "George Crowninshield's Yacht."

2. The *Barge's* US flag is preserved at the Peabody Essex Museum.

3. According to Kemp, *Oxford Companion to Ships,* 926, the water sail was a small sail used aboard square-riggers when running before the wind in calm conditions. It could be set either below the studdingsail or the boom of the driver (an archaic type of studdingsail). Harold Underhill, *Sailing Ship Rigs and Rigging* (Glasgow: Brown, Son & Ferguson, 1938), 115, defines the water sail as a squaresail flown under the bowsprit. David Steel, *Steel's Elements of Mastmaking, Sailmaking, and Rigging from the 1794 Edition* (London: W. & G. Foyle, 1932), 100–102 and 192, defines and illustrates water sails and ringtail sails for

sloops and ships; both are more or less quadrilateral studdingsails used in light winds. W. H. Rowe, *The Maritime History of Maine* (New York: Norton, 1948), 90, further defines the ringtail fitted to a hermaphrodite brig similar in size to the *Barge* as "a light sail bent on a long sliding spar which was fitted to her main boom . . . [and] increased the size of her mainsail by one-third."

4. Morison, *Maritime History of Massachusetts,* xiii, claims to have found this image in Charles S. Stewart's *Voyage to the Pacific Ocean* (i.e., Stewart, *Private Journal of a Voyage to the Pacific Ocean*). However, it does not appear in any of the first several editions of this work.

5. These descriptions are ably collected by Whitehill, *George Crowninshield's Yacht,* 5–8.

6. Chapelle, *History of American Sailing Ships,* 304. The Peabody Essex Museum drawing's catalog number is P3229.

7. H. Percy Ashley's plans of the *Barge* are cataloged as P-359a & b; Perry Shaw's lines drawing is PEM P-3229B.

8. See Crowninshield, "An Account of the Yacht," 93–94.

9. See Kevin J. Crisman, *The EAGLE: An American Brig on Lake Champlain during the War of 1812* (Shelburne, VT: New England Press, 1987), which describes the brigs *Eagle* and *Jefferson* in Lake Champlain. Crisman, chaps. 10 and 11, found much useful information in comparing these inland naval vessels with the oceangoing eighteen-gun sloop *Peacock* of 1813; however, this warship was significantly larger in all dimensions than the *Barge,* preventing close comparison.

10. See J. Richard Steffy, *Wooden Ship Building and the Interpretation of Shipwrecks* (College Station: Texas A&M University Press, 1994), 257–258: "Douglas fir ranges . . . to the Pacific coast . . . from central British Columbia. Contracts for large sailing vessels built on the Pacific coast early in this [twentieth] century specify yellow [Douglas] fir for nearly all construction." Biologist Alex Wiedenhoeft of the Forest Products Lab, in Madison, Wisconsin (personal communication, 18 July 2002), suggested that common timber in the region of the Queen Charlotte

Islands included the softwoods western hemlock, western red cedar, Sitka spruce, and Douglas fir as well as hardwoods.

11. Crisman, *The EAGLE,* 156.

12. See, for example, J. R. Harris, "Copper and Shipping in the Eighteenth Century," *Economic History Review* 19, no. 3 (1966): 550–568; Randolph Cock, "'The Finest Invention in the World': The Royal Navy's Early Trials of Copper Sheathing, 1708–1770," *Mariner's Mirror* 87, no. 4 (2001): 446–459; John M. Bingeman et al., "Copper and Other Sheathing in the Royal Navy," *IJNA* 29, no. 2 (2000): 218–219; Eric A. R. Ronnberg Jr., "Copper Sheathing of Whaleships," *Nautical Research Journal* 20, no. 4 (1974): 183–185, and Ronnberg, "Coppering"; Iver Lunn, *Antifouling: A Brief Introduction to the Origins and Development of the Marine Antifouling Industry* (Thame: BCA Publications, 1974); A. C. Redfield et al., eds., *Marine Fouling and Its Prevention* (Annapolis: US Naval Institute, 1952). McCarthy, *Ships' Fastenings,* 108 ff., cites G. Rees, "Copper Sheathing: An Example of Technological Diffusion in the English Merchant Fleet," *Journal of Transport History* 1 (1971): 85–85, for the 1816 percentage of coppered British merchant ships. His chapter 8 also discussed copper pioneers Williams and Grenfell in greater detail.

13. I am grateful to Michael K. Stammers of the Merseyside Maritime Museum, Liverpool, for tracing the stamp of Owen Williams and Pascoe Grenfell's company through Edward Baines, *History, Directory and Gazetter of the County Palatine of Lancaster with a Variety of Statistical Information . . .* (Liverpool, Wm. Wales & Co., 1824), 370. See also John R. Harris, *The Copper King: A Biography of Thomas Williams of Llanidan* (Liverpool: Liverpool University Press, 1964), 148–183.

14. I am grateful to John Bingeman of West Sussex, UK, for an alternate possibility (personal communication, 5 October 2001): "All the dated copper sheathing I have examined from 1804 up to the 1930s has the thickness measured in 'oz per square foot.' Referring to my Copper Data book: 24-gauge copper is equivalent

to 16 oz/ft² 'Old Birmingham Wire Gauge (approx)' or 16½ oz Imperial Standard Wire Gauge. This is a lighter gauge than the thinnest Royal Navy copper sheathing at 22 oz/ft². The tougher Muntz metal used on merchantmen is thought to have been 16oz/ft²."

15. Ronnberg, "Coppering," 137, and Walter J. Zimmerman, "A Method for Coppering Models," *Nautical Research Journal* 24, no. 2 (1978): 95–99, depict different nailing patterns for metaling hulls.

16. This time estimate is based upon the copper sheathing changes for HMS *Victory,* as detailed in Bingeman et al., "Copper and Other Sheathing in the Royal Navy," 223, table 1.

17. See Geoffrey M. Footner, *Tidewater Triumph: Development and Success of the Chesapeake Bay Pilot Schooner* (Mystic, CT: Mystic Seaport Museum, 1998), 110.

18. On 22 April 1824, Levi Chamberlain recorded that he delivered old sheet copper taken from the hull of the *Ruby* to Captain Blanchard for $10 per hundred pounds; Levi Chamberlain Journal III, 22 April 1824, 40. Two days later, the official Journal of the Sandwich Islands Mission documented the same sale at $11 per hundred pounds; JSIM, 24 April 1824, 498 (ms.). Two years earlier, John C. Jones, in a letter to his employers, wrote: "I have purchased of Capt. de Koven 200 Sheets of Copper at 40 cents per pound, we expect to have the job of repairing the Bordeaux Packet. I can sell the copper at any time for 65 cents"; J. C. Jones to Marshall & Wildes, 10 October 1822, in Morison, "Boston Traders in the Hawaiian Islands," 40–42. This works out to $40 per hundred pounds; the much higher price paid by Jones may reflect either fluctuating prices or perhaps new copper.

19. Camie Campbell [Thompson], *Elemental Analysis of Finds from Hanalei Bay, Kauai.* (Washington: CAL, 1995); report on file. Later, as knowledge of copper, its antifouling properties, and other metals increased, the concentration of the expensive metal in bottom sheathing declined, and by the mid-nineteenth century "yellow metal" (an alloy of ~66 percent copper/~33 percent zinc) or Muntz metal

(~60 percent copper and 40 percent zinc) were more common.

20. Ronnberg, "Coppering," 137.

21. For the use of lead at the ship's bow, see Harland, "Piet Heyn and the Early Use of Copper Sheathing" and Ronnberg, "Coppering," 129.

22. See *The Boston Directory* (Boston: Hunt and Stimpson, 1828) for James Davis & Son. James Davis had a brass foundry in Boston and was a partner of Joseph W. Revere, father of Paul Revere of Revolutionary War fame. See S. T. Snow, *Fifty Years with the Revere Copper Co.: A Paper Read at the Stockholders' Meeting held on Monday 24 March 1890* (Boston: Samuel Usher, 1890). My thanks to James P. Delgado for this reference.

23. Apsley Pellet, "Lighting the Interior of Ships, Buildings, &c," patent no. 3058 (London: British Patent Office, 1807), 2.

24. I am grateful to Dr. Kevin Crisman of the Nautical Archaeology Program at Texas A&M University for supplying copies of the early patent and two student papers on the subject of deck lights. For further information, see his article "Two Deck Lights from the U.S. Navy Brig *Jefferson* (1814)," *Seaways' Ships in Scale* 3, no.6 (November–December 1992): 48–50, and Kendra L. Quinn, "Shipboard Lighting: A.D. 400–1900" (M.A. thesis, Texas A&M University, 1999), 94–98.

25. "Description of a Portable Deck Glass, and Ventilator, By Mr. Grant Preston, of Burr-street, Wapping," *The Repertory of Arts, Manufactures, and Agriculture,* 2nd ser., 32 (1818): 358.

26. See Bingham, *Residence,* 221.

27. There are several good books in which rope, rigging, and masting are discussed at length; some of them were around in 1816 when *Cleopatra's Barge* was built. See William Falconer, *A New Universal Dictionary of the Marine . . .* (London: T. Cadwell and W. Davies, 1815); Steel, *Steel's Elements of Mastmaking;* Blanckley, *Naval Expositor;* George Biddlecombe, *The Art of Rigging* (Salem, MA: Marine Research Society, 1925); Ashley, *Ashley Book of Knots;* Underhill, *Sailing Ship Rigs and Rigging;* H. A. Underhill, *Masting and Rigging the Clipper Ship and Ocean Carrier* (Glasgow: Brown, Son & Ferguson, 1946); John Fincham, *A Treatise on Masting Ships & Mast Making* (London: Whittaker, 1859); James Lees, *The Masting and Rigging of English Ships of War 1625–1860* (Annapolis, MD: Naval Institute Press, 1979).

28. Some of the clearest illustrations of the futtock shrouds may be seen in Lees, *Masting and Rigging,* 54 and 60.

29. For the definition of a ringbolt, see Steel, *Steel's Elements of Mastmaking,* 126. Unfortunately, Steel does not say what the function of the ringbolt was.

30. All of the old seamanship and rigging manuals mention leathering in passing; the most thorough discussion of the subject is Brion Toss, *The Complete Rigger's Apprentice* (Camden, ME: International Marine, 1998), 220–226. For naval leathering, see Louis Bartos, "David Steele's *The Art of Sailmaking* & HMS *Victory*'s Fore Topsail" *Sea History* 111 (Summer 2005): 10–13.

31. I am grateful to Thomas Hulsebosch of the University of Hawai'i's Geology Department for his review of the stone ballast (personal communication, 25 August 1995).

Chapter 4

1. Wagner Surveying, personal communication, 30 July 1998.

2. See Thomas, *Schooner from Windward,* 155–158, 166, 182, 193, 210.

3. See Robert E. Röntgen, *Marks on German, Bohemian, and Austrian Porcelain* (Atglen, PA: Schiffer Publishing, 1997), 479 and referenced marks as specified.

4. Bennett, *Archaeology of Kauai,* 26. Buck, *Arts and Crafts of Hawaii,* 570–571, discusses sand burials throughout the Hawaiian Islands, noting that the present population (1950s) had no knowledge of the custom.

5. For example, see Jean Boudriot, *The Seventy-Four Gun Ship* (Annapolis, MD: Naval Institute Press, 1974), 2:159–160, figs. 192–193, for almost identical trucks. For the estimate of size, see M. A. Edson, "18th-Century Gun Carriages and Fittings," *Nautical Research Journal* 12, no. 3 (1964): 113–116. Edson used a table in the eighteenth-century treatise by John Roberts, *A treatise of such mathematical instruments as are usually put into a portable case: containing their various uses in arithmetic, geometry, trigonometry, architecture, surveying, gunnery, &c.* (London: T. Heath and J. Nourse . . . , 1757), to extrapolate the proportional dimensions of contemporary gun carriages into actual measurements in inches. His figures indicated that the outer diameter of the hind truck of a period four-pounder measured 8.8 in. in diameter × 3 in. thick.

6. See Arthur B. Cohn and Adam I. Kane, Spitfire *Management Plan* (Vergennes, VT: Lake Champlain Maritime Museum, 2002), 122, fig. 6.12.

7. I am grateful to David Moore of the North Carolina Maritime Museum for pointing out the *Carysfort* apron parallel. He also provided information about four other, plainer examples: three having one edge containing parallel cuts (from the wrecks of *Whydah* [1717], so-called *Queen Anne's Revenge* [1718], and *Henrietta Marie* [1700]), and one a simple lead sheet from the Scallcastle Bay cannon site (1690) in England.

8. See Austin C. Carpenter, *Cannon* (Exeter, UK: Halsgrove Press, 1993), 10, table of ordnance weights, lengths, bores, and materials.

9. See John Seymour, "Coopering," *The Forgotten Crafts* (New York: Alfred Knopf, 1984), 86–95, and Kenneth Kilby, *The Cooper and His Trade* (London: John Baker, 1971), 42–53. Kilby, p. 53, provides a table indicating that a powder keg with a $5\frac{1}{2}$ in. head contained five pounds of product.

10. For *Invincible,* see John Bingeman, "Solent: HMS *Invincible* (1758) wreck site," *IJNA* 10, no. 2 (1981): 155, and Bingeman, "Interim Report on Artefacts Recovered from the *Invincible* (1758) between 1979 and 1984," *IJNA* 14, no. 3 (1985): 195 and fig. 8. For *La Belle,* see Chuck Meide, "Preliminary Report on the Staved Container Remains from the La Salle Shipwreck *La Belle,*" in Denise C. Lakey, ed., *Underwater Archaeology 1997* (Tucson: Society for Historical Archaeology, 1997), 135–136.

11. W. Gilkerson, *Boarders Away II:*

Firearms of the Age of Fighting Sail (Lincoln, RI: Andrew Mowbray Inc., 1993), 97–105. Most boat guns lacked barrel bands, but they did have ramrods. See also De Witt Bailey, *British Military Longarms 1715–1815* (Harrisburg, PA: Stackpole Books, 1971), 41–43, and *British Military Longarms 1815–1865* (Harrisburg, PA: Stackpole Books, 1972), 17–19, 30–33.

12. See Ray Riling, *The Powder Flask Book* (New Hope, PA: Robert Halter/ The River House, 1953), 113–114, 151–152. Riling, p. 193, reproduces page V of Frith's catalog, which has an almost identical example to C94 in the upper-right corner of the page.

13. Lead shot similar in size and aspect were found in the late eighteenth-century Boca Chica wreck in the Florida Keys; see Robert S. Neyland and Barbara A. Voulgaris, eds., *The Boca Chica Channel Wreck: An Assessment* (Washington, DC: Naval Historical Center, 2003), 68–71, figs. 25 and 97.

14. Very little has been written about sandglasses, and most of the later sources repeat the earlier ones. Even less has been done with maritime examples. See Joseph Sternfield, *Hour Glasses* (Williamstown, MA: National Association of Watch and Clock Collectors, 1953); Anthony J. Turner, "Sand-glasses," in *Time Measuring Instruments,* vol. 1 of *The Time Museum: Catalogue of the Collection* (Rockford, IL: Time Museum, 1984), 75–113 and extensive bibliography. Examples from wrecks are illustrated from the wreck of a ca. 1700 merchant vessel off Stockholm, Sweden, by Catharina Ingelman-Sundberg, "Preliminary Report on Finds from the Jutholmen Wreck," *IJNA* 5, no. 1 (1976): 57 and fig. 1; four of the six recovered from the 1758 wreck of the British warship *Invincible* are shown by Bingeman, "Interim Report on Artefacts Recovered from the *Invincible,*" 191 and figs. 1–2; two from the 1676 wreck of the Swedish warship *Kronan* are illustrated in Lars Einarsson, "*Kronan*—Underwater Archaeological Investigations of a 17th-Century Man-of-War . . ." *IJNA* 19, no. 4 (1990): 294, fig. 17. Several sandglass fragments are cataloged from the 1781 wreck of the British merchantman identi-fied as the *Betsy;* see John D. Broadwater, *Final Report on the Yorktown Shipwreck Archaeological Project* (Washington, DC: NEH, 1996), 5:59–60. A single sandglass bulb was found in the stern area of the late eighteenth-century Boca Chica Channel wreck; see Neyland and Voulgaris, *Boca Chica Channel Wreck,* 93 and 144, figs. 46 and 97–23 (bottom). A good discourse on the use of the log chip and sandglass is found in Frank Scott, "Speed, Navigational Accuracy and the 'Ship Log,'" *Mariner's Mirror* 92, no. 4 (November 2006): 477–481.

15. See Jeannette Lasansky, *To Draw, Upset, & Weld* (Lewisburg, PA: Union County Oral Traditions Project, 1980), 63 (top).

16. See Ashley, *Ashley Book of Knots,* opp. ix, 19, fig. 85, 22, fig. 101J; and Robert J. Schwendinger, *Maritime Arts & Artisans* (San Francisco: San Francisco Craft and Folk Art Museum, 1989), 31, no. 7.

17. David Malo, *Hawaiian Antiquities* (Honolulu: Bernice P. Bishop Museum, 1951), 47, 77. See also Adrienne L. Kaeppler, *"Artificial Curiosities": Being an Exposition of Native Manufactures Collected on the Three Pacific Voyages of Captain James Cook, R.N. . . .* (Honolulu: Bishop Museum Press, 1978), 91–93.

18. I am grateful to Drs. James Mead of the National Museum of Natural History and Natalie Uhl of Cornell University for this identification.

19. See *Munsell Book of Color* (Baltimore: Munsell Color Co., 1966), 2.54R 5/10; according to the 1970 Kidd and Kidd classification system, the shape is Wic. Kenneth E. and M. A. Kidd, *A Classification System for Glass Beads for the Use of Field Archaeologists* (Ottawa: Department of Indian Affairs and Northern Development, 1970).

20. The number is approximate, as some of the glass fragments recovered were too small or worn to positively identify as gin bottle sherds.

21. See Cecil Munsey, *The Illustrated Guide to Collecting Bottles* (New York: Hawthorn Books, 1970), 84–85, for a fuller explanation of the origins of gin and the case bottle.

22. See Blanckley, *Naval Expositor,* 58, "Forks." Interestingly, the Smithsonian's copy of this volume has inked marginal notes, tables, and other notations, including one next to the definition of flesh fork: "2 ft long." On the same page, Blankley indicates that long forks were also used to hold burning faggots while breaming the hulls of ships to keep them clean. However, in the Hawaiian Islands, breaming, graving, and other large-scale maintenance tasks were done in Honolulu, and there would have been no need to carry a breaming fork as part of the ship's tool chest. Other early meat forks are in Don Plummer, *Colonial Wrought Iron: The Sorber Collection* (Ocean Pines, MD: SkipJack Press, 1999), 39–43.

23. See Seymour B. Wyler, *The Book of Old Silver* (New York: Crown Publishers, 1937), 74–77.

24. The two-prong variety is the oldest type of fork. Although three and four prongs were in use by the seventeenth century, the two-pronged type remained in higher demand until Victorian times. See H. Raymond Singleton, *A Chronology of Cutlery* (Sheffield, UK: Sheffield City Museums, 1973), 4. I am grateful to Anne Serio and Anne Golovin, originally with the Domestic Life Collections of the Smithsonian's National Museum of American History, for their insights into the flatware.

25. See, for example, Ruth Webb Lee, *Sandwich Glass* (Framingham, MA: privately published, 1939), 64 and plate 46; and Jane Shadel Spillman, *Glass Tableware, Bowls, and Vases* (New York: Alfred A. Knopf, 1982), 254 and figure. The National Museum of American History has examples of these shallow bowls as well (Glass Collections, nos. 63.37 and 64.89).

26. See Crowninshield, *Story of George Crowninshield's Yacht,* 230. For examples of box and Shaker stoves, see Tammis Kane Groft, *Cast with Style: Nineteenth Century Cast-Iron Stoves from the Albany Area,* rev. ed (Albany, NY: Albany Institute of History and Art, 1984), 45; Josephine H. Peirce, *Fire on the Hearth: The Evolution and Romance of the Heating-Stove* (Springfield, MA: Pond-

Ekberg Co., 1951), 95-101; Will Curtis and Jane Curtis, *Antique Woodstoves: Artistry in Iron* (Ashville, ME: Cobblesmith, 1974), 11-15, 22-25; and Henry C. Mercer and Horace M. Mann, *The Bible in Iron, or Pictured Stoves and Stove Plates of the Pennsylvania Germans,* 2nd ed. (Doylestown, PA: Bucks County Historical Society, 1941), 146, fig. 263.

27. I am grateful to Donald Fennimore of the Winterthur Museum for his insights into this and other furniture attachments from the wreck site.

28. See Plummer, *Colonial Wrought Iron,* 200, upper right, Latches, 4-112. The copper or brass fixture is identical to the same feature, Lock, 4-113, where it is called a "drop stirrup brass knob." The *Barge* example is $3\frac{1}{4}$ in. square, while Plummers's seem to cluster around 4 in. on a side. Plummer, ibid.: "These are frequently referred to as square, open-faced latches." The *Barge* example is very close to English pieces on 200, top right; 201, bottom, left, and right; and 202, bottom right.

29. See ibid., 184-194, and Albert H. Sonn, *Early American Wrought Iron* (New York: Bonanza Books, 1978), pl. 33; pl. 64, fig. 1; pl. 67, fig. 3; pl. 69, fig. 3.

30. See Thompson, "Historic American Yachts," 6, left column. I am grateful to Dr. Daniel Finamore of the Peabody Essex Museum, for pointing out this image.

31. See Dean A. Fales Jr., *American Painted Furniture 1660-1880* (New York: E. F. Dutton & Co., 1972), 119, fig. 196, for an example of this decorative feature in the frame of an ornate gilded pine looking glass (American or English) dating to 1800-1810 in New York's Metropolitan Museum of Art. Other examples of similarly decorated frames from the same period are on 121-123, figs. 203-205. Interestingly, Fales also devotes an entire spread in this book to the original 1816 furnishings of *Cleopatra's Barge* (168-169)!

32. I am grateful to Sheila Alexander, formerly with the National Museum of American History's Glass Collections, and Anne Serio, formerly with the NMAH Domestic Life Collections, for assistance with this piece.

33. See Wendy A. Cooper, *Classical Taste in America 1800-1840* (New York: Baltimore Museum of Art, 1993), 186, no. 145, for an almost identical but slightly less elaborate brass or side mount of a cupid sharpening his bow. The matching piece shows a cupid hammering an anvil; Metropolitan Museum of Art nos. 68.8.76 and 68.8.77. For examples of how these mounts were applied to furniture in the 1815-1835 Greco-Roman Revival period, see Jonathan L. Fairbanks and Elizabeth Bidwell Bates, *American Furniture 1620 to the Present* (New York: Richard Marek Publishers, 1981), 255-279.

34. See, for example, Ralph M. Kovel and Terry H. Kovel, *American Country Furniture 1780-1875* (New York: Crown Publishers, 1987), 46, and Robert W. Swedberg and Harriett Swedberg, *Collector's Encyclopedia of American Furniture* (Paducah, KY: Collector Books, 1994), 3:57, top. Unfortunately, virtually all of the standard texts, handbooks, and encyclopedias on American and European furniture of the Federal and Classical periods focus on the high-end material rather than the more common everyday items in use by a majority of the population.

35. Fales, *American Painted Furniture,* is an example of this; on page 37 he mentions plain-painted furniture and even discusses red and black as the most common pigments, but he illustrates only a very few examples of monochrome-painted furniture in his 300-page book—all of it lighter and more delicate than the specimens found in the wreck of the royal yacht.

36. Irving Jenkins, *The Hawaiian Calabash* (Hawaii: Kauai Museum and Bishop Museum, 1989), 241-247, has an excellent discussion of contemporary sources on the popularity of puppies in the Hawaiian chiefly diet and for the *luau,* with as many as 400 consumed at a single feast. Dogs raised for food ran around in herds and were fattened on a diet of vegetables and poi; they were not permitted to eat meat. By 1840, the aboriginal or "poi dog" had disappeared through crossbreeding with Westerners' pets in the Sandwich Islands.

37. Dr. Susan Lebo of the Bishop

Museum was kind enough to review and analyze the ceramic assemblage from the wreck site in 2003; most of this discussion is based on her report of 20 January 2004, on file at the National Museum of American History.

38. I am grateful to Dr. Peter Mills of the University of Hawai'i for drawing my attention to the unpublished paper by Dr. Susan Lebo and Ines D. Gordon, "Early Trade in Hawai'i: A Case Study of Metal Adzes from the Bishop Museum Collection," delivered at the April 1998 Conference of the Society for Hawaiian Archaeology.

39. J.-F. G. de la Perouse, *A Voyage round the World, Performed in the Years 1785 . . . 1788, by Boussole and Astrolabe* (London: G. G. & J. Robinson, 1799), 1:343.

40. JSIM, 22 September 1823, 434 (ms.).

41. Lebo and Gordon, "Early Trade in Hawai'i," 4.

42. Patrick V. Kirch, *Feathered Gods and Fishhooks: An Introduction to Hawaiian Archaeology and Prehistory* (Honolulu: University of Hawai'i Press, 1975), 189-193, fig. 170: "awls/picks . . . may have been used to split leaves into strips for mat-making; others are interpreted as picks for extracting shellfish meat."

43. A few other pieces of copper sheathing were found folded over that may have served the same purpose(s). Although some identical pieces are preserved within an artifact assemblage at the National Museum of American History from the 1838 wreck of the French frigate *Herminie* in Bermuda, their purpose is undocumented. Perhaps they were used as sheathing seam patches or stored aboard ship as scrap to be melted down and reused.

44. For a scraper with a grass handle, see Bennett, *Archaeology of Kauai,* 82, fig. 16a; fig. 16b shows a scraper similar in size to the one from the royal yacht.

45. See Buck, *Arts and Crafts of Hawaii,* 107-109, for descriptions and illustrations of kukui nuts and oil lamps. For the most part, the examples in the Bishop Museum collections are more elaborate, smoother, and more finished

than the Hanalei one, although the size is comparable. Similar hollowed-out lava stones may be interpreted as Hawaiian stone bait mortars. Images of small, partially unfinished examples and their descriptions are found in ibid., 354–355, fig. 240a. However, the Hanalei example is extremely rough on the interior, while the mortars in the Bishop Museum are smooth inside.

46. Holmes, *The Hawaiian Canoe,* 119. Holmes claimed that until the introduction of Western cannon, canoe breakers were the most powerful weapons in the Hawaiian naval arsenal. However, his footnoted reference to Bingham is untraceable as cited. Canoe breakers are also discussed and illustrated in Te Rangi Hiroa (Peter S. Buck), "Canoes," sec. 6 of *Arts and Crafts of Hawaii,* Bishop Museum Special Publication 45 (Honolulu: Bishop Museum Press, 1957), 281, fig. 199c.

47. Buck, *Arts and Crafts of Hawaii,* 357–363, describes the squid-luring technique using cowrie shells.

48. Bennett, *Archaeology of Kauai,* 74 ff., and fig. 14b. Bennet's identified example is $7\frac{1}{2}$ in. × 5 in. in size—slightly larger even than the example found in Hanalei Bay. Buck, *Arts and Crafts of Hawaii,* 281, fig. 199a, identifies an example similar to the Hanalei find as a stone anchor.

49. See Buck, *Arts and Crafts of Hawaii,* 281, fig. 199b. This attribution as an anchor is dubious, due to the lack of a high or steep enough shoulder on the protuberance to hold a wet line. For the "bread-loaf" sinker, see 343–345 and fig. 235c.

50. This example is identical to a canoe rubber illustrated in ibid., 257–258, fig. 182d. Buck says smaller ones "were evidently used on wooden bowls." See also Bennett, *Archaeology of Kauai,* 56, fig. 7b.

51. I'i, *Fragments of Hawaiian History,* 66–67, has the best early description of the sport of *maika* and its variants. See also Bennett, *Archaeology of Kauai,* 76–78; Buck, *Arts and Crafts of Hawaii,* 372–374 and, for pitching/quoits games, 373–374.

52. See Donald D. Kilolani Mitchell, *Resource Units in Hawaiian Culture* (Honolulu: Kamehameha Schools Press, 1982), 43–44; George S. Kanahele, ed., *Hawaiian Music and Musicians* (Honolulu: University Press of Hawai'i: 1979), 306–307; Nathaniel B. Emerson, *Unwritten Literature of Hawaii* (Washington, DC: Smithsonian Institution, 1909), 130–132; Dorothy B. Barrere, "Conch Shell Trumpets," *The Conch Shell* 1, no. 1 (Spring 1963): 3–5; Buck, *Arts and Crafts of Hawaii,* 393–394; Helen H. Roberts, "Ancient Hawaiian Music," *Bishop Museum Bulletin* 29 (1926): 45–46.

53. For further information about Smithson's scientific background, see "Who Was James Smithson?" http://www.sil.si.edu/Exhibitions/Smithson-to-Smithsonian/who_04.html.

Chapter 5

1. Marshall Sahlins, in Kirch and Sahlins, *Anahulu,* 1:65–66, relates several contemporary accounts of chiefly extravagance. Laura Fish Judd, in her edited volume *Honolulu: Sketches of Hawaiian Life in the Hawaiian Islands from 1828 to 1861* (Chicago: Lakeside Press, 1966), 202, describes the auction of "Old Governor Adams' things," mostly textiles and clothing of various sorts. I'i, in *Fragments of Hawaiian History,* 66, says of Ka'ahumanu's Honolulu eating house, "And back of this were two storehouses, filled from top to bottom with gunpowder and guns. East of these were some houses in which were stored the belongings of Kamehameha, of the heir to the kingdom, and of the gods of the heiaus." Charles Hammatt's journal for 18 August 1823 states that "these people have an incurable reluctance to part with anything they have stored away. There is now an immense amount of property stowed away in caves & dirty houses which is rotting away, but which the chiefs will not take out of their repositories even to use themselves. The King sometime ago was in want of duck when it was scarce, & bought a few bolts at a very high price, when at the same time he had two or three hundred bolts

which was stored away rotting"; Hammatt, *Ships, Furs, and Sandalwood,* 26.

2. See Peter Mills, "*Neo* in Oceania," *Journal of Pacific History* 38, no. 1 (2003): 53–67, for information about Western ships owned and operated by Hawaiian chiefs.

3. For recent writing on the shipworm *Teredo navalis,* see David M. Platt, "Shipworms: The Wood-Boring Teredo Moves North," *WoodenBoat* 160 (May/June 2001): 45–48.

4. Harry Alden, personal communication, 3 October 2000.

5. Peter Mills, who excavated the Russian fort at Waimea, Kaua'i, indicated that the cannon found there were removed by the British in 1864 for scrap. See Mills, *Hawai'i's Russian Adventure.*

6. For beef in the Hawaiian diet at this date, see Ellis, *Journal,* 291.

7. See *Barge* log, 23 February 1817: "Mr. Baker aboard fitting a set of his patent pump boxes to our pumps." George Crowninshield to Commodore Hull, from Fayal, 24 April 1817, in Crowninshield, *Story of George Crowninshield's Yacht,* 63: "We use Baker's patent Pump boxes— once in twenty-four hours. They fully answer what has been said of them, and I exceedingly regret that Mr. Baker did not forward me the hand pump he promised, as I am in great need of it."

8. Symptoms of lead poisoning in adults may include high blood pressure, abdominal pain, declines in mental functioning, memory loss, mood disorders, and other (see Mayo Clinic, "Lead Poisoning: Symptoms," http://www.mayoclinic.org/diseases-conditions/lead-poisoning/basics/symptoms/con-20035487). See also Christian Warren, *Brush with Death: A Social History of Lead Poisoning* (Baltimore, MD: Johns Hopkins University Press, 2000), 148; Owen Beattie and John Geiger, *Frozen in Time: The Fate of the Franklin Expedition* (London: Bloomsbury Publishing, 1987), 83–85 and 156 ff.

9. Don Hibbard, State Historic Preservation Division, to Carol Lovell, Director, Kaua'i Museum, 3 October 2000.

General Bibliography

Alexander, W. D. "The Story of Cleopatra's Barge." *Papers of the Hawaiian Historical Society* 13 (1906): 24–31.

Ashley, Clifford Warren. *The Ashley Book of Knots*. Garden City, NY: Doubleday, 1944.

Barratt, Glynn. *The Russian View of Honolulu*. Ottawa: Carleton University Press, 1988.

Belcher, Edward. *Narrative of a Voyage round the World Performed in H.M.S. Sulphur, 1836–1842*. 2 vols. London: Henry Colburn, 1843.

Benedetto, Robert. *The Hawaii Journals of the New England Missionaries 1813–1894*. Honolulu: Hawaiian Mission Children's Society, 1982.

Bennett, Wendell Clark. *Archaeology of Kauai*. Bernice P. Bishop Museum Bulletin 80. Honolulu: Bishop Museum, 1931.

Bingham, Hiram. *A Residence of Twenty-One Years in the Sandwich Islands*. 1847. Reprint, Rutland, VT: Charles E. Tuttle Co., 1981.

Birkett, Mary Ellen. "Hawai'i in 1819: An Account by Camille de Roquefeuil." *Hawaiian Journal of History* 34 (2000): 69–92.

Blanckley, Thomas R. *A Naval Expositor, Shewing and Explaining the Words and Terms of Art belonging to the Parts, Qualities, and Proportions of Building, Rigging, Furnishing & Fitting a Ship for Sea. . . .* London: E. Owen. 1750.

Bradley, Harold W. *The American Frontier in Hawaii: The Pioneers 1789–1843*. 1943. Reprint, Gloucester, MA: Peter Smith, 1968.

Buck, Elizabeth, *Paradise Remade: The Politics of Culture and History in Hawaii*. Philadelphia: Temple University Press, 1993.

Buck, Peter H. *Arts and Crafts of Hawaii*. Bernice P. Bishop Museum Special Publicaton 45. Honolulu: Bishop Museum Press, 1957.

Byron, George Anson. *Voyage of H.M.S. Blonde to the Sandwich Islands in the Years 1824–1825*. London: John Murray, 1826.

Chapelle, Howard I. *The History of American Sailing Ships*. New York: Norton, 1935.

Corley, J. Susan. "British Press Greets the King of the Sandwich Islands: Kamehameha II in London, 1824." *Hawaiian Journal of History* 42 (2008): 69–103.

———. "Kamehameha II's Ill-Starred Journey to England Aboard *L'Aigle*, 1823–1824." *Hawaiian Journal of History* 44 (2010): 1–35.

Cottez, J. "Jean-Baptiste Rives, de Bordeaux: Aventurier Hawaien." *Bulletin de la Société des Études Océaniennes* 123 (vol. 10, no. 10, June 1958): 792–812, and 124 (vol. 10, no. 11, September 1958): 819–844.

Crowninshield, Benjamin W. "An Account of the Yacht 'Cleopatra's Barge.'" *Essex Institute Historical Collections* 25, nos. 4–6 (April–June 1888): 81–118.

Crowninshield, Bowdoin Bradlee. *Account of the Private Armed Ship* America *of Salem*. Salem, MA: Essex Institute, 1901.

Crowninshield, Francis B. *The Story of George Crowninshield's Yacht* Cleopatra's Barge *on a Voyage of Pleasure to the Western Islands and the Mediterranean 1816–1817*. Boston, MA: privately printed, 1913.

Damon, Ethel Moseley. *Koamalu*. 2 vols. Honolulu: privately printed, 1931.

Dampier, Robert. *To the Sandwich Islands on H.M.S. Blonde*. Edited by Pauline King Joerger. Honolulu: University Press of Hawaii, 1971.

Daws, Gavin. *Shoal of Time: A History of the Hawaiian Islands*. New York: Macmillan, 1968.

Dibble, Sheldon. *A History of the Sandwich Islands*. Honolulu: Thos. G. Thrum, 1909.

Dodge, Ernest S. "Cleopatra's Barge: America's First Deep-Water Yacht." *Motor Boating,* December 1954, 18–19, 104–5.

Eastman, Ralph M. *Some Famous Privateers of New England*. Boston: State Street Trust Co., 1928.

Ellis, William, *Journal of William Ellis*. 1827 (London) and 1917 (Hawaii). Reprint, Honolulu: Advertiser Publishing Co., 1963.

Felt, Joseph B. *Annals of Salem*. 2 vols. Salem, MA: W. & S. B. Ives, 1845–1849.

Ferguson, David L. Cleopatra's Barge: *The Crowninshield Story*. Boston: Little, Brown and Co., 1976.

Forbes, David W. *Treasures of Hawaiian History from the Collections of the Hawaiian Historical Society*. Honolulu: Hawaiian Historical Society, 1992.

Frankenstein, Alfred. *The Royal Visitors*. Portland: Oregon Historical Society, 1963.

Frugé, August, and Neal Harlow, trans. and eds. *A Voyage to California, the Sandwich Islands and Around the World in the Years 1826–1829,* by Auguste Duhaut-Cilly. Berkeley: University of California Press, 1999.

Gast, Ross H. *Contentious Consul: A Biography of John Coffin Jones, First United States Consular Agent at Hawaii*. Los Angeles: Dawson's Book Shop, 1976.

Gast, Ross H., and Agnes C. Conrad, eds. *Don Francisco de Paula Marin*. Honolulu: University Press of Hawaii for the Hawaiian Historical Society, 1973.

Gibson, Arrell M. *Yankees in Paradise: The Pacific Basin Frontier*. Albuquerque: University of New Mexico Press, 1993.

Gibson, James R. *Otter Skins, Boston Ships, and China Goods*. Seattle: University of Washington Press, 1999.

Gulick, Orramel H., and Ann Eliza Clark Gulick. *The Pilgrims of Hawaii: Their Own Story of Their Pilgrimage from New England. . . .* (New York: Fleming H. Revell Co., 1918.

Hammatt, Charles H. *Ships, Furs, and Sandalwood: A Yankee Trader in Hawai'i, 1823–1825.* Edited by Sandra Wagner-Wright. Honolulu: University of Hawai'i Press, 1999.

Harland, John H. "Piet Heyn and the Early Use of Copper Sheathing." *Mariner's Mirror* 62, no.1 (1976): 1–2.

Hawaiian Mission Children's Society. *Missionary Album. Portraits and Biographical Sketches of the American Protestant Missionaries to the Hawaiian Islands.* Honolulu: Hawaiian Mission Children's Society, 1969.

Hiney, Tom. *On the Missionary Trail: A Journey through Polynesia, Asia, and Africa with the London Missionary Society.* New York: Atlantic Monthly Press, 2000.

Holmes, Tommy. *The Hawaiian Canoe.* 2nd ed. Honolulu: Editions Limited, 1993.

I'i, John Papa. *Fragments of Hawaiian History.* Honolulu: Bishop Museum Press, 1983.

Johnston, Paul F. "Cleopatra's Barge: *Kauai, Hawaii.*" In *Beneath the Seven Seas,* edited by George F. Bass, 213–217. London: Thames & Hudson: 2005.

———. "*Cleopatra's Barge.*" In *British Museum Encyclopedia of Underwater and Maritime Archaeology,* edited by James P. Delgado, 101–102. London: British Museum Press, 1997.

———. "Do They Really Pay You To Do That?" *Increase & Diffusion: A Smithsonian Web Magazine* 1 (September 1996). http://amhistory.si.edu/docs/Johnston_Do_They_Really_Pay_You_to_Do_That_1996.pdf.

———. "The 1824 Wreck of the Royal Hawaiian Yacht *Ha'aheo o Hawaii* (ex-*Cleopatra's Barge*): 1996 Preliminary Results." in *Methods and Techniques of Underwater Research: Proceedings of the American Academy of Underwater Sciences 1996 Scientific Diving Symposium,* edited by Michael A. Lang, 133–135. Washington, DC:

American Academy of Underwater Sciences, 1996.

———. "Hanalei Redux." *Increase & Diffusion: A Smithsonian Web Magazine* 3 (March 1997). http://amhistory.si.edu/docs/Johnston_Hanalei_Redux_1997.pdf.

———. "A Million Pounds of Sandalwood: The History of *Cleopatra's Barge* in Hawaii." *American Neptune* 63, no.1 (Winter 2002): 5–45.

———. "1997 Excavations of the Royal Hawaiian Yacht *Ha'aheo o Hawaii* in Hanalei Bay, Kauai: Preliminary Report." In *Underwater Archaeology 1998,* edited by Lawrence E. Babits et al., 96–103. Tucson, AZ: Society for Historical Archaeology, 1998.

———. "Preliminary Report on the 1998 Excavations of the 1824 Wreck of the Royal Hawaiian Yacht *Ha'aheo o Hawaii* (ex-*Cleopatra's Barge*)." In *Underwater Archaeology 1999,* edited by A. A. Askins and M. W. Russell, 107–114. Tucson, AZ: Society for Historical Archaeology, 1999.

———. "Preliminary Report on the 1996 Excavations of the Wreck of *Ha'aheo o Hawaii* (ex-*Cleopatra's Barge*) in Hanalei Bay, Kauai." In *Underwater Archaeology 1997,* edited by Denise C. Lakey, 113–120. Tucson, AZ: Society for Historical Archaeology, 1997.

———. "The Wreck of America's First Yacht: *Cleopatra's Barge (Ha'aheo o Hawaii)*: 1995 Survey." In *Underwater Archaeology Proceedings from the Society for Historical Archaeology Conference,* edited by Stephen R. James Jr. and Camille Stanley, 61–66. Cincinnati, OH: Society for Historical Archaeology, 1996.

Judd, Bernice. *Voyages to Hawaii before 1860.* Honolulu: University Press of Hawaii, 1974.

Judd, Walter F. *Let Us Go: The Narrative of Kamehameha II, King of the Hawaiian Islands 1819–1824.* Honolulu: Topgallant Publishing Co., 1976.

Kamakau, Samuel M. *Ruling Chiefs of Hawaii.* Honolulu: Kamehameha Schools Press, 1992.

Kame'eleihiwa, Lilika. *Native Land and Foreign Desires.* Honolulu: Bishop Museum Press, 1992.

Kemp, Peter, ed. *The Oxford Companion to Ships and the Sea.* New York: Oxford University Press, 1976.

Keyes, Willard Emerson. "Cleopatra's Barge," *The Magazine Antiques,* January 1930, 29–33.

King, Pauline N., ed. *Journal of Stephen Reynolds.* Vol. 1, *1823–1829.* Honolulu and Salem, MA: Ku Pa'a Inc. and Peabody Museum of Salem, 1989.

Kirch, Patrick V., and Marshall Sahlins. *Anahulu: The Anthropology of History in the Kingdom of Hawaii.* 2 vols. Chicago: University of Chicago Press, 1992.

Kuykendall, Ralph S. *The Hawaiian Kingdom.* 3 vols. Honolulu: University of Hawaii Press, 1938.

Kuykendall, Ralph S., and A. Grove Day. *Hawaii: A History, from Polynesian Kingdom to American State.* Englewood Cliffs, NJ: Prentice-Hall, 1961.

Leavitt, William. "Materials for the History of Ship-Building in Salem, No. V." *Historical Collections of the Essex Institute* 7, no. 5 (October 1865): 207–213.

Linnekin, Jocelyn. *Sacred Queens and Women of Consequence: Rank, Gender, and Colonialism in the Hawaiian Islands.* Ann Arbor: University of Michigan Press, 1990.

Loomis, Albertine. *Grapes of Canaan: Hawaii 1820.* Honolulu: Hawaiian Mission Children's Society, ca. 1951.

Lydgate, J. M. "The Cleopatra's Barge." *Pacific Marine Review,* August 1921, 471.

———. "The Story of Cleopatra's Barge." Kauai Historical Society, 24 November 1919 (reading transcript), 1–7.

Mathison, Gilbert Farquhar. *Narrative of a Visit to Brazil, Chile, Peru, and the Sandwich Islands, during the Years 1821 and 1822. . . .* London: C. Knight, 1825.

McCarthy, Michael. *Ships' Fastenings from Sewn Boat to Steamship.* College Station: Texas A&M University Press, 2005.

McCleery, Maybelle B. *A Voyage of H.M.S. Blond[e] to the Sandwich Islands in the Years 1824–1825. . . .* Honolulu: Dept. of Public Instruction, 1930.

Menzies, Archibald. *Hawaii Nei 128 Years Ago.* Honolulu, 1920.

Mills, Peter R. *Hawai'i's Russian Adventure: A New Look at Old History.* Honolulu: University of Hawai'i Press, 2002.

Morison, Samuel Eliot. "Boston Traders in the Hawaiian Islands, 1798–1823." *Proceedings of the Massachusetts Historical Society* 54 (October 1920): 9–47.

———. *The Maritime History of Massachusetts 1783–1860.* Cambridge, MA: Riverside Press, 1921.

"Mystery of Our First Seagoing Yacht," *New York Times,* 23 August 1914, p. XI.

Nickerson, Thomas, comp. *Early Images of Hawaii.* Honolulu: Law Library Microfilm Consortium, 1986.

O'Leary, Margaret R., comp. *Register of the Grove Farm Plantation Records and Papers . . .* Lihue: Grove Farm Homestead, 1982.

Paine, Ralph D. *The Ships and Sailors of Old Salem.* Boston: Charles E. Lauriat Co., 1923.

Pleadwell, Frank Lester. *The Voyage to England of King Liholiho and Queen Kamamalu: Essay Read by F. L. Pleadwell at the Meeting of the Social Science Association. . . . .* Honolulu: Social Science Association, 1952.

Pogue, John F. *Moolelo of Ancient Hawaii.* Translated by Charles W. Kenn. Honolulu: Topgallant Publishing Co., 1978.

Remy, M. Jules. *Contributions of a Venerable Native to the Ancient History of the Hawaiian Islands.* Reno, NV: Outbooks, 1979.

Ronnberg, Erik A. R., Jr. "The Coppering of 19th Century American Merchant Sailing Ships." *Nautical Research Journal* 26, no. 3 (1980): 125–148.

Ruggles, Samuel, and Nancy Ruggles. "From a Missionary Journal." *Atlantic Monthly* 134 (July–Dec. 1924): 648–657.

Scott, Edward B. *The Saga of the Sandwich Islands.* Lake Tahoe, NV: Sierra Tahoe Publishing Co., 1968.

Silverman, Jane A. *Kaahumanu: Molder of Change.* Honolulu: Friends of the Judiciary History Center, 1987.

Stannard, David E. *Before the Horror: The Population of Hawaii on the Eve of Western Contact.* Honolulu: Social Science Research Institute, University of Hawaii, 1989.

Stewart, Charles S. *Journal of a Residence in the Sandwich Islands during the Years 1823, 1824, 1825.* Facsimile of 3rd (1830) edition. Honolulu: University of Hawaii Press, 1970.

———. *Private Journal of a Voyage to the Pacific Ocean, and Residence at the Sandwich Islands, in the Years 1822, 1823, 1824 and 1825.* New York: John P. Haven, 1828.

Suter, John Wallace. "A Trader on the North-West Coast." Paper read at a meeting of the Club of Odd Volumes, Boston, 17 March 1920. Boston Marine Society.

Thomas, Mifflin. *Schooner from Windward: Two Centuries of Hawaiian Interisland Shipping.* Honolulu: University of Hawaii Press, 1983.

Thompson, Winfield M. "Historic American Yachts, Cleopatra's Barge." *The Rudder* 15, no. 1 (January 1904): 1–15.

Thurston, Lucy G. *Life and Times of Mrs. Lucy G. Thurston, Wife of Rev. Asa Thurston, Pioneer Missionary to the Sandwich Islands. . . .* Ann Arbor, MI: S. C. Andrews, 1934.

Whitehill, Walter M. "George Crowninshield's Yacht *Cleopatra's Barge.*" *American Neptune* 13, no. 4 (October 1953): 235–251.

———. *George Crowninshield's Yacht* Cleopatra's Barge *and a Catalog of the Francis B. Crowninshield Gallery.* Salem, MA: Peabody Museum, 1959.

Whiteman, Maxwell. *Copper for America. The Hendricks Family and a National Industry 1755–1939.* New Brunswick, NJ: Rutgers University Press, 1971.

Woolfenden, John, and Amelie Elkinton. *Cooper: Juan Bautista Rogers Cooper . . . 1791–1872.* Pacific Grove, CA: Boxwood Press, 1983.

Index